Learning Our Way

ESSAYS IN FEMINIST EDUCATION

Learning Our Way
ESSAYS IN FEMINIST EDUCATION

Edited by

Charlotte Bunch and Sandra Pollack

THE CROSSING PRESS / Trumansburg, New York 14886

The Crossing Press Feminist Series

Learning Our Way: Essays in Feminist Education
copyright © 1983 by Charlotte Bunch and Sandra Pollack

Individual essays are copyrighted by their respective authors except as
otherwise noted. Address inquiries to The Crossing Press Feminist
Series.

Book and cover design by Mary A. Scott
Photograph of Charlotte Bunch and Sandra Pollack by Nancy Myron
Typesetting by Martha J. Waters and Ruth Grunberg

Printed in U.S.A.

Library of Congress Cataloging in Publication Data
Main entry under title:

Learning our way.

(Crossing Press feminist series)
Bibliography: p.
1. Women--Education--United States--Addresses, essays,
lectures. 2. Feminism--United States--Addresses, essays,
lectures. I. Bunch, Charlotte, 1944-
II. Pollack, Sandy. III. Series.
LC1757.L42 1983   305.4'07'073   83-15182
ISBN 0-89594-112-0
ISBN 0-89594-111-2 (pbk.)

Contents

Introduction

THIS BOOK comes out of the experiences of women intimately involved with feminist education. They write to share what they have learned so that we do not always have to start over again at square one. They describe various educational environments which women have created to give form to our desire to teach and expand on our feminist visions. Feminist education is a continual process of discovering, changing, knowing, and sharing. The women in this book look at their experiences of this process and describe both the specifics of their activities and the broader understandings that have emerged from them.

The process of producing this anthology has been, like much of feminist education, a process of many phases and changes. The book itself, therefore, reflects our belief that it is possible to build on the work of the past. This book began in the political turmoil surrounding the opening of Sagaris, a national feminist summer institute held in Vermont in the summer of 1975. June Arnold and Parke Bowman, then publishers of Daughters Inc., initially conceived of a book about that controversial school. They asked Charlotte Bunch, one of the teachers at the first session of Sagaris, to collect essays for the book and made similar arrangements with a teacher from the second session.

In time, as the specifics of the Sagaris controversy receded and the editor of the second half of the anthology dropped out, Charlotte decided to reshape the book. She saw that what led to the conflicts at Sagaris was as much a lack of clearheadedness about political and educational issues as it was the specifics of that institute. Further, it also became clear that these same political issues were the ones facing other efforts at feminist education. She therefore solicited and edited (with the help of Sharon Delano) a collection of manuscripts based on a variety of experiences with feminist education. Unfortunately, just as the book, *Not By Degrees: Essays on Feminist Education*, was completed, Daughters Inc. stopped publishing.

The collection then lay dormant for several years until the Women in Print Conference in October 1981, when Barbara Grier of Naiad Press introduced Charlotte to Nancy K. Bereano, editor of the Feminist Series at The Crossing Press. Nancy became interested in the material and revived the project not only by offering to publish it but also by becoming actively involved with the content and by recruiting Sandra (Rubaii) Pollack as co-editor. Sandy provided the new energy necessary to evaluate the old material as well as to help solicit and edit additional manuscripts that reflected experiences with feminist education since the late seventies.

A third of the essays in *Learning Our Way* were part of the collection for *Not By Degrees*. Some we decided to update; others we chose to leave as they were. Our aim was not to provide an accounting of every phase of feminist education but to show the thinking of women at different moments in the development of their feminist education activities. All too often we get caught up in our current struggles and fail to see how they fit into the continuing evolution of feminist education. We have brought perspectives on current problems together with similar issues identified by earlier "second wave" writers on feminist education. The earlier essays provide an historical context for understanding our present situation.

The political context in which feminist education operates has also changed over the years covered by this book. The earliest articles discuss educational efforts that were born amidst the feminist excitement, optimism, and sense of discovery that characterized the mid-seventies. We have moved beyond those first explorations. There is now greater breadth and depth of experiences, of materials, and of perceptions about the enormous task feminist educators undertake in challenging society. The later essays reflect this evolution and complexity. They reflect as well the effects of the increasing attacks on feminists from the New Right and from the ravages of a declining economy. Yet, the consistency of purpose and the questions asked throughout these essays enable us to see those areas in which we have made progress, as well as to identify why we are still struggling with many of the same issues after more than ten years.

The essays in *Learning Our Way* reflect various approaches, but they share the assumption that feminist education is political. The authors are involved in an educational process that is for them consciously feminist. The common denominator is not where they work but their commitment to feminist education. As used in this collection, *feminist education* is not synonymous with *women's studies*, which may, but does not necessarily, operate from a feminist perspective.

Consequently, this anthology is not about whether women's studies should be political and committed to feminism; all the authors come down clearly on the side that sees the task of women's studies as doing feminist education. Such debate, however, has been important to many of the authors and can be found in other books and journals concerned with women's studies. The National Women's Studies Association, founded in 1977, took a stand in this debate when it stated that its purpose was to actively promote feminist education and support feminists involved in that effort at every educational level and in every setting. Much of NWSA's history has involved the struggle to translate this commitment into reality. This has not been easy, particularly as some have sought to separate women's studies from the political "taint" of feminism. Thus, while this struggle and the relationship of feminist education to women's studies programs is a theme, this book is not about women's studies programs per se. Rather, it focuses on what constitutes feminist education, how it is done, and what problems arise in a variety of educational settings.

The authors discuss three interrelated aspects of educating women:

- the teaching of specific skills (from reading and writing to computer technology and filmmaking) and passing on of information to students that will help them to survive better in the existing culture while working to change it;

- the development of feminist consciousness and the educating of women specifically about the women's movement, about women's diverse individual achievements and cultural heritages, and about various feminist theories and strategies for change;

- the creation of space, the encouragement of desire, and the provision of tools for women to develop their ideas, theories, art, research, and plans so that the body of feminist knowledge and action is expanded.

Initially, Charlotte drew up a list of questions that contributors to the book were asked to address. These dealt with the purpose and focus of feminist education, how they vary according to different situations and needs, what approaches can be taken to both curriculum and methodology, how method varies according to content, what the advantages and disadvantages are of different environments, what political responsibility feminist education has toward the movement and vice versa, and what the relationship should be between teachers, students, and administrators.

As the book took shape, these questions were discussed in various ways, but the situations which prompted the essays generally fell into three major categories, and we divided the anthology into three sections accordingly: "Feminist Education Within Existing Institutions," "Alternative Structures for Feminist Education," and "Approaches to Feminist Education."

The first section, "Feminist Education Within Existing Institutions," deals with conducting feminist education within existing structures, particularly in universities. It addresses a recurrent theme in this book: the relationship of women's studies programs within institutions to the activist feminist movement. It asks how many of the probing questions of feminism we drop by the wayside if we rush to respectability, and what happens if we reduce the feminist critique of patriarchy to the study of different lifestyles. The authors explore both how feminism has changed as it has moved from the streets into the classrooms and the reasons why radical feminists need to be within these institutions. Agreeing that women's education and feminist activism should complement each other, the authors discuss ways to overcome the barriers that frequently prevent a productive interaction.

These essays examine the problems involved in trying to shape feminist education in nonfeminist environments that range from hostile to mildly benevolent. They offer useful suggestions to those involved in teaching within academic settings. There are historical accounts of backlashes against feminism in the university, from the SUNY (Buffalo) struggle to maintain all-women's classes to the

New Right's attempt to prevent feminist teaching at California State University in Long Beach.

Several authors look at whether feminist education is reaching and addressing the lives of women from different class backgrounds, or Women of Color, and describe efforts to expand in these areas. The articles in this section demonstrate the tremendous differences between teaching in prison and in elite colleges, between teaching Black working women and white co-eds, between large state universities and small neighborhood-based experimental programs. Yet they also show the common struggles that women face when we seek to take control over our lives and our education. While pointing out the recurring problems of feminist education, the women writing here do not lose sight of the progress and the scope of the revolution we are making as we attempt to drastically alter our society.

The second section, "Alternative Structures for Feminist Education," covers an area about which too little has been written – the successes and failures, the highs and the pitfalls, of feminist efforts to create our own environments for education. It includes information about projects that is generally not available and that is vital to women who are planning to organize or participate in a political education program.

The essays in this section reflect the large amount of attention that alternatives give to questions of process and survival. Unlike existing structures where feminists struggle to prevent the bureaucracy from interfering but can usually assume that the institution will continue, in alternative programs nothing can be taken for granted. This has positive and negative consequences, but above all it demands extreme self-consciousness and constant evaluation.

Highly controversial issues must be resolved in order for an alternative to begin operation. For example, decisions must be made at the very outset about how much, or whether, to pay teachers, how much to charge students, and where to get money to start. Another difficult question for alternatives is who the students will be: where will they be recruited, who will be interested in what issues, who will be able to afford what costs (and what kinds of class and race biases does that assume), what will the incentives be to attend if there is no degree involved, and so on. Perhaps the most difficult problem that alternatives face is the issue of money and how to survive without relinquishing their political goals. Alternatives are important for developing feminist spaces and ideas, and they offer many opportunities for creative experimentation. However, given their economic problems, they are usually unstable and often unable to reach women beyond feminist circles. They tend to exhaust the energies and resources of their organizers and teachers. The authors reflect on these problems and various approaches to solving them.

One of the things we see clearly in this second section is how often involvement in one feminist education project sparks the development of another project. Califia was started by women who had attended Sagaris, and the Califia Women of Color Network is an outgrowth of Califia. The Women's Writer's Center closed in order to be transformed into a new vision – Freehand. Thus, even alternatives like Sagaris that "fail" in and of themselves often lead to the creation of new structures that explore the issues that were unresolved before. In creating alternatives, we build on our past as we learn from previous experiences. These articles seek to expand that sharing and learning process.

This section also demonstrates the variety of ways that one can engage in feminist education. We see women teaching in their homes and on the road. We see women working year-round in buildings that they own and conducting short-term two-week or even one-day educational endeavors. It is a testimony to feminist creativity and to the urgent desire we have to develop our own ways of learning.

The final section of the book, "Approaches to Feminist Education," includes a variety of experiences and issues that do not center on where one works. Most of the authors have taught in more than one setting, and they reflect generally on their approach to feminist education as a distinct process. Here the question of whether there is a feminist methodology gets raised most clearly. Throughout the book there are references to what different authors see as feminist techniques in teaching. Some say only certain approaches are feminist; some adapt ideas from progressive education; others reject the idea that there is a specifically feminist method. All, however, are involved in finding ways to teach more effectively and to break down what they perceive as barriers to women learning.

In this section, women remind us of components we often lose sight of in our discussions of feminist education. There is concern with how feminism can educate women to break down the prejudices of classism, racism, anti-Semitism, and homophobia, as well as sexism. We are asked to look at the relationship of feminist education to the technology of an increasingly computer-oriented society, as well as to the basics of reading and writing. What will it mean for women's struggles for power to change society if we are not literate in both of these areas?

The authors here are aware that feminist education takes place in many forms and is not limited to the classroom. It occurs through feminist publications and conferences; it happens in the mass media where we need to address the shaping of public attitudes; and finally, it is often a matter of how we approach the everyday encounters in our lives.

The essays in *Learning Our Way* build on each other, but they do not lead to a single conclusion: there is no one correct theory of feminist education. Feminist education is an experimental area in which what has previously been defined as fact is questioned, and new theory and process is in the making. While more definitive theory and methodology will no doubt emerge from this exploration, to impose any one approach at this time would short-circuit the process of creating a new kind of education.

The experiences described here reflect the struggle over the past fifteen years to develop feminist education. They are instructive not only to those concerned with women's studies but also to the feminist movement generally and to those involved in other types of experimental education. This book is only a beginning. We have focused on the voices of a sample of women in the United States, and so we do not include many other women throughout the world who are also creating feminist educational spaces and approaches.

Feminist education is an ongoing process, and like the movement that gave it birth, it has only begun to realize the radical transformational possibilities of feminism. We hope that *Learning Our Way* will come to be seen as one of the early recordings of that movement, and that it will nourish and be joined by many more voices on this subject in the coming years.

CHARLOTTE BUNCH
SANDRA POLLACK
July 1983

PART I

Feminist Education Within Existing Institutions

If the Mortarboard Fits . . .
Radical Feminism in Academia

by Sally Miller Gearhart

IN THE FALL of 1976, San Francisco State University offered, for the first time, a Bachelor of Arts degree program in women's studies. The program was the result of almost four years of work and struggle by students, staff, community workers, and faculty — women with a wide range of political points of view. The organizers of the program were influenced by San Francisco State's recent history, particularly the 1968 strike which ended with the establishment of the School of Ethnic Studies. This was a Pyrrhic victory, according to many, since the cost in dismissed faculty members, subsequent restrictions on minorities, and low campus morale more than outweighed the token recognition granted to Black, Asian American, La Raza, and Native American Studies, they argue. Cautioned by the example of the now isolated School of Ethnic Studies, women at SFSU decided to try an inter-disciplinary approach and chose not to form a separate depart-ment. Instead they arranged for a program that provides core courses for its majors and experimental courses which it seeks to "sell back" to the separate departments in the hope that women's concerns will be imbedded in course offerings throughout the university.

Although San Francisco State University is largely a commuter campus with many Third World and working-class students, women's studies here is still predominantly a white middle-class enterprise. The participants are mostly able-bodied women under forty and are, by and large, heterosexual, although there is strong input of both lesbian-feminist and disability politics. In this paper I don't intend only to generalize from my experience at San Francisco State, although clearly that experience has molded my ideas. All over the country there are other radical feminists involved in similar struggles and emerging with similar ideas.

Colleges and universities are playing a prominent part in the development of the women's movement, both through their commitment to women studies programs and through the hiring and training of academicians who are feminists. Radical feminism has moved from the streets into the ivy halls, and in that process its message seems significantly altered. Demands for the end of the system, for instance, have become pleas for equal treatment; foundation or government money, once despised, is discovered to be useful and even necessary; models of collective action fall back into old-fashioned authoritarian forms; lesbian separatist voices join those singing of "liberated" heterosexual marriage. The few women's studies programs in the U.S. with politics close to radical feminism exist in special – usually volatile – conditions.

In this paper, I will argue that though (I) radical feminism as an ideology is incompatible with academia, still (II) radical feminists can survive there. Finally I will show (III) that radical and liberal feminists can together work on reforms in the system through a women's studies program. I have no universal formula for how much a radical feminist can or must compromise her politics inside the institution, but in this paper I will describe some of the factors that have to be taken into account when such compromises are made.

I.

Radical feminism is inherently incompatible with present institutions of higher education in the United States, i.e., with both private and public colleges and universities. By "radical feminism" I mean the belief with the radical left that capitalism must be dismantled (that reform of the system is not enough) and, more important, the belief with cultural feminism that the biopsychological dimension of oppression (sexism and patriarchy) and not the economic one (the class society) is fundamental. Radical feminism thus defined is incompatible with academia in its assessment of individual and psychological values and in its social and political posture.

One of feminism's earliest efforts was to reject societal definitions and to support every woman's definition of herself, but when a woman reaches a college campus, she discovers that any vestige of self-definition remaining in herself or in others is subtly and systematically suppressed. Higher education is, after all, in the business of producing professionals (or wives of professionals), and there are a limited variety of dies from which they can be cut. As in any other factory, the jobs are specialized and standardized for efficient production: write the paper *this* way, type the letter *that*, dispense the funds *this* way, grade the student *that*. If the disabled student can't climb up to the French classrooms, then the disabled student can major in something besides French: elevators and ramps are too costly. Academia brooks only token deviance from its norms, just enough to demonstrate its democratic principles or its "innovative" atmosphere. It offers survival and acceptance (graduation, a job, prestige) to those who will quietly take their place on the assembly line or who are themselves willing to be mutilated into professionals.

Feminism, on the other hand, claims *wholeness* to be possible and desirable. Early on, the women's movement challenged the "myth of the half-person," i.e. the existence of something called "femininity" and something else called "masculinity" in human beings, and it deplored society's overvaluing of rational ("masculine") functions (objectivity, logic, analysis, linearity) to the near exclusion of nonrational ("feminine") functions (subjectivity, emotionality, intuition, synchronicity). Academia – even the woman's college – is based on the myth of the half-person and stubbornly continues to lay out its fragmented disciplines in patterns that perpetuate stereotypes of "men's work" and "women's work" (science-math-we-know-the-list versus nursing-teaching-and-we-know-that-list-too). Academia fears the unpredictability (read "uncontrollability") of nonrational functions. It suppresses countercultures by a simple formula for tolerance: permit nonrational experiences as long as the necessary rational judgments can finally be made. Dream explorations are dandy as long as students can be graded; committee work conducted with "organic flow" is fine as long as it yields an acceptable product and meets the deadline.

Radical feminism is opposed to hierarchies, and radical feminists speak often of "horizontal relationships." They suggest that human beings forsake the habit of governing one another and that experience and knowledge be freely shared. But the system of higher education in the United States, built as it is on supremacist principles, cannot tolerate such values. Trustees (wealthy and powerful) judge chancellors who judge presidents who judge vice-presidents who judge staff/deans/faculty who judge students who, in the grand flow of power from the top down, judge no one on campus and thus at home probably (if male) judge their mates, their children, and/or their pets. Everyone is caught in the squeeze and there is always another higher up to blame, always someone below to inflict anger and resentment upon.

Colleges and universities also foster professionalism, stressing not the virtues of acquiring knowledge and analyzing data but rather the greater value of the person who has done so (Ph.D., publications, grants, a "teacher") over those who have not (mere M.A., no publications, no grants, or "just a secretary"). The faculty preserves the exclusiveness and prestige of the club by allowing in only those who have suffered as we have and who, because of their indebtedness to us, will not threaten our power.

Radical feminism is incompatible with academia, furthermore, because the academy is racist and class-biased as well as sexist and is an institution serving an exploitative economic system. U.S. colleges and universities function according to the stratification, values, methods, and goals of the larger society, those of white-male-capitalism. Women's colleges barely begin to deal with racism or "ethnic" institutions with sexism. The higher the step on the administrative ladder, the paler and maler is the atmosphere, and the more economically comfortable. Faculty members operate in concert with administrators to guarantee a profitable quantity of prestigious research and/or human products to be speeded through graduation lines. The lower the step on the staff ladder, the darker and more female is the atmosphere, and in spite of longer working hours, the less economically comfortable or secure. Wages and benefits, only occasionally regulated by union clout, represent the minimum that the institution can escape with.

Student bodies, initially the consumer and thus the *sine qua non* of academic institutions, fail to achieve any real ethnic or sex balance and express dissatisfaction more or less according to times and issues. Even in the United States, where public education is theoretically guaranteed, colleges and universities are not open to public needs. If lack of money is not a barrier to going to college, another criterion is – evidence of adaptation to the standards of the dominant culture. Without that evidence – English literacy, analytic ability, white middle-class skills and values – the masses of candidates cannot enter, or if they enter, they cannot remain.

Radical feminism assumes that everyone has the right to the necessities of physical survival, good health, and education. It further assumes that everyone should receive in full the benefits of her/his own labor. It finds racism, like any bigoted stance against differences, to be intolerable. It understands capitalism to require profit and profit to require loss somewhere along the line. It thus understands institutions like the academy to be perpetuators of capitalist and racist values as well as of sexist ones.

Academia in the United States is an unnecessarily complex institution, alienated from its avowed work and alienated from the needs of the people it is supposed to serve. Mirroring corporate structure, academia more and more frequently seeks its own bureaucratic fulfillments – continued and exorbitant support of its administrators, maintenance of a staff constantly moving outward to encompass "auxiliary functions," provisions for an increasingly disenchanted faculty intent on survival and/or on individual research – often for the military-industrial complex. Though students are the institution's primary justification, they are far from its primary concern.

Academia as an institution will itself budge only in order to relieve pressure (as in, "Get those crazy women out of my office; tell them we'll review the case"); or to capitalize on a good thing (as in, "Give that new Women's Studies Coordinator a press conference and see to it the EEOC gets the news release," or "My god, she's *black* too. Then *make* a position if you have to").

Radical feminism is committed to the dismantling of present societal institutions and to the formation of organizations operated by and for the people to whom the goods/services go.

II.

While radical feminism is incompatible with academia, radical feminists, either as students, staff, or faculty members, are able to survive there. The circumstance of the radical feminist teacher is the easiest to analyze here as an example, but the analysis is adaptable to radical feminists in any academic capacity. Their situation is similar in some respects to that of all radicals who have survived in academia. Radical feminists, however, are different from other radicals in at least one way: their threat to the system is fundamentally bio-psychological in nature. They challenge, often unconsciously, the holders of power on the most intimate level. An ideology that suggests that change must come in both the class structure and in the attitudes and behavior of half the human species is likely to draw more intense fire once it is taken seriously than is socialist ideology, which by now shows its familiar and even legitimate face in most colleges and universities.

The radical feminist may, for two good reasons, choose to work in a college or university. First, she may have skills that the system will pay for and she may find fulfillment in using those skills. The drive for meaningful work is particularly strong among feminists. It seems high time that women threw off sisterly-bestowed guilt and affirmed the joys of an intellectual life if, and only if, of course, that life is connected to experience, if it carries within it the awareness of potentially collectivized woman-power, if it recognizes the political responsibility attached to its privileges.

The second and more complicated reason for working in the academy is that a radical feminist's political analysis may require that she use her skills within the system. There are, essentially, four avenues of political action for a woman who is committed to radical feminism: (a) reform within the system, (b) revolutionary action against the system, (c) work within organizations that are alternatives to the system, and (d) spiritual/apocalyptic wiping out of the system. If she seeks power within academia in order to challenge higher education's structures or policies, then she's working on reform within that institution but not working for the sake of reforming the institution itself. She may have chosen that option because she tried the others and found them inappropriate for her.

She couldn't, perhaps, even when her rage first struck, bring herself to "terrorist" acts — bombs or kidnappings. She did manage, however, some 3:00A.M. graffiti on the ROTC's armory, for which she spent too many fear-ridden nights. When she began serious political organizing, she found herself struggling in vain against her socialist brothers' (and sisters') rampant sexism until all her zeal wound itself into a tight little ball of counterproductive rage.

The approach of alternative organizations may have been no better for her. Her collective's feminist college failed because the women they wanted to involve were spending their earnings on food and rent while the women who had the money/time to come weren't the women they wanted to involve. Besides, too many students needed accredited degrees and teachers, accepting only minimal pay, began feeling ripped off. When she put her energy in-to the alternative high school, it worked so well that the city paper wrote it up and Ford bought it with a grant.

Disillusioned, she may have turned to the fourth approach, throwing up her hands and declaring that only some apocalypse, some spiritual reawakening among women, would save the world from capitalism/patriarchy. But that seemed a slow and in-dividualistic solution – carried out in the arms of Mother Earth, rocking to the phases of the moon – and even the most ardent of its advocates spoke at the earliest of a "hundred-year plan."

The radical feminist may be in academia, then, working on reform within the system, because other options have been eliminated. Or she may feel that all four approaches work together for change, providing buffers and protection for one another. Or she may see one of the other three as primary but her own role in academia as a part of a necessary buffer zone. Her choice in these cases to devote her energy to institutional changes is a matter of where she can best use her talents.

The radical feminist will operate in academia with the knowledge of the dangers and under certain preconditions. The dangers are familiar by now. First, her working there may inspire hope in the system – if Goldenrod College hired a radical feminist, it must not be so bad. Second, there's that persistent energy drain, not only to herself but possibly to the women who love and support her out-side the workplace. Third, she understands that whoever pays the piper calls the tune, that she can't be paid by one source and expect to remain totally accountable to another for her politics or morali-ty. Fourth, and most important, is the danger that the radical femi-nist will separate herself from other women, not just from students or the clerical staff whose lives, thought, and typing she will be called upon to judge, but also from her women colleagues who are supposed to sharpen their claws, along with her, in the time-honored tradition of competition and the "adversary mentality."

A woman in this situation can become even further divided from her movement sisters. Richer now than many of them in privilege and prestige as well as in salary, the radical feminist edging her way into academia finds the going tough. With each small victory, she reaps benefits – time for research, opportunities for grants, secretarial help, free materials, contracts with the publish-ing/media world. With such tools she can get the radical feminist message out to the public; but with an irony close to cynicism, she discovers that the more power she acquires, the less radical her translation of the message may tend to be. The subtle and insidious identification with the system has begun: there is always one more obstacle to her achievement of "secure" power with which she can fulfill her promise to "make room for others after I get inside." It can become harder and harder to maintain lines of trust with the autonomous women's movement.

Given these dangers, there are at least four prerequisites for the survival of the radical feminist in the academy. First, she must keep her radical politics intact. She must remind herself daily that neither she, nor her women's courses, nor any women's program, nor all the affirmative action in the world can ever save that institution; that indeed that institution can never meet the real human needs; that even a switch to all-female personnel would hardly alter the structure and value system of academia. She must remind herself regularly – like checking her oxygen supply on the moon – that her job is a matter of survival, not revolution; that transformation of the system will come from another source – perhaps from one of the other strategies or from a combination of strategies or from some strategy not yet evolved – but it will not come from the institution itself, nor from those working within it except in so far as they have bought precious time or made some footholds to be used when the time comes for the scaling of the walls from outside.

Second, she must know she cannot survive there alone, and, unfortunately, others who believe as she does are not common in the hallowed halls. She may find allies among other minority groups on her campus – in Ethnic Studies, in groups rallying around civil rights or ecology, among political organizers – but unless those allies believe as she does about the fundamental nature of sexism, they can be no more than part of a potential coalition. She will find other feminists there, but unless they believe as she does about the insidious relationship of sexism to capitalism, an alliance with them is limited, for they stand with the institution in its perpetuation of an inhuman economic system. For her survival, the radical feminist requires other radical feminists working there with her, all of them meeting regularly together, formulating strategies, making evaluations, praising and criticizing, even – let us say it aloud because it is so utterly true – holding and caring together.

Third, the radical feminist within the academy – particularly if she is associated with a women's studies program – will need the courage to risk and a keen sense of when to do so. When does she stop a negotiation to respond to the bigoted implications of a remark? How can she know that it is safe and worthwhile to do so under circumstance A or B but not under circumstance D or E? If she lets the remark pass, is it because it was good tactics to do so (he'll allocate money to women's courses), or because she's becoming identified with the "enemy" (she'll lose her job next year if she seems uppity)? But *is* that "identification with the enemy" or just "part of the strategy to keep the jobs of strong feminists" like herself?

Finally, the radical feminist working within the academy needs to assess daily the "state of my commitment." She must know that she can and will at any given time disengage from the institution. She has to be able to say: "I can walk away from you, Goldenrod State College, and never come back. I give you my energy because I choose to and today may be our last day together." Bold words. Easy to write, harder to say. Even harder to keep genuine in their meaning. The more emotionally and/or politically involved the radical feminist is with the institution, and the more power or prestige she has there, the harder it is to say the words. And the scarcer jobs and money get, the more the words tend to stick in her throat. Good reasons hold her there. ("How else do I support my children?" "I'm doing revolutionary work.") And some rationalizations. ("I have to hold my job so I can keep up my pledge to the feminist health collective." "I am necessary here; no one could do the job I do.") Yet the more difficult it is to leave, the more urgent it is that she be able to do so. She needs a device to remind her of her option: perhaps a morning ritual at the mirror, or a song she can hum on the bus, or a slip of paper that falls out of her billfold (in Celtic maybe, or in code) reading, "You don't have to be doing this, you know."

All her survival tactics – keeping her politics intact, holding to other radical feminist support, maintaining a sense of risk, knowing she can detach herself from the institution – seem ultimately to be a matter of being aware of what she is doing while she is doing it, a matter of sustaining a constant state of reflection upon her actions even while those actions are going on.

III.

Some women, academics all their lives, find that their radical feminism "comes upon them" in the course of their careers. Other radical feminists are in touch with their politics before they choose academia. Hundreds of radical feminists associate with the institutions of higher education in this country strictly for survival (a degree, a job); they hack out that tiny but inhabitable environment that will be safe as long as they keep a low profile. Others, however, work for some explicit meeting of women's needs, either in an existing women's studies program or in the initiation of similar projects and courses. Though she may fear that institutionalizing her politics will devitalize them, the radical feminist won't gain much by declining to participate in that process. Women's studies courses will continue to develop, and she must figure out how this phenomenon may best serve radical interests.

Liberal feminism places a high value on tolerance and individual rights. Moreover, since the liberal feminist characteristically believes that with sexual equality the system can be reformed, the actions acceptable to her as goals may often be the same reforms that are acceptable to the radical feminist as strategies. For example, equal rank for women teachers may be for liberal feminists a goal and for radical feminists a step along the way that will give women more power for future showdowns. This overlap of concerns makes it possible for a radical feminist to work with liberals on specific reforms within academia, most particularly in women's studies programs.

From a radical feminist perspective, a women's studies program is responsible for providing students with an education first in radicalism, and second in the patriarchal/capitalist tools which will enable them to function in society as feminist professionals. To fail at the first of these tasks is to pump into society uncritical automatons and female masters of the consumer system who, at best, envision fifty women in the Senate and clamor for affirmative action. To fail at the second is to cast into the world battalions of women whose lives have been turned upside down but who do not have skills to go much beyond wringing their hands and cursing the system.

Radical women do not find their liberal sisters opposing them in either of these tasks. The very nature of liberalism encourages all points of view, and though she may not champion or like radical postures, the liberal feminist usually stands strong in her support of the radicals' right to representation. It is only when radicals, characteristically much less tolerant, become more demanding ("all our courses should be anticapitalist in their assumption") that serious conflict begins.

Radical and liberal women have a common interest in creating feminist professionals. I think of a "professional" as a person who *has* status but who does not necessarily *seek* status; the arrogance that accompanies status-seeking is professional*ism*. In radical feminist circles, some of us have too often criticized a professional for having particular skills or knowledge which have been denied to others of us. But we must understand that there's nothing wrong with skills and knowledge – even patriarchal skills and knowledge – and that in a just society everyone would have access to them. We need what academia is built to produce: professional engineers, CPAs, teachers, biologists, lawyers who are also feminists. Our hope, of course, is that they will be *radical* feminist professionals.

A women's studies student must be given the opportunity to learn how to survive – to create her own job, to take over a position within the system, and to live with the schizophrenia that often accompanies the job she gets. Part of her education and preparation should help her appreciate the devalued "feminine" qualities of intuition, emotionality, subjectivity, and nonlinear thinking. But those qualities alone are not sufficient for a whole person any more than the so-called masculine qualities (logic, reason, objectivity, linear thinking) are. Women need analytic skills (speaking, writing, critical reading, and thinking) in order to survive, and we do students an injustice if we fail to insist on their acquiring such skills. Analytic tools are valuable, even essential, to any person seriously committed to changing society. We can't understand the complexity of our lives if we can't evaluate what we read, if we can't create new options out of our reflections on experience. We are lost as strategists for the movement unless we can think critically and articulate feelings and thoughts. The capacity to categorize, to break ideas into parts, is an evil only when it fails to allow for any other kind of thinking.

If it is sin to feel that rush of confidence, the tangible rise of self-esteem that accompanies the mastering of computer programming or the intricacies of law, then let's sin and rejoice. Part of the baby we have to rescue from the patriarchal bath water is the exercise of the Greek concept of excellence – to be speakers of words as well as doers of deeds. However vivid our visions are of a world where the tyranny of words and analysis is ended, it's still true that we will survive to reach that world only by making those tools work for us in the present. Women's studies graduates will do little to change the pain of the world if they are not radicalized, but if they leave academia without training in survival within the system, without the tools to think about change, then radicalization will have been for nothing.

Since the academy is the primary training ground for the personnel of an oppressive society — the factory owners, the corporation executives, the medical men, the clergy, the people who will have some minimum of control over their own lives — it is one of the most vital workplaces for radical reform activity. When she commits herself to "producing" radical feminist professionals, the radical feminist teacher can share with students the danger and the pain of living with the contradiction between her politics and her own job in academia. Her students will have to deal with the same contradiction, and together they can explore concrete ways to work and survive with that contradiction.

The second task of a women's studies program, from the radical feminist's point of view, is the maintenance of the program for as long as it is appropriate. Survival of a women's studies program means survival of a bubble of freedom for liberal and radical feminists. The bubble balances precariously between total co-optation by the institution (the liberal tilt) and the repression that could occur if it became too overtly threatening (the radical tilt). In maintaining a tension between these two dangers, there are large territories of agreement among liberal and radical women. They may agree, for instance, that the program must costume itself to fit the institution's dress code: eagerness to "smash the state" must be clothed in euphemisms; overt suggestions that lesbian love or celibacy are pathways of liberation for women must be couched delicately or presented only as "alternatives."

From the radical feminist's perspective, the struggle is not so much to make the program itself radical as to maintain the maximum amount of radical input possible. Except in rare cases (usually where courses and program are largely student-run), the drift of women's studies is toward greater and greater institutionalization and co-optation. When a program exists within hierarchical structures and patriarchal practices, it can probably be only liberal at best, even if its personnel is a hundred percent radical feminist.

There's good reason, then, for radical feminists to take advantage of the liberal stand for tolerance and individual freedom. The best way to guarantee that radical voices will be heard is to work for a program of variety, full of feminists of all persuasions (cultural, socialist, liberal, radical, lesbian, etc.). The radical feminist's role is to watchdog the compromises. She has to raise her voice, for instance, when in the effort to prove the legitimacy of the program, consciousness-raising groups are forsaken for more rigorous academic "content," or when a tight grading policy threatens irrevocably to widen the gap between students and teacher, or when a faculty is too lily-white. She has to see to it that the campus affirmative action office will be concerned about more than just professional women.

While the radicals in a program resist any restrictions from the institution, the liberals – perhaps out of the same tolerance that sanctions radical participation – tend to accept such restrictions more readily. "It won't hurt us," runs the liberal argument, "to comply with the directive to hire only Ph.D.'s." The radicals retort: "*We are the judges of a woman's qualifications and we'll hire kindergarteners if that's what we want!*" The issues underlying this exchange – program autonomy and the proper qualifications of a women's studies teacher – represent the controversies around which struggles are bound to arise.

Where's the bottom line? When does the radical cease struggling? What's the point at which the program begins serving the system better than it serves the women in it? When we apply for a grant from Standard Oil? When a course in lesbianism is turned down? Whan a Fascinating Woman course is proposed? Though the variables influencing that decision are endless, often one of the biggest factors, economic pressure, actually serves a useful function: radicals who in softer times might abandon the program early on to its liberal fate find that job scarcity raises their tolerance for compromise. Hard times make us stay, make us struggle and learn.

The third task of a women's studies program is to make permanent incremental changes within the institution – changes which will be useful to women. Such changes might be in faculty or administrative positions, in some commitment to budget allocation, or in a long-term committee appointment. It is essential that any such openings, once gained, remain as footholds for women where they may rotate or succeed each other. In this goal the liberal joins her radical sister, believing that ultimately the entire system can be humanized in this fashion. Though the radical woman has no such hope, she can still work to maintain the small inroads that women make in the institution.

The conflicts here revolve around questions of who will fill the positions created. The liberal's commitment to equality and greater visibility for women often makes her more concerned with the appointment of "a woman" (any woman) than with the politics of the candidate. Radicals, believing that sex (like race or class background or lifestyle) is no determiner of politics, hold out for someone (possibly even a man) with high radical feminist consciousness and commitment. If small permanent openings are filled by opportunistic women, by gynophobic (woman-fearing, lesbian-fearing) women, or by women without the liberal's tolerance for variety, then the energy put into creating that reform will have been turned against us.

The fourth task of a women's studies program is fundamental to each of the others: creating an environment and a process for struggle and change. In academia, any difference between people can, at the will of the institution, be intensified. Professional women with middle-class backgrounds are particularly vulnerable to such pressure and the polarization that results. We have fought to avoid the perils of socialization – such as the habit of giving more while taking less – and rather than backslide into volunteerism and martyrdom, we change "Approve me," "Define me" to "Move over." In so doing, we unfortunately find ourselves pitted against each other.

Take any group of women, dose them up on competitiveness, and let them practice new-found ego-assertiveness in the preheated oven of academia. It is no surprise that the casserole explodes: feminist teachers seek student followings; students sharing power and even warm moments with a teacher on the women's studies board suddenly find themselves being graded by that teacher; secretaries resent women faculty members who turn out to be more demanding than men; nontraditional hiring committees seethe in the turmoil of class differences or a gay-straight split; a kind of "in" feminist professionalism develops among women who have published ("cashing in on their students"), or who have participated in national events, and that "elitism" tacitly excludes those who have not done these things; students deny that their credibility with faculty should depend on their mastery of traditional academic skills; amid cries of "racism" or "male-identification," uneasiness about ethnic minorities escalates into tooth-and-nail battles; and disabled women confront able-bodied chauvinists for failing to make meetings accessible to those in wheelchairs. It's a wonder that women's studies programs have survived, much less grown.

When it comes to disagreement or decision making, the patriarchy has offered us two alternatives: either fight it out or talk it out. The more acceptable of the two − talking − has traditionally been at best a matter of reasoned discourse, a dialectical process which moves from mutually acceptable statements to acceptable conclusions. Though abstract and disconnected from feelings, dialectic provides a "search for truth," a principled use of "good reason in controversy." We have need of dialectic in our struggles with one another. Our differences as feminists are not just personality conflicts, though they may involve that too. There *are* issues at stake. Political positions can be delineated. Arguments can be formulated. Circumstances can "make sense."

What the dialectical process lacks, feminism seems to have in abundance: feelings, connections with personal experience, the grounding of ideas in reality, and a regard for unconscious motives and processes. If we can use these gifts and strengthen our analytical side, we can begin communicating more effectively.

The power dynamic is exacerbated by the fact that some women, usually teachers, have more skills than others for coping with the institution's demands and practices: with the highly-refined art of promise-delay-renege, for instance; or with the condescension, the humorous apology, the question-hedging, the nit-picking, the buck-passing, and always, of course, the subtle sexist flattery. Because they have these skills, more power centers around them. When there are two rush jobs, No. 1 collating the newsletter and No. 2 negotiating with an administrator, who does which? How and when do those who can only do No. 1 learn to do No. 2? How can those who can do No. 1 and No. 2 learn how not to work alone ("I can do it quicker myself") and still be efficient? How is it possible in this hierarchy to place an equal value on all work?

On top of this, the public image of the program is constantly at issue. If there are too many visible lesbians, then straight Third World women may avoid association with women's studies; if there are too many exclusively heterosexual projects, then lesbians may feel unwelcome; too much Marxist language, and middle-American women are turned off; too many women in their early twenties, and older women aren't interested; too much "spirituality," and socialist women turn their backs. I believe there's a process, still in an embryonic stage, developing among feminists in women's studies which may unite the academician's rational discourse with the emotional, relational qualities of feminist experience. This new process has not yet been adequately explored or described,* yet there's evidence that women of vastly different political persuasions are participating in it.

Although there are women's studies programs which are totally co-opted and have no radical input, a healthy number of programs work with cooperation among radical and liberal feminists. In these, liberal feminists have come to doubt the system that they believe can be reformed, and they are often willing to make rigorous demands of it. They are discovering in themselves a respect for their own rage and the rage of other women – not an ingredient that is compatible with their usual tolerance. Under radical pressure, liberal women can question and deal with the professionalism and hierarchical attitudes they've fought so hard to achieve as women in a man's system. Radical women, for their part, are learning the satisfaction of concrete accomplishments, however small (a reform is not a revolution but it's a lot more tangible in the here and now). Further, radicals can come to understand that liberal feminism is not just a stage along life's way but a viable political position: they can stop implying that today's liberal is necessarily tomorrow's radical. They frequently have come to the realization that some feminists consciously change from radical to liberal politics.

Since programs do move toward institutionalization and a more conservative mold, it's incumbent on the liberal feminist to put her power behind radical issues and radical feminists, thus to ensure their *presence* on the academic scene. She needs to acknowledge the value of a radical presence in the program even when such a presence challenges her own politics. But not even a good liberal feminist is going to beat the bushes for radical participants. The radical woman will have to come on her own to the hallowed halls.

---

* The process, the subject of another paper, involves a coming together in *dialogue* of the techniques of fair fighting (used in resolving interpersonal conflict) and those of dialectic. For a political difference to be engaged, each party must (1) seek not to change the other but to contribute to an atmosphere in which change (for both parties) can take place; (2) feel equal in power to the other; and (3) be willing on the deepest level to yield her position to the other. What emerges is not win-and-lose but some third thing, unexpected by either party and acceptable to both.

She has hard work to do there, not just in radicalizing the atmosphere or in providing students with a twofold education. Her work there is not simply to watchdog the program's maintenance or the small changes in the system. The hardest and most crucial work for the radical feminist is to learn patience and tolerance for the process of struggle and change through which she and other women will deal with the realities of their different political positions.

As radical feminists we'll never be comfortable in academia. We can't expect completely to transform it or even to find in it an open political arena. If we work or study there, we'll have to be satisfied with compromises and small changes, and we'll be opening ourselves to constant frustration, a host of dangers, and even some deep pain. But if we do cast our lot with that time-honored institution, there are satisfactions and joys too. As a place to put to work our skills and our politics, academia is as good as any other. It's satisfying to learn, and to learn through teaching, and to be in an atmosphere where knowledge is available. It's especially rewarding to be part of a place where women's lives are changing, in which their pain is becoming more manageable and their strengths more useful. It is good to be working with women. Period.

NOTES

I'm particularly indebted to the following people/articles/occasions:

The Women Studies Committee of San Francisco State University.

The Women's Studies Group of the preconstitutional San Francisco Women's Union.

The California State University, Sacramento, May 1973 Women's Studies Conference, "Women Studies: Survival in the Seventies."

A position paper with Jane Gurko for the San Francisco State University Women Studies Program, December 1, 1976.

The Women's Studies division of the Western Social Science Association's convention in Denver, April 22-24, 1977, particularly Anne Boylan of the University of New Mexico's History Department.

Charlotte Bunch, "The Reform Tool Kit," in *Quest: A Feminist Quarterly*, volume I, no. 1 (Summer 1974).

Ann Leffler, Dair L. Gillespie, and Elinor Ratner, "Academic Feminists and the Women's Movement," unpublished, April 1973.

Cynthia Secor, "Cynthia Secor of HERS – Mid-Atlantic," interview in *Anima: An Experimental Journal*, volume II, no. 1 (Fall Equinox 1975).

Women's Studies Program: Three Years of Struggle, publication of Inside the Beast, California State University at San Diego, May 1973.

The Politics of
Black Women's Studies*

by Gloria T. Hull and Barbara Smith

MERELY TO USE the term "Black women's studies" is an act charged with political significance. At the very least, the combining of these words to name a discipline means taking the stance that Black women exist – and exist positively – a stance that is in direct opposition to most of what passes for culture and thought on the North American continent. To use the term and to act on it in a white-male world is an act of political courage.

Like any politically disenfranchised group, Black women could not exist consciously until we began to name ourselves. The growth of Black women's studies is an essential aspect of that process of naming. The very fact that Black women's studies describes something that is really happening, a burgeoning field of study, indicates that there are political changes afoot which have made possible that growth. To examine the politics of Black women's studies means to consider not only what it is but why it is and what it can be. Politics is used here in its widest sense to mean any situation/relationship of differential power between groups or individuals.

Four issues seem important for a consideration of the politics of Black women's studies: (1) the general political situation of Afro-American women and the bearing this has had upon the im-

---

* This article was originally written as the Introduction to *All the Women Are White, All the Blacks Are Men, But Some of Us Are Brave,* edited by Gloria T. Hull, Patricia Bell Scott, and Barbara Smith (Feminist Press, Old Westbury, New York, 1982).

plementation of Black women's studies; (2) the relationship of Black women's studies to Black feminist politics and the Black feminist movement; (3) the necessity for Black women's studies to be feminist, radical, and analytical; and (4) the need for teachers of Black women's studies to be aware of our problematic political positions in the academy and of the potentially antagonistic conditions under which we must work.

The political position of Black women in America has been, in a single word, embattled. The extremity of our oppression has been determined by our very biological identity. The horrors we have faced historically and continue to face as Black women in a white-male-dominated society have implications for every aspect of our lives, including what white men have termed "the life of the mind." That our oppression as Black women can take forms specifically aimed at discrediting our intellectual power is best illustrated through the words of a "classic" American writer.

In 1932 William Faulkner saw fit to include this sentence in a description of a painted sign in his novel *Light in August*. He wrote:

> But now and then a negro nursemaid with her white charges would loiter there and spell them [the letters on the sign] aloud with *that vacuous idiocy of her idle and illiterate kind.*[1] [italics ours]

Faulkner's white-male assessment of Black female intellect and character, stated as a mere aside, has fundamental and painful implications for a consideration of the whole question of Black women's studies and the politics that shape its existence. Not only does his remark typify the extremely negative ways in which Afro-American women have been portrayed in literature, scholarship, and the popular media, but it also points to the destructive white-male habit of categorizing all who are not like themselves as their intellectual and moral inferiors. The fact that the works in which such oppressive images appear are nevertheless considered American "masterpieces" indicates the cultural-political value system in which Afro-American women have been forced to operate and which, when possible, they have actively opposed.

The politics of Black women's studies are totally connected to the politics of Black women's lives in this country. The opportunities for Black women to carry out autonomously defined investigations of self in a society which through racial, sexual, and class oppression systematically denies our existence have been by definition limited.

As a major result of the historical realities which brought us enslaved to this continent, we have been kept separated in every way possible from recognized intellectual work. Our legacy as chattel, as sexual slaves as well as forced laborers, would adequately explain why most Black women are, to this day, far away from the centers of academic power and why Black women's studies has just begun to surface in the latter part of the 1970s. What our multilayered oppression does not explain are the ways in which we have created and maintained our own intellectual traditions as Black women, without either the recognition or the support of white-male society.

The entry entitled "A Slave Woman Runs a Midnight School" in Gerda Lerner's *Black Women in White America: A Documentary History* embodies this creative, intellectual spirit, coupled with a practical ability to make something out of nothing.

> [In Natchez, Louisiana, there were] two schools taught by colored teachers. One of these was a slave woman who had taught a midnight school for a year. It was opened at eleven or twelve o'clock at night, and closed at two o'clock a.m. . . . Milla Granson, the teacher, learned to read and write from the children of her indulgent master in her old Kentucky home. Her number of scholars was twelve at a time and when she had taught these to read and write she dismissed them, and again took her apostolic number and brought them up to the extent of her ability, until she had graduated hundreds. A number of them wrote their own passes and started for Canada . . . .
>
> At length her night-school project leaked out, and was for a time suspended; but it was not known that seven of the twelve years subsequent to leaving Kentucky had been spent in this work. Much excitement over her night-school was produced. The subject was discussed in their legislature, and a bill was passed, that it should not be held illegal for a slave to teach a slave . . . . She not only [re]opened her night-school, but a Sabbath-school . . . . Milla Granson used as good language as any of the white people.[2]

This document illuminates much about Black women educators and thinkers in America. Milla Granson learned to read and write through the exceptional indulgence of her white masters. She used her skills not to advance her own status, but to help her fellow slaves, and this under the most difficult circumstances. The act of a Black person teaching and sharing knowledge was viewed as naturally threatening to the power structure. The knowledge she conveyed had a politically and materially transforming function, that is, it empowered people to gain freedom.

Milla Granson and her pupils, like Black people throughout our history here, made the greatest sacrifices for the sake of learning. As opposed to "lowering" educational standards, we have had to create our own. In a totally antagonistic setting, we have tried to keep our own visions clear and have passed on the most essential kind of knowledge, that which enabled us to survive. As Alice Walker writes of our artist-thinker foremothers:

> They dreamed dreams that no one knew – not even themselves, in any coherent fashion – and saw visions no one could understand . . . . They waited for a day when the unknown thing that was in them would be made known; but guessed, somehow in their darkness, that on the day of their revelation they would be long dead.[3]

The birth of Black women's studies is perhaps the day of revelation these women wished for. Again, this beginning is not unconnected to political events in the world outside university walls.

The inception of Black women's studies can be directly traced to three significant political movements of the twentieth century. These are the struggles for Black liberation and women's liberation, which themselves fostered the growth of Black and women's studies, and the more recent Black feminist movement, which is just beginning to show its strength. Black feminism has made a space for Black women's studies to exist and, through its commitment to all Black women, will provide the basis for its survival.

The history of all of these movements is unique, yet interconnected. The Black movements of the 1950s, 1960s, and 1970s brought about unprecedented social and political change, not only in the lives of Black people, but for all Americans. The early women's movement gained inspiration from the Black movement as well as an impetus to organize autonomously both as a result of the demands for all-Black organizations and in response to sexual hierarchies in Black-and white-male political groupings. Black women were a part of that early women's movement, as were working-class women of all races. However, for many reasons – including the increasing involvement of single, middle-class white women (who often had the most time to devote to political work), the divisive campaigns of the white-male media, and the movement's serious inability to deal with racism – the women's movement became largely and apparently white.

The effect that this had upon the nascent field of women's studies was predictably disastrous. Women's studies courses, usually taught in universities, which could be considered elite institutions just by virtue of the populations they served, focused almost exclusively upon the lives of white women. Black studies, which was much too often male-dominated, also ignored Black women. Here is what a Black woman wrote about her independent efforts to study Black women writers in the early 1970s:

... At this point I am doing a lot of reading on my own of Black women writers ever since I discovered Zora Neale Hurston. *I've had two Black Lit courses and in neither were any women writers discussed.* So now I'm doing a lot of independent research since the Schomburg Collection is so close.[4] [italics ours]

Because of white women's racism and Black men's sexism, there was no room in either area for a serious consideration of the lives of Black women. And even when they have considered Black women, white women usually have not had the capacity to analyze racial politics and Black culture, and Black men have remained oblivious or resistant to the implications of sexual politics in Black women's lives.

Only a Black *and* feminist analysis can sufficiently comprehend the materials of Black women's studies; and only a creative Black feminist perspective will enable the field to expand. A viable Black feminist movement will also lend its political strength to the development of Black women's studies courses, programs, and research, and to the funding they require. Black feminism's total commitment to the liberation of Black women and its recognition of Black women as valuable and complex human beings will provide the analysis and spirit for the most incisive work on Black women. Only a feminist, pro-woman perspective that acknowledges the reality of sexual oppression in the lives of Black women, as well as the oppression of race and class, will make Black women's studies the transformer of consciousness it needs to be.

Women's studies began as a radical response to feminists' realization that knowledge of ourselves has been deliberately kept from us by institutions of patriarchal "learning." Unfortunately, as women's studies has become both more institutionalized and at the same time more precarious within traditional academic structures, the radical life-changing vision of what women's studies can accomplish has constantly been diminished in exchange for acceptance, respectability, and the career advancement of individuals. This trend in women's studies is a trap that Black women's studies cannot afford to fall into. Because we are so oppressed as Black women, every aspect of our fight for freedom, including teaching and writing about ourselves, must in some way further our liberation. Because of the particular history of Black feminism in relation to Black women's studies, especially the fact that the two movements are still new and have evolved nearly simultaneously, much of the current teaching, research, and writing about Black women is not feminist, is not radical, and unfortunately is not always even analytical. Naming and describing our experience are important initial steps, but not alone sufficient to get us where we need to go. A descriptive approach to the lives of Black women, a "great Black women" in history or literature approach, or any traditional male-identified approach will not result in intellectually groundbreaking or politically transforming work. We cannot change our lives by teaching solely about "exceptions" to the ravages of white-male oppression. Only through exploring the experience of supposedly "ordinary" Black women whose "unexceptional" actions enabled us and the race to survive, will we be able to begin to develop an overview and an analytical framework for understanding the lives of Afro-American women.

Courses that focus on issues which concretely and materially affect Black women are ideally what Black women's studies/feminist studies should be about. Courses should examine such topics as the sexual violence we suffer in our own communities; the development of Black feminist economic analysis that will reveal for the first time Black women's relationship to American capitalism; the situation of Black women in prison and the connection between their incarceration and our own; the social history of Black women's domestic work; and the investigation of Black women's mental and physical health in a society whose "final solution" for us and our children is death.

It is important to consider also that although much research about these issues needs to be done, much insight about them can be arrived at through studying the literary and historical documents that already exist. Anyone familiar with Black literature and Black women writers who is not intimidated by what their reading reveals should be able to develop a course on rape, battering, and incest as viewed by Black female and male authors. Analysis of these patriarchal crimes could be obtained from the substantial body of women's movement literature on the subject of violence against women, some of which would need to be criticized for its conscious and unconscious racism.

In addition, speakers from a local rape crisis center and a refuge for battered women could provide essential firsthand information. The class and instructor could work together to synthesize the materials and to develop a much-needed Black feminist analysis of violence against Black women. Developing such a course illustrates what politically based, analytic Black feminist studies can achieve. It would lead us to look at familiar materials in new and perhaps initially frightening ways, but ways that will reveal truths that will change the lives of living Black women, including our own. Black feminist issues — the real life issues of Black women — should be integral to our conceptions of subject matter, themes, and topics for research.

That politics has much to do with the practice of Black women's studies is perhaps most clearly illustrated by the lack of positive investigations of Black lesbianism in any area of current Black scholarship. The fact that a course in Black lesbian studies has, to our knowledge, yet to be taught has absolutely nothing to do with the "nonexistence" of Black lesbian experience and everything to do with fear and refusal to acknowledge that this experience does in fact exist.[5] Black woman-identified-women have existed in our communities throughout our history, both in Africa and in America. That the subject of Black lesbianism and male homosexuality is greeted with fearful silence or verbalized homophobia results, of course, from the politics of institutionalized heterosexuality under patriarchy, that is, the politics of male domination.

A letter written in 1957 by Black playwright and political activist Lorraine Hansberry to *The Ladder,* a pioneering lesbian periodical, makes clear this connection between homophobia and the sexual oppression of all women. She wrote:

> I think it is about time that equipped women began to take on some of the ethical questions which a male-dominated culture has produced and *dissect and analyze them quite to pieces in a serious fashion.* It is time that 'half the human race' had something to say about the nature of its existence. Otherwise — without revised basic thinking — the woman intellectual is likely to find herself trying to draw conclusions — *moral conclusions* — based on acceptance of a social moral superstructure which has never admitted to the equality of

women and is therefore immoral itself. As per marriage, as per sexual practices, as per the rearing of children, etc. *In this kind of work there may be women to emerge who will be able to formulate a new and possible concept that homosexual persecution and condemnation has at its roots not only social ignorance, but a philosophically active anti-feminist dogma.* But that is but a kernel of a speculative embryonic idea improperly introduced here.[6] [italics ours]

Hansberry's statement is an amazingly prescient anticipation of current accomplishments of lesbian-feminist political analysis. It is also amazing because it indicates Hansberry's feminist and lesbian commitments, which have previously been ignored and which will best be investigated through a Black feminist analysis of Black women's studies. Most amazing of all is that Hansberry was speaking, without knowing it, directly to us.

An accountable Black women's studies would value all Black women's experiences. Yet for a Black woman to teach a course on Black lesbians would probably, in most universities, spell career suicide, not to mention the personal and emotional repercussions she would inevitably face. Even to teach Black women's studies from a principled Black feminist perspective might endanger many Black women scholars' situations in their schools and departments. Given the difficulty and risks involved in teaching information and ideas which the white-male academy does not recognize or approve, it is important for Black women teaching in the white-male academy always to realize the inherently contradictory and antagonistic nature of the conditions under which we do our work. These working conditions exist in a structure not only elitist and racist, but deeply misogynist. Often our position as Black women is dishearteningly tenuous within university walls: we are literally the last hired and the first fired. Despite popular myths about the advantages of being "double-tokens," our salaries, promotions, tenure, and general level of acceptance in the white-male "community of scholars" are all quite grim. The current backlash against affirmative action is also disastrous for all Black women workers, including college teachers.

As Black women we belong to two groups that have been defined as congenitally inferior in intellect, that is, Black people and women. The paradox of Black women's position is well illustrated by the fact that white-male academics, like Schockley and Jensen — who work in the very same academy — are trying to prove "scientifically" our racial and sexual inferiority. Their overt or tacit question is, "How could a being who combines two mentally deficient biological identities do anything with her intellect, her nonexistent powers of mind?" Or, to put it more bluntly, "How can someone who looks like my maid (or my fantasy of my maid) teach me anything?" As Lorraine Bethel succinctly states this dilemma:

> The codification of Blackness and femaleness by whites and males is seen in the terms "thinking like a woman" and "acting like a nigger" which are based on the premise that there are typically Black and female ways of acting and thinking. Therefore, the most pejorative concept in the white/male world view would be that of thinking and acting like a "nigger woman."[7]

Our credibility as autonomous beings and thinkers in the white-male-run intellectual establishment is constantly in question and rises and falls in direct proportion to the degree to which we continue to act and think like our Black female selves, rejecting the modes of bankrupt white-male Western thought. Intellectual "passing" is a dangerously limiting solution for Black women, a nonsolution that makes us invisible women. It will also not give us the emotional and psychological clarity we need to do the feminist research in Black women's studies that will transform our own and our sisters' lives.

Black women scholars must maintain a constantly militant and critical stance toward the places where we must do our work. We must also begin to devise ways to break down our terrible isolation in the white-male academy and to form the kinds of support networks Black women have always formed to help each other survive. We need to find ways to create our own places – conferences, institutes, journals, and institutions – where we can be the Black women we are and gain respect for the amazing depth of perception that our identity brings.

To do the work involved in creating Black women's studies requires not only intellectual intensity, but the deepest courage. Ideally, this is passionate and committed research, writing, and teaching whose purpose is to question everything. Coldly "objective" scholarship that changes nothing is not what we strive for. "Objectivity" is itself an example of the reification of white-male thought. What could be less objective than the totally white-male studies which are still considered "knowledge"? Everything that human beings participate in is ultimately subjective and biased, and there is nothing inherently wrong with that. The bias that Black women's studies must consider as primary is the knowledge that will save Black women's lives.

BLACK WOMEN'S STUDIES AS AN ACADEMIC AREA

Higher education for Black women has always been of serious concern to the Black community.[8] Recognition that education was a key mechanism for challenging racial and economic oppression created an ethic that defined education for women as important as education for men. Nearly 140 Black women attended Oberlin College between 1835 and 1865, prior to Emancipation, and Mary Jane Patterson, the first Afro-American woman to receive a B.A., graduated from Oberlin in 1862. The only two Black women's colleges still in existence, Spelman in Atlanta, Georgia, founded in 1881, and Bennett in Greensboro, North Carolina, founded in 1873, played a significant role in the education of Black women, as did those Black colleges founded as coeducational institutions at a time when most private white colleges were still single-sex schools.

Although Black women have long been involved in this educational work and also in creating self-conscious representations of ourselves using a variety of artistic forms, Black women's studies as an autonomous discipline only began to emerge in the late 1970s. At the moment, it is impossible to gauge definitely how much activity is going on in the field. There have been few statistical studies which have mapped the growth of women's studies generally, and there have been no surveys or reports to establish the breadth and depth of research and teaching on Black women.

One of the few sources providing some documentation of the progress of Black women's studies is *Who's Who and Where in Women's Studies,* published in 1974 by The Feminist Press. This book lists a total of 4,658 women's studies courses taught by 2,964 teachers. Approximately forty-five (or less than one percent) of the courses listed focus on Black women. About sixteen of these are survey courses, ten are literature courses, four are history courses, and the rest are in various disciplines. The largest number of courses taught on Black women was in Afro-American and Black Studies departments (approximately nineteen) and only about three courses on Black women were being taught for women's studies departments. Approximately nine Black colleges were offering women's studies courses at that time. None of the forty-five courses used the words "feminist" or "Black feminist" in the title.

More recent relevant comment can be found in Florence Howe's *Seven Years Later: Women's Studies Programs in 1976.*[9] She states:

> . . . Like the social movement in which it is rooted, women's studies has tended to be predominantly white and middle-class, in terms of both faculty and curriculum, and there is a perceived need for a corrective . . . . The major strategy developed thus far is the inclusion of separate courses on Black Women, Chicanas, Third World Women, etc. Such courses, taught by minority women, have appeared on most campuses with the cooperation and cross-listing of various ethnic studies programs. For the most part, it is women's studies that has taken the initiative for this development.

However, as Howe proceeds to point out, more seriously committed and fundamental strategies are needed to achieve a truly multiracial approach.

Clearly, then, if one looks for "hard data" concerning curriculum relating to Black women in the existing studies of academic institutions, we are seemingly nonexistent. And yet, impressionistically and experientially it is obvious that more and more study is being done about Black women and, even more importantly, it is being done with an increasing consciousness of the impact of sexual-racial politics on Black women's lives. One thinks, for instance, of Alice Walker's groundbreaking course on Black women writers at Wellesley College in 1972, and how work of all sorts by and about Black women writers has since blossomed into a visible Black female literary "renaissance."

It seems that after survey courses (with titles like "The Black Woman in America") which provide an overview, most courses on Black women concentrate on literature, followed by social sciences and history as the next most popular areas. An early type of course that was taught focused upon "famous" individual Black women. Partly because at the beginning it is necessary to answer the basic question of exactly who there is to talk about, this is the way that materials on oppressed people have often been approached initially. Printed information written about or by successful individuals is also much more readily available, and analytical overviews of the field do not yet exist. Nevertheless, such focusing on exceptional figures is a direct outgrowth of centuries of concerted suppression and invisibility. When the various kinds of pedagogical resources which should exist eventually come into being, teachers will be able to move beyond this ultimately class-biased strategy.

The core of courses on Black women at colleges and universities has grown slowly but steadily during the 1970s. And increasing interest in Black feminism and recognition of Black women's experiences point to the 1980s as the time when Black women's studies will come into its own. Perhaps this may be seen less in teaching than in the plethora of other activity in Black women's scholarship. Some essential books have begun to appear: the Zora Neale Hurston reader, *I Love Myself When I Am Laughing* . . . (Old Westbury, N.Y.: The Feminist Press, 1979); and Sharon Harley and Rosalyn Terborg-Penn's *The Afro-American Woman: Struggles and Images* (Port Washington, N.Y.: Kennikat, 1978), to name only two. Special issues of feminist magazines – like *Conditions* and *Heresies* – are being devoted to Black/Third World women. Workshop sessions and entire conferences on Black women (e.g., The Third World Lesbian Writers Conference in New York City and the National Council of Negro Women's national research conference on Black women held in Washington, D.C. – both in 1979) have been organized.

Other indications that Black/Third World women are talking to each other and carving out ways of thinking, researching, writing, and teaching include the founding of *Sojourner: A Third World Women's Research Newsletter,* in 1977, and the founding, in 1978, of the Association of Black Women Historians, which publishes the newsletter *Truth.* Finally, research and dissertations by young Black female scholars for whom the developments of the past few years have opened the option of studying Black women have begun to produce the knowledge that Black women's studies will continue to need. These scholars – many of them activists – are working on a wide range of subjects – including revising the Black woman's role in slavery, recovering Black female oral and popular culture, and revamping the reputations of earlier Black women authors.

At this point, we are on the threshold – still in our "Phase One," as it were. There are still far too few courses and far too few Black women employed in institutions where they might have the opportunity to teach them. Although people involved in women's studies are becoming increasingly aware of issues of race, the majority of white women teachers and administrators have barely begun the process of self-examination which must precede productive action to change this situation. The confronting of sexism in Black studies and in the Black community in general is a mostly unfought battle, although it is evident from recent Black publications – e.g., *Black Scholar's* Black Sexism Debate issue – that the opposing anti-Black-feminist and pro-Black-feminist forces are beginning to align.

Ideally, Black women's studies will not be dependent on women's studies, Black studies, or "straight" disciplinary departments for its existence, but will be an autonomous academic entity making coalitions with all three. Realistically, however, institutional support will have to come from these already established units. This will be possible only in proportion to the elimination of racism, sexism, and elitism.

VISIONS AND RECOMMENDATIONS

Our visions and recommendations for the future of Black women's studies are myriad. Countless projects and areas of research concerning Black women have not even been conceptualized. The following are merely examples:

Many of our visions require financial and institutional support. We would like to encourage:

• Funding of individual research by Black women scholars.

• Funding of teaching projects and curricular materials.

• Funding of summer seminars for college teachers, like those sponsored by the National Endowment for the Humanities.

• Funding of a directory of who's who and where in Black women's studies.

• Funding of a Black women's research institute at an institution with significant holdings on Black women.

• Funding of a national interdisciplinary Third World women's studies conference.

• Funding to allow the creation of our own publications, including both academic and Black feminist movement journals.

Already existing institutions can/must respond to the following needs and recommendations:

• That university departments provide a climate open and supportive to the teaching of materials on Black women.

• That universities and individual departments make hiring, promotion, and tenure of Black women faculty a priority and fulfill affirmative action directives.

• That universities implement more programs for "reentry" women, with particular outreach to Third World and working-class communities.

• That Black women's studies programs be made accessible to all Black women, not only those who are in universities.

• That Black women's studies programs be implemented on the elementary and secondary levels.

• That journals make a serious effort to identify and publish the work of Black women scholars, particularly their research on Black women.

• Accreditation of women's studies programs on the basis of their approach/inclusion of Third World women's studies.

• Accreditation of Black and Third World studies programs on the basis of their approach/inclusion of Third World women.

All of our visions require fundamental social, political, and personal change. For Black women's studies to flourish, we call for:

• The eradication of racism in the white women's movement through a serious examination of their own racism and a recognition of Black history and culture.

• The eradication of antifeminism and homophobia in the Black community and particularly among Black women academics.

• A strong Black feminist movement supported both by white feminists and by the Black community.

NOTES

1. William Faulkner, *Light in August* (Modern Library, New York, 1932), p. 53.

2. Laura S. Haviland, *A Woman's Life-Work, Labors and Experiences* (Publishing Association of Friends, Chicago, 1889; copyright 1881), pp. 300-301; reprinted in Gerda Lerner, ed., *Black Women in White America: A Documentary History* (Vintage, New York, 1973), pp. 32-33.

3. Alice Walker, "In Search of Our Mother's Gardens," *Ms.* (May 1974): 64-70, 105.

4. Bernette Golden, Personal Letter, April 1, 1974.

5. J.R. Roberts, *Black Lesbians: An Annotated Bibliography* (Naiad, Tallahassee, Florida, 1981) contains over three hundred entries of books, periodicals, and articles by and about Black lesbians and provides ample material for developing a variety of courses.

6. Quoted in Jonathan Katz, *Gay American History: Lesbians and Gay Men in the U.S.A.* (T.Y. Crowell, New York, 1976), pp. 425.

7. Lorraine Bethel, " 'This Infinity of Conscious Pain': Zora Neale Hurston and the Black Female Literary Tradition" (Feminist Press, Old Westbury, New York, 1982), pp. 176-88.

8. Most of the material in these first two paragraphs about Black women in higher education was gleaned from an unpublished paper by Patricia Bell Scott, "Issues and Questions in the Higher Education of Black Women: Taking a Brief Look Backwards."

9. This is a report of the National Advisory Council on Women's Educational Programs published in June 1977. Another study sponsored by the National Institute of Education, "Involvement of Minority Women in Women's Studies," promises additional data.

Teaching Writing in Prison*

by Andrea Loewenstein

WOMEN WHO BEGIN to write creatively under the auspices of a women's studies department or in a feminist seminar usually do so with the idea of discovering something about themselves. "Am I anybody special?" they ask. "Do I have anything to say?" "Am I even worth getting to know?"

The women who begin to write with me at the Framingham Correctional Institution, near Boston, have similar goals. Their life situation, whether they are "free" or in jail, simply makes this need more desperate. One of my students told me: "You may not understand this since I have so many other problems [at the time, the custody of her three children was being transferred to the state, and she faced a long term in prison on various counts], but to write this book is the most important thing in my life. I don't even care if it's any good, or if no one but me and you reads it. I just have to write it." A feeling of desperation is not the worst thing to start out with as a writer. More than any other group I have worked with, the women at Framingham are *ready* to write.

The prisoners I teach fall into three broad categories. One group includes hustlers of all kinds – pickpockets, bank robbers, prostitutes, dealers in drugs or goods. Most of the women in this group have been involved in several of these occupations at different times in their lives. For them, both drug use (with the likelihood of addiction) and periods of time spent in jail are occupational hazards.

---

* All the names used in this article are changed, and I have sometimes attributed various quotations to the wrong people in order to maintain confidentiality.

Another group is made up of women whose repeatedly self-destructive, seemingly unprovoked, violent, or bizarre behavior causes them to be labeled by staff and inmates as "off," or "the crazies." These women are in prison – rather than in the mental hospitals they also frequent – because they have hurt or scared someone a little too much. Their aberrant behavior is sporadic, often developed because institutional busywork and respectful politeness to prison authorities are not demanded of a "crazy person who can't help it." On the few occasions when it is more advantageous to be sane, and when the women are not under medication, the bizarre behavior may be discarded.

The final group consists of women who have not previously been involved in crime, but whose lives have been shattered by some violent and usually, even to them, inexplicable act. These women tend to be "model prisoners" and are often shocked or offended by the language and behavior of the others. They are also the ones who are generally serving the longest terms, although unlike the women in the first group, they probably will not return to prison once released.

The women in all three of these groups exist at a knife-edged concentration of American womanhood. They are 70 percent nonwhite, so their oppression is at least twofold. But in addition to a background of oppression and a sense of having lost control of their lives, these women share the unique position of living within an institution which has assumed total responsibility for them. While in many ways this system continues the work of the families/employers/pimps/government/teachers/husbands who made the decisions and assumed the power before, it also frees the women from responsibility over their day-to-day lives. In jail they cannot be expected to provide for a family or earn enough money to maintain a habit, whether theirs or anyone else's; a drug habit is possible in jail, but very difficult and expensive to keep up. Except for visits, one is separated from one's significant others, and while that is one of the most painful aspects of imprisonment, it is also one of the most freeing. Framingham is an 80 percent female society, and most of the women seem to find it relaxing and liberating to be surrounded by peers instead of by men and children.

While it is nearly taboo to mention anything but the bad parts of being in jail, Judy tells me in the privacy of my office: "I don't admit it to anyone, of course, but these times in here is all the rest

I get." "Who got the time to stop and think out there?" Candy says. Grace begins each writing session by reading aloud the poster on my wall that says, "I am a woman giving birth to myself." "I'm thirty years old," she tells me, "and it took being in jail for me to get to know me." Jail is not a day camp, yet it can be refuge from the lovers and pimps and tricks and cops and kids and welfare or job which are waiting to grind a woman down on "The Outside." It is a unique time-out, and for some women, the only chance they will have to write.

While women who are caught in exploitative or destructive marriages, or deadening and programmed lives, still have some stake in maintaining the illusion that everything is fine, this is no longer necessary or possible in prison. "I can't let myself really feel," women on the outside reason in order to maintain the status quo. "I'm afraid of what might happen." For the woman in prison, it has already happened. Much is shut off in Framingham; feelings are not.

In the cafeteria at any meal, one can watch a woman sitting alone at a table, shouting and singing to herself in alternately mocking and anguished poetry. At another table, a group of women are doubled over laughing and throwing food at someone who is doing imitations of them and of the staff. At a third table, someone is busily spreading rumors about someone else, hoping to spark off a fight; while at a fourth table, a deeply depressed woman is weeping, cradled by her friends. In the serving area, a woman is cursing an officer and throwing dishes. In the entrance hall, two lovers are passionately embracing. Feeling, and expressing one's feelings, are essential first steps in learning how to write. Framingham is a place where writing can happen.

At Framingham, where the women are largely uneducated and sometimes illiterate, writing exists as an integral part of daily life. Oral and written poetry, songs, plays, and stories made by the women themselves were intrinsic to the life of Framingham well before "Andrea the writing teacher" came along. But the most important pieces of writing are letters. They provide vital ties to the outside, and in many cases must substitute for actual contact. They are also needed for communication with friends and lovers on the inside with whom telephone communication is forbidden. During the course of her imprisonment, a woman may be transferred to and from a variety of settings — from the dungeonlike maximum security cells, or "Max," to the "cages" in the hospital (used for women when they "go off" and for newly returned escapees), to a graded series of locked and unlocked cottages, and finally to a "Prerelease Center" which is forty-five minutes away in Boston. Letters are the only means a prisoner has of communicating with others in different parts of this web.

Often when a woman gets a letter, she shows it to her friends, who may then help to write the response. For example, an arrangement existed between two women: June, who could not write at all but was known for her wit and ability with words, and Pat, who wrote neatly and correctly, but had trouble expressing herself well. June composed Pat's letters for her, and Pat wrote down June's. A group tended to gather during this process, and the letters created were truly communal.

Letters often contain poetry and may be written completely in verse. The first time I saw Janet engaged in the writing of a very reproachful and passionate poem to "her man" I was bewildered, for I knew Janet had a woman lover on the inside to whom she was completely committed. Janet explained that she was writing the poem "for" her friend Nicki. Nicki wanted to make her man feel guilty for not visiting her, and so Janet tried to remember similar experiences in her own life. Once she got in touch with these feelings, she explained to me, it was easy; she pretended to be Nicki and wrote the poem. Neither woman felt the need to tell the man in question about this dual authorship. If an appropriate poem had been found in a book, or in the words of a popular song, it too would have been used. The individual authorship was not important – the message was.

Poems travel up and down from the cells of Max, in the care of a friendly officer or teacher, and are sometimes shouted out the barred windows to a listener below. Max, a place where there is nothing at all to do, inspires unusual creativity. The poems always have a purpose – they are love poems, "I'm breaking up with you" poems, "Why did you treat me so mean?" poems, or, occasionally, "Help, I can't stand it" poems. As my influence as an instructor became more widely felt, the poems were no longer invariably rhymed. They often consisted of more immediate thoughts, memories, or feelings, but the use of poetry itself was established well before I came. Janet and I call the rhyming, very communicative poetry that is sent in and out of Max and which she writes for friends with such facility, "bebop" poetry. Being able to compose such verse is a valued skill. Poems are needed, and if a woman can produce them, she has something to offer; just as someone who can do hair, fight very well, or teach pool or crocheting has something to offer. The position of the prison poet is like that of the popular poets or scribes of an earlier, less sophisticated time. They are not set apart as a distrusted intellectual elite but treated as people with a skill to be bartered, or given as a favor, whose best efforts are memorized and passed into oral tradition.

TEACHING WRITING — FLEXIBILITY AND SUBSTANCE

At Framingham, much of the cushioning of everyday life is absent, and the student-teacher interaction, like everything else, is intensified. I may arrive in the morning prepared to teach a large class and end up, instead, with only one student, or have an afternoon's individual tutorial session suddenly blossom into a fifteen-person workshop. Even if I have been carefully leading up to a certain exercise in a writing class, I must be able to discard it instantly if, when my class gathers, they are completely preoccupied with something such as the elimination of all furloughs or a classification meeting which will determine their futures. I must be able to modify the assignment so that it centers on the current concern, and I must be able to accept the fact that on certain days the group needs to talk and not to write.

This flexibility applies also to the individual tutorials. If a student who has been writing a day-to-day journal on prison life comes in immersed in the past, I must help her temporarily shift the focus of the writing. When a usually calm student comes in threatening to break all the windows in the corridor, she is making it clear that her anger must be translated onto paper that day. With other students, I have to provide a fairly rigid schedule and a study plan which must not be broken. Some women use the hours with me each week to be functional writers, no matter what else is raging in their heads or lives, and if this is the case, I must respect their need.

Yet a flexible teaching technique is not enough. I am at Framingham because I have more than sympathy and good listening skills to offer. Effective teaching consists of a balance between responsiveness and something more substantial than a collection of ideas which "work" to get people writing. During the years I have taught writing, at Framingham and in more conventional situations, I have asked myself what circumstances and what kind of support have enabled *me* to function as a writer. I want to try to give my students what has been given to me.

For me, becoming a writer meant beginning to write from the center of myself. Many writing teachers tend to teach from the outside in instead of from the inside out. "Writing well," we are told again and again, "is not magic. It has nothing to do with inspiration. It is a skill which can and must be learned." While there is a certain truth to this (especially after the initial stage), to deny the magic, the inspiration part of our process, is to force it into a sterile mold; to collaborate with the men in the Massachusetts Department of Corrections who, while trying by a cost/benefit analysis to determine the value of my work, kept asking me how many inmates I "serviced" per week.

Writing, when taught from the inside out, is a process by which a woman's magical, creative ability is tapped. My job is not to "teach her to write." Instead, our job together is to allow her to find what it is she needs to say and how to say it. Although I have a few times (and never at the prison) worked with women for whom the risk of truly experiencing themselves was so great that they were not able to write, I have never worked with someone who had nothing to say. Unless I affirm this faith in and respect for my students, I will inspire little as a teacher. I believe that each of my students has countless books, plays, poems, stories, and songs inside her, waiting to be released – and I also believe that learning to write is part of the more important process of learning that one is not invisible.

THE FIVE-STEP PROCESS

My approach to teaching writing can be broken down into a five-step process; this process is a fluid one, and although all of the five steps must be dealt with at some time, the order in which the steps will be taken varies from student to student. Many students have already accomplished most of the steps on their own and will need help from me on only one or two. Here again, the teacher's flexibility and ability to listen are vital. If, like many students at Framingham, a woman comes in knowing exactly what she wants to write about, it is pointless to insist on the early steps.

The first step consists of acknowledging one's real feelings. There is no shortage of feelings among my students at Framingham, but there *is* often confusion. Sadness, anger, or fear may be expressed by: "I feel icky today," "I can't sit still," or "Why don't you forget about this stupid writing and give me money so I can get high?" I don't think these words are simply something a woman tells whitey to get her off her back, for they come from women who know and trust me. What they do express is the woman's confused sense of her own feelings. One of my students, Gladys, came into my office every week holding up newly burned or cut arms and hands, saying at the same time that nothing was wrong. Another woman, Faith, came in clearly depressed: her skin was broken out, she had deep shadows under her eyes, and she moved sluggishly. When I asked her what was wrong, she was bewildered. "Everyone's been asking me that," she said. "I know I haven't been sleeping well, but nothing's *wrong*." In all these cases, the women were also blocked in their writing. "It's all jumbled," I often heard. Gladys and Faith, trapped in the contradiction between their actual feelings and their understanding of them, would sit blankly, unable to produce a word. My job in such cases is to provide a safe space for feelings to come out. This can happen by just sitting quietly, or frequently, by talking together. It can also happen through written or oral exercises using free associations, memories, dreams, fantasies, listening to one's inner and outer voices, conversations with oneself or absent others, and real and fantasy letters to oneself or to others.

When none of these processes work, I sometimes write a few words down myself, taken either from the woman's own conversation or from my perception of her appearance. If these words strike a chord, they may open the way to the expression of feelings, and if they are very different from what the woman is feeling, the need to correct the misperception sometimes results in an unblocking. Another exercise that is helpful is to have the student write down everything that comes to mind for five minutes, without censoring or stopping to think. Afterward she can go over what she has written, circling the words or phrases which feel especially "right." This unblocking exercise often results in the beginning of a poem or a larger project. Some students feel more comfortable if I also participate in the exercises, while others prefer my undivided attention.

At this point, one may well ask whether it is teaching writing, or therapy, that I am talking about. I must emphasize, however, that it is impossible to write unless one is in touch with one's feelings. When the self is temporarily lost, there remains nothing to write from. And in this process, the feelings uncovered are uncovered for one specific purpose – to write with. The purpose of this uncovering is made clear during my first contact with each student, when we enter into a contractual teaching arrangement. Feelings are used by their owner, for herself.

Step two is a natural corollary to step one. In step two, the writer must not only experience herself as herself, but herself as a separate person. When one writes one must be alone, not only physically but emotionally as well. If one is merged with another person so that something is not really experienced until it is recounted to the other, it is not possible to write. I have noticed that there are times my office, like my person, becomes associated with the ability to write. While I tend to encourage this *kind* of associative ritual which all writers use, I feel that it is important that the student find her own aids. A private journal or notebook, a certain place, or a specific time set aside for writing are possibilities, depending upon their availability. When a student insists that she can only write when I am there, I sometimes disappear for ten minutes or so once she has begun to write to counter the feeling that it is really the teacher, and not the student, who has somehow magically done the writing. At this stage, I stress journal writing, which must be completely uncensored and need be shown to no one.[1]

Once the student is able to experience herself as a separate, feeling person, she is able to begin to write. It is in step three that she decides which mode of expression feels best. While some students like to write in a variety of genres, others grasp the play or the short story as their medium; yet others are clearly poets. Exposure to writers who use a variety of forms is helpful here. Most of my students have few models to refer to, and it is difficult to write a play without ever having seen or read one. Examples of successful works utilizing a theme or a form which a student is working on are useful. I do not feel, as some writing teachers do, that this leads to imitation. The student who has come to step three through steps one and two will have little need to imitate. It is in step three that the student begins to work on more formal pieces instead of, or in addition to, her journal entries. Long-term projects may be begun. Some students move away from autobiographical writing, creating characters and scenes outside of themselves, while others stick to their own lives.

The teacher's role in step three is mainly an enabling and supporting one. Some students choose to use their time with me to come in, sit down, and quietly write for an hour, sometimes reading the results to me afterwards. If a student has a great deal of difficulty with the actual process of writing, I can serve as secretary and take dictation. A tape recorder is another valuable tool in such a case. Other students no longer feel the need to work with me regularly but will give me pieces of work to read. They no longer want to sit in my office; they do need some kind of affirmation. I try to retain unscheduled time in my week when I can work more informally with women who prefer this.

I hesitate to discuss step four because it is the place where many writing teachers start, and it is a step frequently misused. It involves perfecting one's work. For many, this evokes fears of rejection and negative criticism. But there *is* a point where every writer needs and wants supportive criticism. It is important here to distinguish between criticism of authentic writing and recognizing inauthentic writing, which comes not from the writer's center but from a desire to please, from habit, or from fear. The writer herself, if she has proceeded through the earlier steps, is often well aware of the difference. Students who experience difficulty writing authentically may need to return briefly to steps one and two so that the progression continues to be fluid.

When we are refining authentic work, the job is to help the student get in touch with her own sense of what works and what does not. The teacher can help elicit this sense. Such questions as: "Can you hear them really talking here? Can you hear their voices? Are you supposed to or not?" or "Where in that description did you feel yourself leaving and wandering off? Anywhere?" or "Where does that poem really end? Where does the line break when you read it to me?" are helpful. Sometimes the general inquiry "Is there something that doesn't fit or feel right here?" is called for. I find reading the work aloud, usually by the author but sometimes by myself, invaluable. If something doesn't sound right, it will be noticed.

It is also at this stage that the musicality of words can be emphasized. Style and sound are not separate. If a piece has a feeling, that feeling must have a speed and rhythm; there must be particular sounds and words for it; and it will be complex or simple in expression. Just as the first aim was to find the feeling which was already there inside the writer, the aim is now to find the form which is already there, inside the particular piece.

The final stage of the process consists of providing the student with the opportunity to share her work. While it is not essential to share the first three stages of the process, I feel that it is important to share writing from step four in some way beyond showing it to the teacher and friends. Formal or informal readings are an excellent mechanism for doing this, with each author reading her own writing. Publication is also a possibility, for seeing one's work in print gives it an almost magical credence.

THREE STORIES

To illustrate some of the ways this scheme of teaching writing actually works, I will briefly describe three examples of my teaching at Framingham, two of them involving individuals and one with a group.

Gladys is a good example of a woman labeled as "crazy" inside the institution. She is young, white, overweight, and her dragging steps bespeak the number of institutions she has frequented during her life. Her burnings (of buildings and of herself) are what brought her to Framingham instead of the State Hospital. When Gladys began to work with me, extreme passivity was her most noticeable trait. She would arrive punctually twice a week, show me her latest scars, and then refuse to initiate anything, either in words or in writing. She would reply to my questions only in monosyllables.

Our first real contact came when I wrote a piece describing her and guessing some of the things I imagined she might be thinking. Although she did not respond verbally to my reading of this piece, she did smile and asked whether she could look at a collection of one-act plays which she had been eyeing on my desk. I began our next meeting by asking whether she would like to read the plays aloud, and she agreed. For several months we read plays, each taking several parts. Gladys' only indication that she enjoyed what we were doing was her willingness to continue. She read each part in the same monotone, refusing to comment beyond her slight smile when a character expressed angry or murderous feelings.

One day Gladys stopped short in the middle of her reading the part of Amanda in Tennessee Williams' *Glass Menagerie*. She told me the mother shouldn't have spoken the lines she had read and went on to say what she thought should have been said instead. The next day we began to write plays. Gladys insisted that I do "my share of the work," and so we followed a pattern in which each of us composed a part. At first, setting pen to paper was too much of a commitment so I wrote down both parts; later, Gladys decided to write down her own. I tried to follow her cues as much as possible in the writing of my parts in the first play which was about "a sad, lonely girl, in jail."

Gladys often spoke of her depriving mother, and she decided that the second play would have only two parts – a mother and a daughter. During the writing of this long play, over a period of about a month, she became much more assertive. She would rush in saying, "I have to tell you what's happening to them today!" One day, when she was fed up with the "wrong" lines I kept putting into the mother's mouth, she decided to take over both parts: my job became limited to participation in the reading aloud. The play Gladys eventually finished was realistic and intense. It was circulated widely, and everyone was surprised that "crazy Gladys" had written it.

After this, Gladys did her own writing. She began to write poems using the "word exchange" method in which, after talking together for a while, each of us would write five words for the other based on what we heard and use these words in a poem. Again, Gladys soon began to give herself her own words to write from and then to plunge into poetry without aids. Her anger, which had been well hidden behind her passivity and self-destructiveness, emerged as a powerful force in her poetry. It has a stark, rhythmic quality, and uses a great deal of dream and fantasy material. Gladys eventually decided that she worked best on her own, and we used the hours together to discuss the work she brought in or to sit and talk, something which would have been impossible for her when we first began working.

It would be deceptive to present Gladys' progress as a writer as easy. She was subject to severe and sometimes very long-term depressions during which she would miss meetings, and sometimes she struggled to my office only to sit, wordless. Once, the demons she brought with her were so tangible that I began to experience them too, and we spent the hour fighting them together. Gladys did not stop cutting and burning herself, and although her behavior changed, she did not become "cured" through our work together. However, she did become a writer.

When I met Grace, a Black woman of thirty, she was slumped in a chair in the hospital, exhausted and disheveled, fighting off the combined effects of heroin withdrawal, strong medication, and entry into prison. She immediately asked whether I was the writing teacher she had heard about because she wanted to write a book. A few days later, I returned to the hospital with a friend and coteacher, Linda DiRocco, who works with video. Grace suggested that I interview her with Linda taping the interview as a way to begin the book. During the interview, using a series of self-portraits in chalk which she had done the previous day, she named and described her different selves. One of these selves had come into existence the first time her father raped her as a child. The whole interview was amazing in its courage and clarity.

Both Grace and I were surprised when, after this beginning, the writing of the book did not proceed as smoothly as we had hoped. Grace immediately became involved in the life of the institution and began to miss meetings. Then her guilt at having, once more, proven herself to be undependable and "no good" made her miss more meetings. Much of our work during the first months involved working out a system that allowed us to meet regularly, but where Grace was free to break the appointments as long as she told me in advance.

Once the writing began, other problems came up. Grace had become deeply involved with one of the men in the prison and, as she told me: "I can't write when Jay's around. Even when he's not here in person, it seems like he gets inside my head and takes up too much room!" When she did manage to expel Jay from her head, she felt confused and fragmented; the early writing she did consisted of oddly flat lists of seemingly unconnected events. She was frustrated both with the "shit" she felt she was writing and with the unsatisfied feelings she was left with after the writing sessions. We began to spend the first part of each meeting working on centering or, as Grace put it, on concentrating on one thing at a time. She would talk to me about herself at random until we were able to focus upon one particular feeling. I would then ask her to return to a day in the past in which she had felt the same way. Slowly, "The Book" took on a structure, with each chapter beginning with Grace in the present and then turning to a corresponding emotional point in her childhood. While at first Grace's writing lacked the spontaneity and wealth of detail of her speech, it is evolving from a fragmented list of tragic events into a well-woven, highly charged series of scenes.

Grace and I will meet over coffee or under a tree. We have had more than one shouting match up and down the corridors, with Grace yelling out that I might as well forget about her and the book can go down the toilet, and me yelling for her to stop the shit and come in and get to work. The writing proceeds slowly, and it is still hard for Grace to write when I am not present, but I predict that she will soon move on to working independently. The fact that she can come in and tell me when Jay is inside her head and she has to get him out first, or when she is ready to write about her father, or when she needs to just talk and not write at all, makes my job easier. Grace has never had trouble experiencing her feelings, and she knows both what she needs from me and what she wants to write. Everytime I work with her, I believe more strongly that there are poems and books waiting inside all of us, and that the writing teacher should be a midwife.

Acting, including both imitation of people and scenes, and polished and dramatic storytelling, is another creative form which existed at Framingham before I came. Role playing and improvisational drama have always been important in my teaching. For these reasons, our first play had gone into rehearsal before anyone was quite aware of what was happening.

One woman had written a short story about her first day at Framingham, and she and I decided to act it out. More people were needed, so she brought some friends to our next meeting, and Linda brought her video camera.[2] Because each member of the group had been through a similar experience of entry and initiation, different women took turns playing the main part, each adding elements from her own experiences. Most wanted a chance to take off on the superintendent and different officers, and everyone wanted to play the judge at least once, so the cast revolved for the first few weeks. After each run-through, we would watch the tape together, everyone commenting on the best and worst elements of the different performances. "Freeze that, that's good," several people would say, or "It's slow there. Got to get rid of all that talk." Gradually, the play took shape (although changes were still being made on the night of the performance), and it was agreed that certain people were best at certain parts. A few of the original group had dropped out. We were left with seven women, all of whom had written the play communally and all of whom were able to take any part. This flexibility of the cast proved important when the woman who was to play the judge in the first play escaped the night before the performance and, in later plays, when important actors were suddenly released early, or locked in Max on the day of the performance. We tried to write down the first play but found that this process limited improvisation and change and excluded good actors who were bad readers. The subsequent plays remained oral, recorded only on video tape.

Because of the emotional climate at Framingham and the frustration in the actors' lives, the course of each play is dramatic. A few actors consistently forget that they are acting and treat allegiances and quarrels between characters as real. The play wavers between drama and life and, in early stages of rehearsal, there are always at least two actors who will not trust themselves in the same room with one another. Each time, however, about two weeks from the performance date, the women's attitudes change. "The Play" suddenly becomes a common child of the group, to be nourished tenderly and treated with care, and the members begin to treat each other in this way also. Up to this point, I usually do a fair amount of directing, as well as arbitrating and coaxing. Now I am able to sit back, play my part (I usually act in the plays, preferably playing someone as far removed from myself as possible), and watch it all happen. The night of the performance itself is exciting and satisfying because of the large audiences (usually made up of members of the women's community in Boston, and families and friends of the actors) and because, for many of the women, acting in the play is their first experience of public approval and affirmation.

The process of making "The Play" embodies the aim of my teaching at Framingham; it is creative work which is born of the women themselves and which nurtures them in the process of its creation. The other day, one of the women asked me why I stay on at Framingham in the face of a gradual reduction of salary and hours by the Department of Corrections and an unwillingness on their part to contract me for more than two months at a time. My first answer was that I stay because I love the work. There is something in the climate of intense emotions and personal interaction, and teaching that is not divorced from living, which appeals to me. I have become addicted to the place.

"But do you succeed very often?" Pat asked me. I questioned what she meant by success, and she said, half mockingly, half hopefully, for she is one of my students, "Do the people you work with straighten up? Do they stay off drugs? Do they go back to school when they get out? You know — do they make it?" I thought for a while. Gladys wrote to me recently from the mental hospital where she now lives. In the letter she tells me about her loneliness and says that she thinks she will always keep on writing, but now has no one to share her work with. Grace has not written for a while; she has been locked in her cottage because of a fight she had with someone who is also in the cast of our current play, and she has not yet learned to write on her own. I am working with Janet again, one of my most talented students, because she was arrested on a drug charge after escaping two months before the date of her early release. When I looked at it that way, the success rate was low. Yet I still believe in the process.

Teaching writing from the inside out is no life solution for women who are imprisoned and oppressed in so many ways. But it *is* one way of taking back a little of their lost power and of regaining a sense that one exists.

NOTES

1. Keeping a private journal is almost impossible in prison, where your possessions are always subject to a search. Still, some of the students have selected to take the risk.

2. The use of video in coordination with creative writing has proven to be extremely valuable and opens up many new possibilities. At Framingham, Linda DiRocco and I worked for a while as a team.

College for
Neighborhood Women:
Innovation and Growth

by Terry L. Haywoode

How can I go to school? I have kids to take care of.

I haven't been inside a classroom in thirty-nine years.

I went to school down south, you know; they weren't so particular
about how much Black children learned in those days.

I work all day and attend meetings at night and I have a family to
take care of.

We need all our money for the kid's education. I can't think about
myself.

My husband won't let me.

I'm scared.

THIS REPRESENTS just a small fraction of the problems which
were standing in their way. Beginning in 1974, however, groups
of poor and working-class women, working through the National
Congress of Neighborhood Women, developed college programs
for themselves, attended and were graduated with accredited
A.A. degrees from the City University of New York, and later
from the State University of New York.

Their story is a remarkable one which has much to tell us about
women, about feminism, and about education. The college program these women created has had to take into account their own
fears, scarce resources, the doubts and reluctance of the educational establishment, the questioning attitudes of families and
other neighborhood people. Yet the outcome has been not merely

49

a college program, but one which might well be envied by some who have had a more privileged education: what substitutes for money, space, and resources is the sense of a community of learners. Participants in the programs support each other, help each other, counsel each other, and quell their own fears as they tell their friends: "You can do it, I know you can."

To understand the nature of their achievement and why it is important for feminist education, we must start at the beginning. In 1974, the National Congress of Neighborhood Women (NCNW) was founded, claiming as its constituency the large number of working-class and poor women who found little to identify with in the main stream feminist movement which they saw as addressing only the needs and issues of middle-class women. NCNW women were faced with many "women's issues" in their lives, but these issues did not seem to be identified as women's concerns by the movement.

At the same time, various ethnic identity groups had been coalescing, modeled on the Black nationalist movement of the late sixties. These ethnic movements helped break down the polite fiction of the "melting pot" and allowed ethnic groups to claim their own identities and their heritage. For the most part, however, they were male-dominated organizations which glorified a male model of ethnic identification and achievement. Yet another movement which touched the lives of these women was the neighborhood movement. Such organizations as the National Association of Neighborhoods were beginning to recognize that the thousands of neighborhood-based organizations throughout the country constituted a social movement. Once again, the movement was male-dominated, with women doing the quiet, patient day-to-day work of organization building while most of the leadership positions went to men. Finding themselves on the periphery of three movements, feeling excluded by class in the women's movement and by gender in the other two, some of these women decided to start a movement of their own.

The headquarters of NCNW were in Williamsburg, a multi-ethnic working-class and poor neighborhood in Brooklyn, New York. Many of the women attracted to the organization were local neighborhood activists who had spent years fighting to preserve their communities as the housing deteriorated and the bureaucratic complexity of government and industry increased. People in Williamsburg and similar neighborhoods felt a sense of loss and bewilderment. Services were cut, amenities were removed, and deterioration settled in. Some neighborhoods just seemed to fall apart.

Women defended their neighborhoods with the same intensity as they protected their families, but they felt unsure of their course of action. What was the right city agency to approach? How could you get local politicians involved? How could you design a long-range strategy instead of just reacting to current developments? Could the federal or state governments be useful? How could people figure out what they were entitled to, and then how could they go about getting it? What factors encouraged families to stay in a neighborhood, and what factors forced them to leave? How could people develop an awareness of the threats to neighborhood life and the potential for developing new levels of community consciousness and participation, both to preserve what already existed and to build a new level of community cohesion?

The women in NCNW, some of them veterans of battles for housing, childcare, and other issues, came together to develop a program. Many issues were discussed, but one theme seemed to keep reemerging: the women wanted more education. At first, they talked about sewing classes and driving lessons, but gradually a new idea developed. They wanted to go to college. Higher education, they believed, would help them understand the forces behind the social changes in their neighborhoods. It would give them the skills to analyze policy and develop organizational initiatives. It would give them the confidence to deal with government officials, bureaucrats, and executives. But could they fit classes into their busy lives? Would their rusty academic skills be adequate? Some had not written more than a shopping list in twenty years. What college would want them anyway?

In spite of the problems, once the idea was voiced it gathered force and momentum. Long-ago dreams were recalled. Women, who as young girls had thought about college, realized how they had been taught instead that:

- A girl's education is a waste. She will only get married and not "use" it.

- Boys get first priority in financially hard-pressed families.

- You have to go to work. The family needs your salary. There are younger children to be provided for.

- You don't need an education, honey. We'll get married and I'll take care of you.

Without support or encouragement, these young women had folded up their dreams and placed them in dresser drawers with the good linen and other fading treasures. They marched off instead to factories and offices. Many had married young, become mothers, and submerged themselves in the lives of their families and communites. Now those buried dreams emerged. They were dusty and timeworn but increasingly real, and maybe even possible to achieve.

But the women who now gave voice to these early dreams were different from the young girls they had once been. They wanted to go to college as the active shapers of their own educational model rather than the passive recipients of someone else's idea of education. In this respect they agreed with many other feminists who were developing new educational programs. A fruitful collaboration began as sympathetic educators were drawn in, not as authority figures but as colleagues in this educational experiment. Many of these academic women were working-class and poor in origin. Their scholarly interests were rooted in understanding people's actual experience, not in imposing an outside framework on it. They were eager to participate in a nonhierarchical educational community.

These academics and neighborhood women attempted to understand why conventional colleges did not meet their needs. In the United States, especially among working-class people, higher education is viewed as an avenue of social mobility. When working-class and poor people attend college, they are expected to shed the particular identities which link them to the families and communities of their youth and to develop the universalist frame of reference of middle-class culture. A working-class person goes to college to learn "subject matter," but also to learn how to be middle class. Working-class identities are hidden as students come to recognize that the price of admission to the great American success sweepstakes is not only the understanding that John Donne is "better" than Harold Robbins, but that one hundred percent cotton is superior to polyester blend. The price of this transition for many working-class college students is a painful internal split between the sweet memories of an un-self-conscious youth and the current reality of a carefully wrought "dressed-for-success" persona. The lure of upward mobility claims the "best and the brightest" of working-class and poor youth. It constitutes a "brain drain" from working-class neighborhoods, pulling off the potential leadership of the next generation into corporate life and suburbia. The NCNW program was for people who would stay, for people who wanted to improve their lives by building their communities, not by leaving them.

Thus the goals of the program emerged: education for community people and education for leadership. The program would help people move ahead, but it would not require that they relinquish their basic identities. It would not result in people who were split between their ethnic, neighborhood, family selves, and their middle-class, achievement-oriented, individualistic selves. The college experience was to be one in which self-identity, community ties, and women's roles would be affirmed and strengthened; growth would not be paid for by a denial of one's past.

As these ideas emerged both from the neighborhood women and their academic collaborators, the question of how these goals could be realized in a workable structure became crucial. The process of discussing goals was the beginning of the larger process of institution building. The college program would be an institution consciously created to meet the needs of its participants rather than those of the institution.

The first principle about which everyone agreed was that the program would be community-based. It would be located in the neighborhood; classes, offices, and other support systems would be local and on-site; class scheduling would reflect the needs of the community women. Classes were given in a specific block of time, rather than scattered throughout the day, and the timing took account of school closings and family dinner hours. Second, it meant that the curriculum would grow out of people's concern for the neighborhood and be geared to facilitating people's understanding of forces which shaped neighborhood life. It also meant that the neighborhood would be used as a resource, that research projects and fieldwork would focus on the community. As the neighborhood was to be a resource for the college, so the college would be a resource for the neighborhood. The college would generate data and information that would be helpful to neighborhood residents. New ideas for neighborhood preservation and renewal would also be a product of the college program. The program itself would be an important community institution. Finally, the program would generate new community leaders whose individual and collective community development work would contribute to various aspects of community life.

Cooperation and collaboration were viewed as basic to the program. These adult women did not wish to be treated like children. They wanted to be partners in their own education. Students, staff, and faculty cooperated to develop institutional structure and curriculum. Selecting faculty was then and still remains a difficult problem. The students' strong wish to play a role in this area often collides with well-established academic traditions.

An important concern is the relationship of the NCNW community to a cosponsoring academic institution. NCNW has worked with a number of institutions to implement the program. These relationships have been productive and positive but have also raised many questions. Each institution brings a specific set of resources to the program – its own faculty, curriculum, and support systems. They provide academic accreditation and issue the degree. NCNW students meet the same degree requirements as do all students of these institutions.

A number of problems, however, are inherent in the nature of the collaboration. The decision-making process and the communication system in NCNW, as in most community groups, is informal and personal, and it contrasts sharply with the structured, formal, and hierarchical processes of the larger academic institution. The community people have to learn to relate to both the formal hierarchy of the academic structure and to its informal power structure. Cooperation between the academic institution and the NCNW program needs to be translated into cooperation among the actual individuals who must work together. It is a process that is not without pain and frustration on both sides.

Practical concerns play an increasingly large role in the life of the college program. Two areas of central concern are establishing and maintaining relations with an academic institution and funding for the program. Funding has proved to be an especially difficult problem in this period of diminishing resources for education and other social programs. Many students are eligible for various financial aid programs; for those who are not, paying even the relatively modest tuition of the public colleges is a real hardship. Innovative programs are able to secure funding for their experimental phase, but few government agencies or foundations will fund the normal operations of an ongoing program. Community-based programs therefore need to maximize their ability to utilize existing resources in the university and in the community. Local fundraising – "selling" the program to local corporations, community groups, and government officials – could help provide the funding needed to stabilize NCNW's financially precarious position.

Curriculum development was central in the original formulation of the program. Women voiced strong concerns about what they wanted to learn and about general curriculum principles. Although the curriculum was to be innovative, it was to be encompassed within the traditional liberal arts framework. It was not to be only vocational training or leadership training. We believed that the depth of analysis, the sense of continuity, and the broad humanistic perspective that we wanted could come only through the liberal arts. Too often, working-class and poor people are offered "training," which may be adequate for their immediate needs, and not "education," which could satisfy their long-range goals.

The curriculum was to be interdisciplinary, flexible, and problem-oriented, rather than broken down into discrete subject areas. Women wanted to learn about themselves and other women's lives, their families, their community, and the larger society. They wanted to learn about the government and the economy and other institutions which shaped the conditions of their lives. The women wanted to explore art, theater, and literature, to develop a deeper appreciation of these areas and to be able to create their own works. The initial curriculum focused on the social sciences and the humanities, and included math and science in recognition of their importance in modern society and women's general weaknesses in these areas.

The curriculum was also to be practical, hands-on and product-oriented. One example of how these two goals were brought together was the Williamsburg-Greenpoint-Northside Colloquium. In this unit, women undertook community-oriented projects which included both creative work and original research in the community. The projects were closely linked to the academic subjects the women were studying. Thus, a video group produced a video study of the college program; a creative writing group produced stories and poems about life in the neighborhood; a local history project produced multimedia family and neighborhood histories. In the social sciences, a legal studies group produced a survey of the legal needs of working-class neighborhoods, and a medical studies group learned about alcoholism and its treatment in the community. Both of these groups included recommendations for future action. A gala "college night" was held at the local public library, and neighborhood residents were invited to share in the results of these projects.

We learned that a curriculum which seemed perfect for one class does not necessarily meet the needs of the next group. For example, the discovery of various ethnic literary works enabled us to supplement the dominant Anglo-American works of many standard reading lists. It is a moving experience for women to find books written with power, insight, and beauty about people with lives similar to their own. Building curriculum, with its accompanying debates and discussions, contributes to a sense of unity and power in each class.

Women often come into the program with great doubts about themselves and with many practical problems. Could they actually do college-level work? They question their ability, their preparation, their general suitability. It is important to create space for women to voice these doubts. Counseling is available and peer-support systems are encouraged. The counseling approach assumes that the college program is a positive and important element in the women's lives, and the focus of the support is to enable women to remain in the program. In this "directive counseling," counselors never suggest leaving the program as either a temporary or permanent solution for problems. Women are urged to make adjustments in other areas of their lives, instead, even when doing so is very difficult. The lives of working-class and poor women *are* difficult and are not apt to get any simpler in the future. In spite of the hardships, the program represents a lifeline and a positive element in the women's lives.

A key part of the program is the development of a working system of peer support. Women helping women and reaching out into the community is the central theme. Many participants have led relatively isolated lives, defining themselves primarily in terms of their families, as housewives and mothers. Others have been employees and/or been active in community organizations; still others are leaders in the neighborhoods. Breaking through the isolation of the housewife is as important as supporting the leadership of the active woman. Women are also divided by differences of age, race, ethnicity, and class. If the program is to work, trust and support have to develop in this diverse group. Women struggle together to understand how social forces keep them divided. The results are not always tranquil, but people learn about each other and about themselves with honesty and clarity. One woman stated that she was closer to her class than to any group except her family, and she added: "I have revealed things in this setting that even my family doesn't know about me."

Courses such as group dynamics, psychology, and sociology of the family help create occasions for people to examine their own experiences and those of people different from themselves. However, peer support comes primarily from structures which students create for themselves out of their care for each other. Each one recognizes that her strength and continued participation strengthens others. Many women have said, "There were many times I thought that I couldn't go on, but I knew I couldn't let the others down – so I stayed." These students are not attending school as their primary life activity. Family life goes on – with its attendant illnesses, economic hardships, and personal strains – but the majority of the students have remained in the program and graduated. The valedictorian of the first graduating class, a grandmother in her sixties, required surgery in the middle of one term. She was able to keep up with her academic work with help from her teachers, but her music classes seemed an insurmountable obstacle because they required participation. Classmates took turns recording the class, bringing her the tape, and accompanying her while she practiced her musical instrument.

Support systems developed to emphasize the continuing connection between the students and the community. Community people are invited to participate in special events and graduations. Family nights are held for husbands and children who might fear that college is removing "mama" from her accustomed role. The support of husband and children is precious to many of the participants, who delightedly report children helping them with homework and a new, serious level of conversation with spouses. When family support is not available, or when family opposition is, in fact, the case, women turn more to the group for support. In one instance, four classmates accompanied a woman whose husband had threatened not to permit her to leave the house.

The college program creates a place for women to learn, to question, to develop new skills, to develop new relationships with people. It provides time and space for reflection and the possibility of change for women who had believed that their lives were pretty well set. It opens up new possibilities for women who do not choose to declare their independence from families and communities, and who want to be able to grow and change — to acquire power and to use it — to save themselves and their neighborhoods.

The number of working-class and poor women who attend college is pitifully small. This program demonstrates the ability and the eagerness of this group to take advantage of higher education, if it is made available to them in a way that makes it possible for them to utilize the opportunity. Neighborhood women are a great resource: their energy, creativity, and full potential is still unrealized. Programs such as NCNW provide the opportunity for neighborhood women to define themselves as thinkers, doers, and powerful people; to come together to both preserve and change their world; and to build new social institutions.

All-Women Classes and the Struggle for Women's Liberation*

WOMEN'S STUDIES COLLEGE at the State University of New York (SUNY) at Buffalo is a program that has tried to be responsible to the autonomous women's liberation movement while remaining a part of the university. We have come to understand that the university does not serve our needs. So we have begun to struggle to create our own program for education, an education for liberation. While developing this program, we have had to fight to maintain as much control as possible. In the past we offered some courses that were open to women only. In December 1975, however, after waging a public fight for over two years, we lost the right to the selective use of all-women classes. This article is an analysis based on that experience.

I

The women's liberation movement of the past ten years has demanded education for, about, and by women and has encouraged the development of independent women's schools and women's studies programs. Although generated by the women's move-

* The original article, written in 1978, is the product of collective work. It was written primarily by Deborah Gnann, Ilene Krzystek, Kathleen McDermott, and Abbe Tiger. It was built on the work of Lucy Campbell, Angeliki Keil, Dana Naparsteck, Rena Patterson, Marie Sebastiano, and Billie Warden. It was also assisted by the critiquers, polishers, and members of Women's Studies College Governance Assembly. The 1982 update was written by Mary C. Gentile with revisions and assistance from Judy Gerich, Sharon Leder, and Ruth Meyerowitz.

ment, these schools and programs have maintained quite different relations to it. Independent women's schools vary in form and politics, but all hold in common a concern for serving women and see themselves as responsible to a women's liberation movement. In contrast, women's studies programs in universities are of two kinds: those which have cut or lost their ties with the movement and see their primary responsibility as serving the university, its traditions and goals; and those which see themselves primarily as a project of the women's liberation movement and therefore are responsible to it as well as to the university. The second form is much less common than the first, given the many forces that act to maintain traditional education which is opposed to education that is responsible to liberation movements.

How the issue of all-women classes is understood in various kinds of programs is a good measure of their differences. Independent women's schools assume that all-women classes are vital for most, if not all, of women's education and are necessary for achievement of their goals. Since these schools are not part of another institution, they can determine their own educational policy and can incorporate what they have learned from the movement into their teaching programs, e.g., that all-women classes are necessary.

Women's studies programs in universities are in an entirely different situation. Educational policy there is set by the administration and, to our knowledge, no administration has been friendly to all-women classes. In fact, most have been openly hostile. The women's studies programs that see themselves as responsible to the university, with no direct ties to the women's liberation movement, explicitly prohibit all-women classes. Some of their instructors might de facto have all-women classes; others may want them but bow to the pressure of the university. In any case, women's studies programs that do not have direct ties to the women's liberation movement must, at least publicly, ignore the value of all-women classes.

In contrast, women's studies programs that see themselves as responsible to the women's movement have to take into account that these classes have been proven to be the best situations for women to learn in. Many such programs therefore establish and maintain all-women classes while at the same time meeting the requirements of their university. This creates a situation of permanent tension with the institution which is sometimes only resolved by open conflict. At other times, it is a question of developing strategic ways for getting around a hostile administration.

In this article, we want to show that the fight for all-women classes is an example of institutional struggle revolving around the right to organize women autonomously in our classes. As such, it challenges the power relations of capitalism and patriarchy. We are organizing to gain more control over the education provided by the university. We must have this control in order to have a quality education that meets our needs as women. We know that education which is defined by the ruling class and by men serves their interests alone and perpetuates our oppression.

II

The political activity generated by the civil rights movement, antiwar and student movements, autonomous women's liberation and gay liberation movements of the late sixties and early seventies contributed a general political framework on which Women's Studies College bases its work. Some of the important tenets are: capitalism is dependent on a class society; patriarchy oppresses women; women, the working class, gay, and Third World peoples are oppressed and/or exploited in this society. To end women's oppression, and that of all people, the systems of capitalism and patriarchy that uphold that oppression must end. These ideas have guided our work in the university, a state institution. We do our work within such an institution because there is a natural base of women here.

In the late sixties and early seventies, women's liberation movement projects sprouted everywhere: women's centers, self-help clinics, consciousness-raising groups, and women's studies programs. Buffalo Women's Liberation (BWL), an antiracist, anticapitalist, autonomous women's organization, took on women's education as one of its several projects. Largely through the efforts of women involved in BWL, Women's Studies College (WSC) was formally constituted as a unit of the Collegiate System of the State University of New York at Buffalo in the spring of 1971.

The Collegiate System was designed to provide experimental, multidisciplinary, non-degree-granting educational units. It was used by the university administration as a concession to the increasingly militant demands of students for a more relevant education. In similar ways, administrations across the nation tried to harness and channel the force of the rising student movement. As part of the Collegiate System, WSC was given: (1) a budget; (2) a building to work out of; (3) credit for courses, allowing women students to get academic credit for doing work in the women's movement; (4) the opportunity to have both community people and supervised undergraduates teach courses; (5) the opportunity to develop internal structures that allow a large measure of student participation and control; and (6) encouragement for doing work in the wider Buffalo community as a part of the Collegiate System's efforts to break down the ivory tower image of the university.

The Collegiate System provided the particular crack in the institution that allowed a project of the women's movement to become a legitimate educational unit within the university. Even though BWL dissolved, our origins in the movement and our continued responsibility to it provided us with a set of goals that form the foundation and direction of the work we do. These goals are:

1. to involve women in the women's movement through education;

2. to serve as a focal point for developing a body of knowledge about women;

3. to act as a base for institutional struggle around sexism;

4. to be a center of resources which can be tapped by the movement for the community.

Our primary intellectual goal is the creation of an educational process by, for, and about women. Traditional education neglects an in-depth study of women; it neither challenges stereotypes nor analyzes the contradictions between these stereotypes and our own lives. This neglect of women in the curriculum strengthens the dominant cultural perspective that we are passive, dependent, unintellectual, and unable to analyze our own position in society. This "education" has denied us the fullness of our history and the skills we need to understand, in a critical way, how society operates.

In order to create our own education, one that will begin to meet our needs as women, we have to expose and counteract existing power relationships. WSC is organized as a nonhierarchical, participatory democracy, and the collective structure encourages social relationships that are cooperative and allow for growth and development of the individuals involved. The effectiveness of the program is reflected in some of our concrete achievements. For example, we've developed a curriculum of twenty-five to thirty courses a semester, serving approximately 500 students, and have a governing structure that encourages the greatest possible amount of student participation and responsibility. Our collective structures have allowed working-class, middle-class, Third World, white, gay, and straight women to work together and to understand each other's lives better.

III

The university is traditionally supposed to be a place removed from society where ideas are openly discussed and where the governing concern is the development of human intellectual potential. In our work, however, we have come to see the university as representative of the system that maintains the exploitation and oppression which cause real suffering in our society. The forces at work here are generally the same forces that are at work in every major institution.

As part of the women's movement, and as individual women, we saw that concern for women's education is not, to say the least, a university priority. In fact, the needs of most people associated with the university − students, staff, and faculty − are not met. While many of these people are getting together to articulate their discontent, to analyze their situation, and to act, making changes that end oppression and exploitation is not easy. High-level administrators have power. To keep that power, they will use the resources of the institution, the ideology of the society, and the support of others whose interests are also being maintained.

Even though our sphere of work is education within a state university, Women's Studies College measures that work by how much closer it brings us to the liberation of all women. Responsibility to the women's movement has made us see that we have no choice but to engage in institutional struggle. In the short run, institutional struggle means fighting to wrest some control from those in power so that we can stay alive and work toward our goals. In the long run, it means fighting in this institution as part of the struggle to change society.

We have often asked ourselves whether WSC should leave the university and set up an independent women's school where we can teach what we want as we want. But as we came to understand institutional struggle better, we understood that we do not have that choice. Women are in all major institutions and are deeply affected by them. We have to learn to force *them* to meet *our* needs, and to transform the institution as part of the struggle for social change.

In our discussions about leaving the university, the women who thought the work was no longer worthwhile were people who had worked with WSC for more than a year. New people, on the other hand, would say, "We can't leave; WSC is important. It's changed my life." This taught us that while individuals may choose to set up an independent women's school, an institution such as WSC, which developed out of the struggle of women to end oppression, cannot just pull out. If our work or conditions here are unsatisfactory, the only real option is to transform WSC into something else so that it can carry on institutional struggle in a different form or from a different base.

Involving ourselves in institutional struggle means: (1) keeping in touch with social reality. The harassment we face makes us continually aware of power relations; (2) keeping in touch with our constituency. The tenuous nature of our existence in the university makes it critical that we be in contact with our base. Unless we have that support, the administration could cut our program with little repercussion; (3) maintaining the program and making tiny cracks in the institution. We channel some of the university resources available to us into the community by funding projects like the Buffalo Women's Prison Project. Another example is the precedent set by the formal approval of five all-women classes that was initially wrung from the administration; and (4) building socialist-feminist leadership in women. Through our courses, women are drawn into program maintenance – in both its internal development and its external defense. Undergraduate women not only work on our curriculum committee but also meet and argue with high-level administrators as representatives of WSC.

We get hassled because the work we do and the analysis of society that we put forth threatens and attacks what the university stands for. However, we have support precisely because we offer that critique; people respond to our work because it changes and improves their lives.

IV

In 1970, when our introductory course "Women in Contemporary Society" was taught for the first time, the class had both men and women in it. The men found it hard to relate and seemed to "gum up the works." In the following semesters, all-women classes were encouraged, and they became integral to the success of the program. This change was happening all over the country for two reasons: men simply did not see it in their self-interest to register for women's studies courses, and women were beginning to realize the importance of autonomy.

To understand this dynamic, we looked at how the classroom operates. Part of the myth of education, as most of us have known it, is that knowledge is given and received in the classroom, with all students having an equal chance to do well. The reality of the situation, however, is just the opposite; the classroom operates as a microcosm of the larger society, reinforcing social privileges and destructive stereotypes. Education as the pusher of a sexist social perspective trivializes women's experiences. In a classroom with both men and women, the real differences among women are minimized, and the gender differences predominate. Women are inhibited by the male presence, which inevitably provokes social competitiveness and produces hierarchical forms – both of which have been historically detrimental to women. In mixed classes, we recognize male power and respond, either by contesting it or withdrawing. This response cuts off the possibility for a full and truthful examination of our lives and oppression.

Working autonomously in the classroom, we are released from the dominant male view of reality and can begin to form our own social analysis. Men have little to contribute to the exploration of women's realities since they haven't experienced them. We understand that men need to learn that their lives do not reflect the whole world, but even those men who sincerely wish to do this find it difficult to accept a perspective that challenges their use of privilege to oppress women. Again, experience has shown us that men participate better in courses based on more objective material, where there is a common, already developed subject, rather than in courses where subjective appraisal is an integral part of the learning.

All-women classes enable us to openly study the material conditions of our lives and evaluate them in the light of current theory. Through such study, we develop an analysis based on both personal experience and general theory. In the absence of hierarchical jockeying, we can all develop leadership skills and can experience women as initiators in nonoppressive leadership roles. Free from the threat of loss of privilege or male backlash, women can learn to express themselves, take control of their education, and work in a collective way.

V

The fight for the selective use of all-women classes spanned two full years. It began in 1974, when administrative harassment of WSC and the Collegiate System took the form of a "chartering" process in which each unit of the Collegiate System was forced to defend the validity of its program. The purpose of chartering clearly was to eliminate courses, programs, and instructors that countered traditional university education. For WSC, this meant that the administration would try at least to transform us, at most to discontinue our program completely. Some of us feared co-optation, and we discussed whether or not we could remain with the university. Finally, after discussing both the advantages and disadvantages of being in the university, our governance body decided to go through with the chartering process. We agreed that we would try to stop any infringements on the integrity of the College.

Many aspects of our program – undergraduate teaching, a governance system based on a collective participatory democracy, and noninstitutionalized participation of faculty – were matters of contention between WSC and the administration. There was also concern about some of our classes excluding men. As the chartering process developed, the Dean of the Colleges questioned whether all-women classes were in violation of the new federal antisex discrimination legislation (Title IX).

From the beginning, WSC intended to create an "education, by, for, and about women." The "all-women character" of the program was achieved by counseling men into courses they could relate to more easily. There were never any grievances lodged against us, and we never forced a public debate about all-women classes because we did not know how it would develop.

After an open hearing on all the issues, where we received broad support from the university and the community, the one issue which remained in contention was all-women classes. We were surprised. We had forgotten what a powerful threat the autonomous grouping of women is. As soon as we realized that this was going to be the central issue, we discussed it fully with each of our classes, for it was apparent that we should consider fighting only if the majority of students considered the issue sufficiently important. Although there was disagreement within the college over whether or not an open fight with the university was worth it, or even possible, the majority of our students voted to put up a strong fight if necessary. This struggle took shape through letter-writing campaigns, petitions, rallies, and demonstrations of support, culminating in negotiations with the president of the university.

In January 1975, student demands forced President Ketter to approve the selective use of all-women classes where proven educationally valid. Our courses were approved for this purpose by the appropriate university committee in the spring of 1975. Winning administrative recognition of the principle that all-women classes can be valid and educationally sound was a substantial victory which established a precedent for other women's studies programs. However, it has traditionally been a tactic of the Ketter administration to take away during the summer gains which have been hard fought for and hard won in the spring. In June 1975, when few students were on campus, the administration reversed its position and served us with an ultimatum: we were told that we were in violation of Title IX and would have all funds cut off by August 15 unless we dropped our "exclusionary" courses. It did not bode well that a few days after its passage, anti-sex-discrimination legislation was being applied *against* a women's studies program. The issue of Title IX had been raised first during the chartering process, and although we were prepared to make our case at that time, the administration had avoided legal questions and chose to make their attack primarily on educational grounds.

We began a letter campaign to extend the deadline, arguing that this was an arbitrary and unfair action. It allowed no time for fair open hearings, which were provided for in the one-year self-evaluation outlined in the rules and regulations for compliance with Title IX. The campaign was successful, and the deadline was extended until October 15 when students would be back on campus to prepare a defense and support the program. At this time, there were contradictory legal interpretations of Title IX. Our position was that WSC was a program with an affirmative action thrust and, as such, Title IX did not bar the exclusion of men.* The administration refused to see us as a program in-

---

* Section 86.3b of Title IX reads: b) Affirmative Action. In the absence of a finding of discrimination on the basis of sex in an education program or activity a recipient may take affirmative action to overcome the effects of conditions which resulted in limited participation therein by persons of a particular sex. Nothing herein shall be interpreted to alter any affirmative action obligations which a recipient may have under Executive Order 11246.

volved in affirmative action for women. In fact, they did not see that sex discrimination referred to discrimination against *women,* and that women had a right to affirmative action.

We had the option of going to court but decided not to for several reasons: (a) there was a good chance that the College would be closed during litigation; (b) it would be much harder to bring the issue to the public's attention; (c) we would be relying on one judge to act in our favor, rather than on mass political action to win a victory, and (d) court action would be a money and energy drain. In essence, we saw the real issue as co-optation or termination of our program. Raising the question of the legality of all-women classes was just a tactic to divert us from our primary goal – the education of women.

At this point, our main task was to build mass support. We had to clarify for ourselves, as well as for our constituency, the importance of all-women classes and expose the university's faculty implementation and interpretation of Title IX. This process entailed mobilizing students, community women, national contacts, and people who were concerned with the education of women. What we were demanding, primarily, was that the President (whose office was the initiator of the offensive against us) be responsive to the educational needs of women on campus and to the voices of our supporters. If the President was really concerned about our compliance with Title IX, we should have been allowed the year of self-evaluation outlined in the federal rules and regulations. Instead, he declared us illegal on his own authority and gave us a month to comply, under the threat of loss of funding and cancellation of all our courses. To gather the support necessary to force the administration to give us time, we held educational rallies, started a petition drive, picketed the administration building, and met with various officials to convince them that our arguments were sound. We were also instrumental in getting the faculty senate to pass a resolution supporting our position.

The President's office would not answer our arguments or acknowledge our support. Finally, it was a matter of raw power, and since the administration had more of it than we did, we now had to work to ensure the very existence of the program. The pressure and strain took a tremendous toll. In the hectic two weeks before we had to make the decision to keep fighting or give up, there was much discussion, disagreement, and division. We decided that rather than lose the courses, we would officially open them to men.

Throughout our struggle, WSC had responsible and legitimate arguments. The administration responded by constantly shifting the grounds of their own arguments among the various legal, educational, and moral issues involved, never directly answering our points. They had the power to define and redefine arguments as they pleased. Our arguments were labeled irrational. The following shows some of this process and, briefly, the points at issue:

We Said	**They Said**
All-women courses are a vital part of women's education.	
	All-women courses aren't educationally valid.
We proved validity through academic channels.	
	Your courses violate academic freedom because of basic assumption that women are oppressed.
That assumption is real. Would the geography department say the world is flat?	
	You're just doing consciousness raising.
No, we are looking at women's personal experiences to understand them in a social context.	
	Educational experience is impoverished by excluding male participation and contribution.
Men's and women's experiences are different due to power relations. Men have little to contribute in this context. The administration's overwhelming emphasis on "male exclusion" is due to its protection of its interests as men and fear of women's autonomy.	
	No exclusion is allowable on the basis of sex regardless of which

one. Title IX Subpart D 86.34, Access to Course Offerings: "A recipient shall not provide any course or otherwise carry out any of its education program or activity separately on the basis of sex, or require or refuse participation therein by any of its students on such basis . . . ."

Historically, it is women who have been "excluded" and we must have affirmative action. Clearly all-women classes are an educational format designed to redress the effects of past discrimination and constitute Title IX Subpart A 86.3b, Affirmative Action: "In the absence of a finding of discrimination on the basis of sex in an education program or activity, a recipient may take affirmative action to overcome the effects of conditions which result in limited participation therein by person of a particular sex. *Nothing herein shall be interpreted to alter any affirmative action obligations which a recipient may have under Executive Order 11246.*" [italics added]

Morally, this is reverse discrimination.

Discrimination has to do with social power. Women as a group do not have the power to discriminate against men. As a concept, "reverse discrimination" negates the institutionalized oppression of women, Third World, working class, and gay people.

If you have all-women classes, then the Blacks will want all-Black classes, the Poles will want all-Polish classes, and the homosexuals will want all-homosexual classes.

Every oppressed group should have autonomy.

Open courses to men, or we'll close the College.

You can't destroy a strong educational program.

Open courses to men, or we'll close the College.

CONCLUSION

Capitalism, patriarchy, and racism are inseparably intertwined. Because these are the major systems of social organization that perpetuate oppression in our society, an analysis of them must provide the framework for developing strategies to resist them. Organized resistance can take many forms. In fighting to make the institution of the university more responsive to the needs of women, Women's Studies College engages in institutional struggle. The issue this time was the fight for all-women classes. Embodied in the issue was a demand for more autonomy, more control over our educational experience.

Some major points that arise from an analysis of this situation are:

1. Since capitalism and patriarchy are inseparably intertwined, you cannot have a strategy based on an analysis of one and not the other. These systems are supported by an ideology that says everybody is equal and ignores power relations, repression, and resistance. In the all-women classes, we gave a critique of capitalism, patriarchy, and racism, thereby exposing and undermining this ideology. Fighting for all-women classes publicly was a further threat because people were organizing around a recognition of our oppression. Organizing as students, the bottom of the educational heap, was bad enough; organizing as women, who should be seen and not heard, was a double threat. We threatened not only the class nature of the university but also its male-supremacist nature.

2. The existence of patriarchy and male supremacy as a system was brought home once again. In addition, the need to document and develop a theoretical understanding of this system – like the existing theory of capitalism and class relations – was made clear. All-women classes, as an issue, zeroed in on the differences between men and women and the relations between the sexes. The virulence of the attack and the harsh treatment that we received, both individually and collectively, pointed up the depth of misogynous sentiments and the consolidation of male power. By denying the need for affirmative action that redresses the historic oppression of women, the administration denied the fact of that oppression and the male power that enforces it. They could and did say that sex discrimination did not necessarily refer to discrimination against women. Thus, a law written to end sex discrimination in education (Title IX) was, as far as we know, used first *against* a women's studies program. This reversal of the explicit intent of these laws and the legal concept of affirmative action made male power over women clear. The other side of this recognition was a realization of the depth of our oppression.

3. Institutional struggle is inevitable for our program because we are in the university *and* responsible to the women's liberation movement. It is our ties to the movement that direct us to the theories and strategies that help us provide the best education for women – an education that aids us in our struggle for liberation. We feel that for women's studies programs to be responsible to their constituency, and to survive without being co-opted, they must retain their ties to the women's movement. This commitment means engaging in institutional struggle. However, programs will receive the support necessary for this struggle if they meet the educational needs of women: women move to protect what is in their interests. For example, at Women's Studies College at Buffalo, thirty to forty people do the core maintenance work of the program. There is no way that we could attempt to challenge the power of the administration by ourselves. It has always been the hundreds and thousands of students who support our work who have provided the force behind our demands.

We learned that there are few decisive losses or victories in institutional struggle. The institution will change only as the society changes. Even though we had to give up temporarily the selective use of all-women classes as a publicly recognized principle, we reached many people with our views about sexism and oppression. And in organizing and waging the battle, we all learned a great deal about resistance.

4. The relationship between the fight for all-women classes and the struggles of other oppressed groups became clear. We realized that what we were asking for was, in a broad sense, self-determination. An important precedent would have been set had we won; thus, the viciousness of the attack. In the administration's own words, if you have all-women classes, then the Blacks will want all-Black classes . . . . The university would have been forced to acknowledge for one oppressed group the right to develop its own education, one that would work as a tool for liberation. The potential of the precedent was the power of the threat.

1978

WOMEN'S STUDIES AT SUNY/BUFFALO: AN UPDATE

Women's Studies College at the State University of New York at Buffalo (WSC) continues to recreate and reshape itself to serve the changing needs of women and to survive the opposition of a traditional educational system. In the seven years since 1975 and the struggle for all-women classes, WSC has lived and relived the lessons of that fight: each victory, however small, is hard won; no victory is ever secure; the struggle for change must be a reward in itself – educating and motivating women to recognize their own strengths. Our work in recent years reflects this determination, these goals, and these frustrations.

THE B.A. IN WOMEN'S STUDIES

As the annual budget for the SUNY system decreases, as student activism fades and a concern for individual career opportunities grows, WSC has faced new problems. The university no longer feels the pressure to provide alternative, student-designed curricula. Since 1981, WSC has existed as an elective program within The Colleges, one of several such alternative educational units. Our faculty members, however, have traditionally held their positions and/or tenure in the Department of American Studies within the Faculty of Arts and Letters. This has placed us in an uncomfortable position of dependency within two administrative structures.

In order to decrease time spent on bureaucratic tasks and to encourage an administrative and financial commitment to our program, we decided four years ago that preserving women's right to a feminist education means formalizing our curriculum and creating a degree-granting program in Women's Studies. Students in this program will be able to maintain a personal commitment to their academic major and their career training, while learning the skills and the theory necessary to feminist political endeavors. This move to a degree-granting program is our way of responding to a changing political climate when more students are without prior experience in the women's movement, when women are increasingly committing themselves to personal career goals, and when Women's Studies programs across the country are also implementing B.A. programs.

To this end, we worked to extend our contacts within the several university faculties. We drafted a B.A. proposal that has made the rounds of various faculty, administrator, and student committees. We designed a degree program which allows students a maximum of flexibility within their curriculum while requiring a specific, often career-oriented concentration. Practicums are built into the program, providing students with the chance to secure actual job experience and the practical application of their studies. The B.A. proposal received wide support from the faculty review committee and is now with the SUNY offices in Albany awaiting final approval. We expect its implementation in the near future.

While we believe the B.A. proposal will secure our Women's Studies program within the university, we realize that doing so involves certain compromises. Departmental status means greater institutionalization in our process. We will be drawn even further into the hierarchy and the politics of the university, and energies devoted to maintaining the program and its values will limit our efforts to sustain our radical critique. This realization has been painstakingly discussed within the program; but we realized that the increasing budget cuts Women's Studies has experienced are already crippling our ability to act as a collective, student-run program. For example, we no longer are able to pay student and community-women staff to serve as coordinators. This jeopardizes one of our strongest program elements: the training of women to take control of their own educational process and to develop leadership and administrative skills.

In 1981, the university administration refused to maintain the student and community-women staff positions and to hire the full-time Third World women's faculty member we requested. Instead, we received a one-year full-time faculty coordinator who would eventually become half-time coordinator and half-time women's history faculty member. We were not happy with this decision, for it compromised both the structure of our program's governance and the program's ability to offer full-time faculty commitment to Third World women. We had to find strategies for coping, however, so we implemented a small, collectively-run Steering Committee to manage the day-to-day maintenance of the program. The committee is composed of American Studies/Women's Studies faculty, Women's Studies graduate students, and volunteers from the student body. Although this committee somewhat circumvents the traditional hierarchy our program faced with the elimination of student staff, our student training is now limited to funded students, internships, and volunteers. The development of working-class leadership suffers, and we are concerned that we ourselves contribute to the overwork and exploitation of women who voluntarily give of their time and energies to maintain the program.

These problems, as well as diminishing funding for community instructors, less political awareness on campus, and the individual burnout that results from such constant struggle, are all contributing factors in our decision to become a degree-granting undergraduate program. We hope that the compromises and struggles we face in our attempts to preserve collectivity, student instructors, and a radical critique of society and the academy, will be balanced by the greater security provided by our new place in the university.

THIRD WORLD WOMEN

Some of our most difficult and most important work in recent years has included efforts to develop a coherent and comprehensive critique of the effects and interrelations of racism and sexism within the university and within our society; to offer this critique through a varied and well-structured curriculum; to provide intellectual resources and support for Third World women on campus through the Third World Women's Caucus; and to actively combat racism in the university as a whole and within our own program. The Third World Women's Caucus, composed of a faculty coordinator and Third World students, has produced a variety of courses including "Latin American Women," "Women in the Middle East," and "Black Child in America"; and now a student teaching collective is developing to teach the introductory course, "Minority Women in the U.S." Together with the course, "Women in Contemporary Society," also taught by a student teaching collective, this course has become an integral part of the Women's Studies degree core courses. The enrollment in these Third World courses has grown steadily and, interestingly, they attract a significant number of Third World men who can find this critical attention to other cultures and to racism nowhere else on campus. In addition to courses, the Caucus has been active in organizing and presenting papers at the National Women's Studies Association conferences.

One of the most painful and difficult aspects of our work is the recognition of and struggle against racism in ourselves and in our practice. The courage of various women from the Third World Caucus to speak out has triggered the genuine efforts of other women to see their own racism. Especially at a time when the university is less responsive to Affirmative Action complaints and more willing to cut minority and women's programming, the lines between personal racism and institutional racism begin to blur. It is easier for the university to ignore a group of threatened or divided women, and therefore it is all the more important that we try to openly admit our own biases and to learn to work together solidly for our common benefit. This is an ongoing struggle, and the organization of speak-out meetings and workshops on racism is part of our strategy to forge new understandings.

OUTREACH

WSC has also tried to maintain its ties with the larger women's movement and to reach out beyond the university. Diminishing resources have severely limited this work, but we do continue to work actively with the Regional and the National Women's Studies Associations. Faculty and students from our program serve regularly as delegates and conference organizers, as well as participants on panels and in workshops. We also cosponsor community and university programs for women. Our funds are now too limited to provide monetary support, but we offer publicity and womanpower where we can. Finally, our building, our library, and the women who work in the program serve as valuable resources for community members and for students in other departments who are working on women's issues.

In the years since 1975, WSC has suffered setbacks, many of them reflections of the country's growing conservatism and cuts of social programs. We also continue to reach hundreds of women each year, however, to introduce them to an active critique of their society and their education; to develop a new awareness of the interrelations between sexism, racism, and economic realities; and to provide women with a context, a guide, and the motivation to actively change their education and their lives. Our struggle will be to continue this outreach in the coming years in the face of diminishing resources.

1982

The New Right Challenges Women's Studies: The Long Beach Women's Studies Program

by Betty Willis Brooks and Sharon L. Sievers

> Until left liberals and leftists recognize that New Right politics is fundamentally about the familial and sexual structuring of society, they will remain ineffective in the politics of the 1980s. It will be feminists who will have to "fight the Right."
>
> Zillah Eisenstein[1]

WHEN EISENSTEIN'S article appeared last spring, faculty and students in the Women's Studies Program at California State University Long Beach (CSULB) were learning firsthand the bitter truth of that statement.

Though evangelical Christians had appeared in the Women's Center the previous September to demand that anti-ERA literature be distributed there, none of us paid much attention. When some of the same people arrived on campus in March to monitor W/ST 101 ("Women and Their Bodies: An Introduction to the Biology and Sexuality of Women") and gather "evidence" against the program, a chill settled in that is still with us.

The specific chronology of attacks on the CSULB Women's Studies Program can be found in the Appendix. What we would like to discuss here are our reactions to these events and some of their implications for feminist teaching.

A number of years ago, we made a decision to offer the introductory courses in Women's Studies in two parts – one dealing with issues of sexuality and health, and the other with issues related to the progress and status of women in contemporary

78

society. Both courses have done well, but the sexuality course has been controversial (from the university's standpoint) from the beginning, arousing strong patriarchal reactions on and off the campus. There have been telephone calls from irate fathers who find our teaching daughters about their bodies – particularly teaching self-examination – repugnant and objectionable. Male administrators have been suspicious of the content and intent of the course; in one instance, an administrator assumed that self-help meant teaching women how to satisfy themselves sexually, and thus made the course a training ground for lesbians.

Eventually, we found it necessary to establish firm, university-approved guidelines for self-examination in the classroom, and everyone who teaches the course adheres to them. We also stress the importance of taking responsibility for dealing with sensitive subjects in such a course. In spite of a few complaints and the disgruntled utterances of administrators, there was never a serious challenge to the course or the program until March 1982.

What accounts for the change?

According to Rosaline Petchesky, "What feminists for generations have been urging – that issues related to the family, sexuality and reproduction are political at their roots, that they ramify on every level of public and social life – has been squarely brought home to everyone by the staunchest foes of feminism."[2] But it has not been brought home to everyone.

From the beginning, the university's failure to protect Women's Studies with the same enthusiasm it might have generated for Biology or History stemmed from two related sources: first, a long-standing hostility to Women's Studies that has denied us a single tenure-track position, though we have been around for a decade; and second, the institution's inherent sexism made it impossible for administrators to accept the fact that an attack on women or women's issues might *really* be political. As a result, the university was completely unprepared to take our critics seriously and deal with them. This is still the case.

Faculty and students in the program were left with the responsibility of educating themselves, the press, hostile administrators, and skeptical colleagues. People in the community became our earliest and most knowledgeable allies in this fight, though some of our colleagues did ultimately come through for us.

The initial point of attack on W/ST 101, and later on Betty Brooks' teaching of extension courses, was predictably focused on "lesbian bias" and the encouragement of "deviance." To no one's surprise, university administrators were themselves suspicious enough of these issues to be pushed into extraordinary curricular reviews and basic violations of academic freedom. In spite of the failure of investigations to find any substance in right-wing complaints, attacks on Brooks and her teaching about sexuality continue to insinuate that the content of her teaching is "lesbian indoctrination."

Why does the New Right view a course like 101 as such a threat? The class provides an overview of women's biology, health, and sexuality. What is disturbing is that the course encourages women to comment on what they read, to react to what other women have to say about what constitutes a healthy woman in this society, and to gain permission to take steps to remedy long years of sexual repression. It addresses the current health care system and what it does to women — when and where "the fear and flesh loathing" Adrienne Rich speaks about become institutionalized in such a way that we are obsessed with body consciousness and a repressed sexuality.

The course allows women to define the problem, to struggle, and point to solutions. Most of us who teach 101 use lectures, films, speakers, and assignments designed to raise consciousness. Students are responsible for a final research paper or project dealing with topics covered during the semester. The selection might typically include anything from hysterectomy to sexual-object choice repression to questions raised by Fat Underground. Students are asked to learn to value their opinions by reacting to lectures, readings, and other assignments. We keep journals, menstrual charts, and exercise logs. We interview people around us on the questions raised by the class. It is all standard feminist teaching designed to value a woman's observations about life as a woman — living in a body defined as Body in a patriarchal world. Some of it is new; a lot of it is old.

What I (Brooks) found when I started teaching this class is that, as women, we were simply ignorant of having any choices at all. So I began by trying to provide a thorough review of all the options in the range of human sexuality as they are typically expressed in all cultures. I now present all of the sexual object choices, but I do not present all the ways that people express themselves. I attempt to give an overview of sex-role socialization and sexual-object choice selection against the backdrop of cultural influences and the power relationships that exist between men and women. The idea that we have choices, and that we can learn about ourselves sexually on our own (with the help of other women), has been made possible by the pioneering work of Sherfey, Barbach, Dodson, and others. But it has not been made easy.

It is very difficult to convince women that sexual behavior is normal and that having less or more sex does not define you as an ethical or moral person. Because we are judged by what our bodies look like, and our sexual behavior has for so long been regulated by moral injunctions or the fear of pregnancy, it is problematic for us to see ourselves as assertive sexual beings. Most of us still end up in dependent situations sexually.

Part of what the Bodies class is about is providing a safe space for women to talk without shame, without fear of having their anxieties, activities, and fantasies judged. In discussions designed to inform students of various sexual lifestyles and the persecution that often accompanies those lifestyles, I try to get them to understand their own positions – their power, privilege, and their prejudices. In a sex-negative society that is especially judgmental of women, it is difficult, however, for women to hear other points of view without thinking they are being asked to make a choice that is not their own. There is so much fear among women and such a residual oppression around sexuality that finding a safe place to talk is both imperative and almost impossible. It is one reason why it is so difficult to teach with men in the classroom: whether they like it or not, they symbolize the power many women are struggling with in sexual relationships.

How does one achieve some measure of honesty in the classroom? Talking "sexually" out loud in class is frightening for most people. I use shocking language. Sexual language, like religious language, denotes and connotes significance and power. To dare to say the words out loud, to reclaim their power for women, is dangerous. Most of the derogatory terms used to shock and hurt women are sexual, and/or they relate to body functions. When I take the words back – use the term *cunt*, for example – I run the risk of being labeled "insensitive" or "vulgar," as has happened in the last few months. But the important thing is that my students understand what we are doing, and that they feel secure enough in that classroom to grapple with the issues.

I take strong positions, and I tell my students the first day of class that I welcome their dialogue with me. My right to be myself in the classroom is not intended to infringe on their right to make different choices and to come to different conclusions. I think it is imperative that in a women's sexuality/health class, students see an honest model: a woman who has lived through various experiences and who tries to be truthful about them, who wants to share her experience (with all its ambiguities) with them. I would like to have taken a class from a woman who allowed her feelings as well as her ideas to energize the classroom. That's the kind of teacher I try to be.

I hope when a woman leaves my class, she will feel good about her body and will know that there are a range of options available to her. She will know that a patriarchal definition of the world splits her off from herself, and that she may have to fight for the right to make choices in a society that often tries to say that she has none. These are goals of feminist teaching around issues of women's sexuality; they speak to the control of women's bodies by women. No society has ever really agreed to that.

Of course the New Right finds such a course objectionable. Among the moral absolutes they favor, few rank higher than the notion that a woman's body is not her own. Woman is ordained to be a homemaker and reproductive agent; there is a right way for her to live, a right way to have sex, an eternal moral order that requires women to submit to their husbands. As one of the women who spearheaded the attack on Women's Studies at Long Beach explained:

> I'm not by nature particularly domestic. It didn't come naturally for me to be a homemaker. But instead of becoming a feminist, I became a Christian. The extreme feminist viewpoint that I see reflected in textbooks used in Women's Studies is against male leadership in the home and that male leadership was given by God . . . . It's against the traditional family as God established it in scripture. So to be an extreme feminist and a Christian, I think you'd have to give up one or the other. I don't think they're compatible.[3]

We think the New Right first attacked a women's sexuality class and then Betty Brooks not because they were ends in themselves. Sexuality and uppity women are relatively easy targets, but the real goal is broader than that: to disrupt, dilute, or perhaps even do away with feminist teaching on a college campus. We don't think they anticipated how simple the administration would make it for them. By the same token, we would expect other programs to be able to fend off such attacks without having to resort, as we did, to an American Civil Liberties Union (ACLU) suit to protect our right to teach from a feminist perspective.

Still, it is clear that the New Right intends to attack women's studies throughout the decade and hopes to implement elements of the Family Protection Act on college campuses wherever possible. They will act in public institutions first because it allows them to argue that taxpayer money should not go to support "unbalanced" women's studies programs or universities that allow "pornographic" or "subversive" books to be used in the classroom.[4]

Feminism *is* being targeted as the subversive ideology of the decade. "Feminism," according to one member of the Grace Brethren Church, "is an intense desire to undermine the very freedom of our government."[5] It is a palpable evil to be exposed, and it is also in the eyes of the New Right, connected to "left-wing" causes. That this connection is made became obvious to us during the summer, when neatly drafted posters appeared all over campus with the following slogans: Abort Brooks!, Nuke the Anti-Nukes!, Nuke the Commies!, and (are they serious?) Stop Brooks' Madness! Sondra Hale, a socialist feminist who was director of the program, received an unsigned, uncancelled postcard in campus mail suggesting that she resign and go the way of all "commies and commie sympathizers" who mislead the young.

The tactics of the New Right are already well documented. They are not squeamish about character assassination or a carefully placed lie or two. They understand better than most the anti-intellectualism that runs deeply through the country, and they know how to manipulate the fear and irrationality surrounding both sex and religion. They do not value abstractions like "academic freedom," but they will pretend to appreciate the intellectual tolerance that is the lifeblood of any university – up to the moment they have the power to deny it to their enemies. They are, as Richard Viguerie, the New Right's political fundraiser says, "true revolutionaries,"[6] the leaders of a moral crusade that will transform the country. Apparently women's studies is important to that transformation because such programs can be used to educate women to their proper roles. But first one must purge women's studies of its feminist content. That is exactly what is being attempted on the Long Beach campus.

You may have thought that women's studies without feminist content was a contradiction in terms. Not so. According to State Chairman JoEllen Allen of Eagle Forum, Phyllis Schlafly could teach a women's studies class that would have the proper balance. The Long Beach program, she said, was based on "academic fraud . . . it is not just women's studies with classes about feminism . . . . Feminism is all that they teach. A program should be balanced. A young woman shouldn't be indoctrinated. The title's a lie. They should call it 'feminist studies.' "[7] Evangelical Christians complain that *all* the women's studies books in the bookstore contained feminist bias; they were shocked, they said, to learn that women's studies courses at Long Beach were being taught exclusively from a feminist perspective!

In recent weeks, the New Right in Long Beach has turned to a petition drive, assisted by various fundamentalist groups and churches. The petition asks for a university classroom ban on films depicting explicit sex and textbooks "detailing how to practice sadomasochism, sex with animals and sex with body wastes." This demand, sure to get the public's attention, refers to a recommended text for 101 (Pat Califia's *Sapphistry*)[8] designed to introduce students to a primary source in the current debate over sexuality and pornography in the women's movement. One of the New Right's typical ploys has been to suggest that Brooks advocates what the book contains, just as they suggest she advocates lesbianism because she teaches about it and presents it to students in a positive way. Classroom instruction about lesbianism, according to one of our critics, should include "bringing forth a gal who's tried it and had her life wrecked by it."

The petition also asks the university to prohibit classroom demonstrations of gynecological self-examination by health care professionals, or "at the very least," to remove lesbian students from the classroom during the demonstrations.[9] By focusing on lesbianism and "sexual deviance," they can avoid entirely the fact that they are attempting to undermine the most basic elements of tax-supported higher education.

Given these circumstances, our survival (more or less intact) represents a triumph of rather large dimensions. But we are painfully aware, as classes begin, that survival is not enough. Somehow, those of us who remain in the program now need to find a way to teach effectively as feminists in a threatening, intimidating climate. We have to learn, for example, how to trust and respect our students when we know some of them will now be enrolling simply to gather information that will be used by the New Right. We need to share responsibility with our students for learning about women in an untrammeled atmosphere – one that recognizes the reality of the attack without giving in to it. Somehow, we must see to it that things in the classroom remain pretty much the same when we all know that everything has changed.

August 1982

APPENDIX: CHRONOLOGY OF THE ATTACK ON CSULB WOMEN'S STUDIES

Phase I: During the 1982 spring semester, a small group of women, at least one of whom is connected with the Grace Brethren Church in Long Beach, began to collect information about Women's Studies courses, especially W/ST 101, "Women and Their Bodies." In a visit to the Associate Dean for Educational Policy and to the Program Director, complaints were made about the alleged lesbian emphasis of Women's Studies courses and the lack of courses which espouse "traditional American values." A letter reiterating this complaint was sent to the Program Director, with copies to campus administrators and conservative group and legislators.

During spring break, this group of self-styled defenders of morality (including JoEllen Allen, State Chairman [*sic*] of Eagle Forum, the antifeminist group organized by Phyllis Schlafly), accompanied by aides from the offices of Senators Speraw and Richardson, and Assemblyman Dennis Brown, met with President Horn, Vice-President Drake, Associate Vice-President Haller, and Dean Crowther. Women's Studies faculty were neither invited nor informed of the meeting. Following and apparently pursuant to this meeting, a curriculum review of W/ST 101 was ordered.

On May 12, the Dean informed Vice-President Drake that the course had been favorably reviewed by the School Curriculum Committee.

Phase II: Since the course came through this unprecedented review intact, the next step was to attack one of the faculty members who teaches the course, Dr. Betty Brooks. Senator Speraw's office sent to the campus statements apparently gathered by his staff with the assistance of the same self-professed evangelical Christian who initiated the first complaint, Jessica Reynolds Shaver.

As a result of three unfounded complaints being lodged against Brooks, she was removed from her summer teaching duties and was reassigned to other duties. Her class was cancelled, despite evidence of high enrollment.

Phase III: On June 17, the Dean informed the Women's Studies Advisory Committee (the governing body) that: (1) the two-year lectureship, the only full-time position in Women's Studies, was being suspended; (2) he would do all hiring; and, (3) if there was no one qualified to teach a course (by his criteria rather than the criteria of the Women's Studies faculty most familiar with the discipline), the course would be cancelled.

Phase IV: Dr. Betty Brooks was notified on June 18 that three of her Fall Continuing Education courses were being cancelled. She was further informed on August 2 by Dr. Donna George, Dean of Continuing Education, that her name had been removed from the catalogue listing for four of the courses which she had been regularly teaching.

Phase V: In a statement to the press (first published on July 2 in the *Long Beach Press-Telegram*), Vice-President Drake and Associate Vice-President Haller announced their plans to "restructure" the Women's Studies Program and to drastically alter the direction of the University Women's Center. These announced plans, which included soliciting the advice of an outside consultant, had not been discussed with the Women's Studies faculty.

Phase VI: On July 22, the University Women's Center was abolished, effective September 1, 1982. In announcing the dismantling of the Women's Center and its replacement by the "Center for Continuing Education for Women," no mention was made of continuing some of the basic services provided by the Women's Center, like rape-victim and sexual harrassment counseling.

On August 4, 1982, a lawsuit was filed by the ACLU on behalf of the Women's Studies Advisory Committee, core faculty, and students. The suit charges the university administration with interference with First Amendment, due process, and equal protection rights.

UPDATE: As the result of the filing of the lawsuit and of the public outcry from women's studies professionals, liberal legislators, concerned faculty, students, and community members, some concessions have been made. Dr. Sondra Hale was reappointed to the two-year lectureship, although she was stripped of the directorship.

Women's Studies classes have been cancelled in the fall semester for what we see as primarily political reasons. Although the university was forced to drop the investigation into complaints against Brooks gathered by the New Right, they have never made a public statement exonerating her and refused to allow her to teach both sections of 101. They cancelled "Women and Mental Illness" after refusing to hire Linda Shaw, a highly qualified teacher who is a founder of the Long Beach Women's Studies Program, and who was described by an administrator earlier this year as an "ideologue."

Though full-time and part-time women in the program have agreed to the appointment of advisory board members as directors of the program on a rotating basis during this struggle, it is clear that the administration will make most of the major decisions about the program's future.

At this writing, the university has not responded to the New Right's announced intention of continuing its attack on the program. In fact, it has not made a single public statement in support of either the program or academic freedom since May 1982.

NOTES

1. Zillah Eisenstein, "The Sexual Politics of the New Right: Understanding the 'Crisis of Liberalism' for the 1980s," *Signs,* vol. 7, no. 3 (Spring 1982), pp. 569-570.

2. Rosaline Pollack Petchesky, "Antiabortion, Antifeminism, and the Rise of the New Right," *Feminist Studies,* vol. 7, no. 2 (Summer 1981), p. 208.

3. William Orton and Vicky Hendley, "A Voice from the 'right,'" *Union Daily,* July 6, 1982, p. 7. Or, from Jerry Falwell's "A Day in the Life of a Christian College Student's Life," a housewife's prayer: "Lord, it's been one of those mornings again . . . I stumbled around getting everyone's clothes in order and then faced my closet . . . as my husband's wife, I feel compelled to look my best . . . . It's raining and the windshield wipers won't work. 'You should have told me!' he says. I did tell him Lord, but he's so busy and I am told not to nag. (Didn't some spiritual leader tell me that nagging is like being nibbled to death by a duck) . . . . He'll be out of school

soon, and maybe I can stay home again and be everything I'm told to be as a wife and mother. I just feel that he'll be full spiritually and I'll be drained . . . Help me to hang on." William R. Goodman and James H. Price, *Jerry Falwell: An Unauthorized Profile* (Parish and Associates, Lynchburg, Virginia 1981), pp. 136-137.

4. For example, Gordon Browning, legislative aide to the ultra-conservative Senator H.L. Richardson, said at one point that he had "about 25 educational items, including books, films, and slides from [Brooks'] course" that he found "questionable." Since the legislature is spending millions of dollars on the university, he said, there is "nothing wrong with looking at the way you are spending your money and seeing you get your money's worth." Ina Aranow, "A Problem Course At CSULB," *Los Angeles Times,* May 11, 1982, Part 5, p. 3.

5. Maura Dolan, "Evangelicals Confront Feminism," *Los Angeles Times,* Southeast Area Edition, August 26, 1982, p. 1.

6. "We are no longer working to preserve the status quo. We are radicals working to overthrow the power structure of this country. We organize discontent and must prove our ability to get revenge on people who are against us." Quoted in Suzanne McCorkle, "Richard Viguerie and the New Right on Women's Issues," unpublished paper presented at the National Women's Studies Association, June 16-22, 1982, p. 4.

7. Doreen Carvajal, "Women's Studies in Turmoil at CSULB," *Long Beach Press-Telegram,* August 23, 1982, p. A3.

8. Naiad Press, Tallahassee, Florida, 1980.

9. Dolan, "Evangelicals Confront Feminism."

Teaching the
Feminist Minority*

by Barbara Hillyer Davis

IN WOMEN'S STUDIES conferences during the past few years, I
have heard many descriptions of pedagogical approaches to
specific student groups – working women, displaced home-
makers, business majors, and so on. I admire and learn from
these presentations and at the same time I am uneasy. For some
reason my classes are never like those described. The longer I
teach them, the less homogeneous they seem. I am working out
my role as a women's studies teacher in a university in which –
as in most others, I suspect – no class consists of *just* working-
class women, *just* reentry women, *just* Native American women.
It is time to discuss the work of the feminist teacher in a *mixed*
classroom, where any constituent group may be a minority – and
the smallest consistent minority group is feminist students.

When the field of women's studies began its phenomenal growth
about ten years ago, teachers and students alike were beginners in
a process of self-education. Most of us had been socialized as
"traditional women"; we learned together what that meant. By the
time women's studies classes were offered in our region – the Bible Belt – there were valuable resources, printed and experiential,
to facilitate this reeducational process. Our first classes were
demanded by women who had learned feminism from books and

---

* This article was first published in the *Women's Studies Quarterly,* vol. 9, no. 4
(Winter 1981).

xeroxed essays and who had experienced its practical necessities in the state legislature, in marriage, in consciousness-raising groups. These women, self-educated feminists like their teachers, filled our first classes.

My own first Women in Literature course was very conservative in its content: it focused mainly on Victorian literature and included such male authors as George Meredith, Thomas Hardy, and D.H. Lawrence. My students and I, however, were very well informed about the legal and sociological situation of women in our own time. We brought our personal and political experience into a conventional university classroom and examined the relationship between the two worlds. Together we reread traditional literature in the light of our experience and in the light of contemporary feminist theory. Our expectations of the university classroom itself were traditional; we had no idea that conventional class discussions would soon be inadequate in terms of feminist process. What was radical in our approach was our collective questioning of course *content.*

That was in 1972. By now the situation has almost reversed itself. Gradually the course has changed, literally one volume at a time, so that it now includes "nontraditional" forms, and only women authors, for example, Zora Neale Hurston, Harriette Arnow, and Sarah Wright. A much smaller percentage of the students are feminists, and their awareness of the legal and sociological situation of women in our society is less specific and exact. Less well informed about sexual politics, the majority now are reading nontraditional literature from a more traditional perspective than the earlier students, who had lobbied for the ERA before they petitioned for women's studies.

Both traditional and feminist students are with us still, but their proportions are reversed. This is a sign of our success. Women's studies enrollments are much larger: women from a much wider range of backgrounds now see the study of women as appropriate to university classrooms. The class, therefore, is not for an initiated group only, but for all women and some men. In these circumstances the norms of the university are much more influential. The challenge to me as the teacher is no longer to explore with feminist colleagues the relationship between the legal-sociological condition of women and the literature I learned in graduate school but to educate students who know relatively little about either.

The "traditional" woman assumes as she enters my class that she will spend her life in conventional subordination to men (boyfriend, husband, professor, boss) and, because she has not examined the implications of this assumption, she believes this to be a desirable outcome, freely chosen. "Feminists" share an impatience with the traditional perspective and a belief, ironically similar to that of the traditional students, that women who accept traditional subordination have freely chosen to do so. I am in fact less a peer of these students than I was of the earlier ones; I know more about women's literature and about feminist theory than they do, and I embody the contradictions fostered by the institution in which we work.

The university has taught us well how learning should be done. Because I do "know more" than most of my students, I am easily persuaded that I should impart knowledge for their reception. The institutional pressure to do so is reinforced by the students' well-socialized behavior. If I will tell them "what I want," they will deliver it. They are exasperated with my efforts to depart from the role of dispenser of wisdom.

On the other hand, what I know about feminist process makes me feel an obligation to renounce the professional role, to serve instead as a role model for sisterhood, disclaiming any stance of superiority and presenting myself as one who learns instead of teaching. Struggling to maintain myself between these conflicting pressures, I work out a role as teacher which leans toward a peer relationship but includes enough of the professor to reassure those students who feel comfortable in a more traditional classroom.

In their midst sits a feminist minority — women who have rejected the condescension of the professoriat and who have themselves read some feminist theory. What they want from me is a model of sisterhood and, from the other students, emotional and intellectual support.

Every year, then, I am teaching, at the same time in the same classroom, "kindergarten" and "graduate school," though it is sometimes very difficult to tell which is which. Some students who consider themselves "advanced" in women's studies are separatist/elitist; some who have never before given feminism any thought have a sort of instinct for sisterhood.

Teachers of women's studies have standard devices for bringing these buried contradictions to group or individual consciousness: class journals, small group discussions, readings of feminist essays. The problem is using these tools on two (or ten) levels at once – starting where the individual student is "here and now" when collectively they are in many places. Initially designed to encourage the development of consciousness among traditional women, these devices still seem to work more effectively with that group. We use them in institutions which assume that students-as-beginners and the teacher-as-expert are the norm. Students or teachers who do not share these expectations will seem out of place, even to themselves.

It is a commonplace among us that studying women is a painful experience for women, and that women's studies classrooms should provide an environment in which women can support one another through this pain. But there is also joy in the process, as we discover mutual support and rejoice in the recovery of women's past and women's culture. My recent experience is that this pleasure comes more frequently to "traditional" than to "feminist" students. The process is not, initially at least, so helpful to the small minority whose "consciousness has already been raised." They come to the women's studies classroom with higher expectations, gained especially from feminist literature and also from some limited work in women's groups. They expect, for example, that as they meet the emotional and intellectual needs of other women, their own needs will be met – that their growth into more complex feminist modes will also be supported by the group. But the majority do not know how to support people whose pain is over factions in the women's movement instead of housework.

A traditional student, asked to examine the sexual politics in literature or history, very quickly sees its relationship to her own life. She will grow and change and learn faster in small group discussions with other women who are already clear about their feminism. As traditional students learn from feminists how to analyze their lives as women, they also develop some respect – perhaps even admiration – for the feminists' nontraditional choices. But the feminist students, however "advanced" their intellectual and emotional grasp of feminist issues, often lack empathy with or respect for the hard choices and important conflicts of traditional women.

It is as important for feminists to learn to listen as to be heard – to understand the complexity of traditional women's lives as to present the alternatives of their own. Otherwise, no one is "advanced"; we are all still in first grade. The challenge to us *as teachers* is to keep these two groups together long enough to facilitate their forming relationships and beginning to listen to each other.

The challenge is complicated by the ambiguities in the feminist teacher's dual roles as sister-peer and professor. We may have a commitment to the sister-peer role that makes the conservative majority's obedient cooperation with the professorial role problematic. Our experimental solutions confusingly encompass both roles. We may use professorial power to "require" disclosure, to control group formation, to "facilitate" communication.

This is not all bad. People have to write journals for a while before they understand their importance; they have to stay in a group to develop its effectiveness. To provide structure may be the best way to encourage growth. Having acknowledged this, we wish that we could do better for the feminist students. Precisely because their reasons for making additional demands are feminist ones, we want to meet them.

One of the easiest ways to alleviate the distress of feminists in a conservative classroom is to permit students to segregate themselves into "beginning" and "advanced" subgroups. If we permit or encourage such segregation, we may in the guise of "freedom" be encouraging a decision to avoid a more difficult but potentially more rewarding choice. If, on the other hand, we insist that the groups remain "mixed," we must beware of oppressing the feminist minority. We don't want feminist students to go away, nor should we expect them to become adjunct teachers whose own needs for growth and support are not met.

The most typical ways of helping the desired female bonding to take place are variations on traditional women's roles. We may choose to play superwoman, wife, or mother. Superwoman is a feminization of the professorial role: by adding responsibilities for interpersonal relationships to our work as discussion leaders, evaluators, role models, and paper graders, we "humanize" the classroom. Feminist students encourage the teacher's superwoman role because they, too, have been taught by the educational system that learning is transmitted from teacher to student. Anticipating a different quality of learning from the women's studies classroom, they expect to be reinforced and supported as feminists, not "just as women" (I quote a student). Since (because the institution shapes the way we expect education to take place) even feminists are more comfortable with being *told* than with being *shown*, they expect, like the majority, a better experience through conventional forms, and therefore prefer additions to those forms, not substitutes for them. So we play the role of superwoman, killing ourselves with overwork and denying the students' responsibility for their own relationships.

The role of wife is more insidious. "Let me help you be more comfortable," we suggest. "You're OK, dear, and I will work to reassure you." The role is closely related to that of mother – the role both we and our students probably prefer. I want to meet the student's needs and she wants me to – nurturing, protecting, loving. The catch to these two solutions is that the proper correlative roles are those of husband and child, neither of which seems appropriate to a feminist classroom.

None of these responses to the plight of the feminist student works very well, but all are serious efforts to work as *women* – not in the professorial father role. What we need – and what I believe we are learning to do – is to develop a new role for teachers of these mixed groups, another way of learning, which blends realism about the institutional context with belief in the feminist future.

A more effective, more intellectual, and more feminist role than that of superwoman, wife, or mother is that of simultaneous translator. This role involves hearing and giving back in other words what another person has just said, and at the same time presenting an explanation in another language which will illuminate the issue for a second group without alienating the first. A statement from a still traditional student will, in this model, be fed back to the speaker in a way that tells her she is indeed being heard and understood while at the same time an explanation in theoretical feminist language is provided for another member of the group. This is a practical illustration of the slogan that decorates many of our office doors: Feminism Spoken Here.

The translator intends to teach the "second language" at the same time that interpretation is occurring and the discussion is being advanced to its next stage. The translator works in both languages, without making value judgments about either, but with sensitivity to the nuances of each.

Feminist students have access to a descriptive vocabulary, drawn from their reading of Adrienne Rich or Mary Daly or Susan

Brownmiller, which will be new to other students. The concept of translation may enable them to apply this vocabulary to their own behavior in new ways, as that behavior is interpreted to the others.

For example, when some feminist students threaten to drop out because they can't bear listening to women who conventionally affiliate with men, what they are doing is dichotomizing: dividing women into "good" and "bad" categories on the basis of lifestyle, much as antifeminist groups have done (naming dependent housewives "good" and women's libbers "bad"). Recognizing the dichotomy in the context of feminist analysis of masculinist reasoning is useful both for the students who make such announcements and for the listeners who will be surprised and probably threatened by them. Both groups need to consider how and why such reasoning is masculinist and integral to the institution in which their discussion is taking place.

When students complain that "women are our own worst enemy," the statement can be explored in terms of what Mary Daly has said about women as the enforcers of mutilation (foot-binding, for example) and also as a further example of dichotomizing. The use of Daly's language, which engages us in her analysis, reassures the feminist student that we do speak feminism while asking her to see the connection between her own vocabulary and that of traditional women.

Although the immediate goal of the teacher who performs such philosophical or linguistic analysis may be to alleviate or confront the students' immediate distress, the eventual goal is a change in the teacher's relationship to both groups. As group members learn the second language, they will begin to use it, becoming translators themselves. And as the teacher shares this role, she becomes more like the sister-peer of her ideology. Although her knowledge may remain greater in quantity, it will have become similar in kind. All will be bilingual.

The translator has to have two vocabularies which are consistent with each other and must be able to slip back and forth in response to nonverbal clues as well as words and other symbols. She connects the philosophical with everyday experience. Students who have already read Mary Daly and Susan Griffin may learn much by developing a sensitivity to the language and perspective of women who have never heard of either. It is seriously feminist, after all, to recognize that some women's values are important and different from men's and that traditional women's language and culture are valuable in their own right.

Students who enter a class with the rigid ideology of the university, believing that good teachers dispense wisdom and good students absorb it, learn only with difficulty how to think critically. Those who condemn past attitudes as less valuable than present ones, or beginners as less deserving of respect than those who have rejected their beginnings, will also learn only with difficulty how to think in other ways. Both groups share a cultural expectation that there are right answers and that they can be learned from good teachers. Since we want students to struggle with questions that do not have "right" answers, we are ourselves struggling against that deeply acculturated expectation.

Recognizing this may enable us to understand the paradoxes of our own behavior as teachers. My own teaching strategies, for example, have become more conservative even as my feminism has become more radical. This reflects the conservatism of my students and my belief that within a conservative institution only carefully constructed support will permit the transition to other modes. At the simplest level this may require me to *explain* how women's experience is devalued in our economic and social system, or to *state* that a group's frustration may come from the difficulty of attempting a nonhierarchical relationship in a political context that enforces hierarchical norms, so that what we attempt and the ways we fall short become conscious. At a more complex level, what is effected by the process of translation is awareness of the shaping power of language: that understanding of the crucial life experiences of women involves learning to "think like" other women.

Literature is often used to develop students' empathy for women whose lifestyles are different from their own. Class members' experiences can be used in the same way, though the teacher may have to interpret as the novelist has done. When some students describe their own inclination to "mother" their husbands, their dilemma can be interpreted to others who cannot imagine being so male-dominated by references to Adrienne Rich and Nancy Chodorow, but it can also be presented to both groups as illustrating women's values. The feminist student is thus asked to appreciate the skills involved in balancing the emotional needs of husband and children, while the traditional student comes to understand how the institution of motherhood limits people. This can be accomplished by echoing the language of the traditional students and the language of feminist theory in the same discussion, thus expanding both vocabularies while affirming both.

Citation of feminist theory meets everyone's expectation that wisdom will be dispensed in the classroom. Translation of that theory into the languages of several populations of the class helps meet the needs of students who want a more personal satisfaction from a women's studies course. To the extent that this strategy succeeds, both traditional students and the feminist minority will learn to understand a wider range of women's experience and the consciousness of both will be gently raised.

Feminist Scholarship:
The Extent of the Revolution*

by Florence Howe

WHEN I WENT to college in the forties, I could not have imagined questioning the teacher, the syllabus, or the texts I was given to read. I was at Hunter College, in those days still a women's college, with a high percentage of women faculty, even a few women administrators. None of these persons, however, seemed concerned about the fact that the entire curriculum taught women that their education would carry them into domesticity. If they were to work, it would be because they had to, and only in the few fields open to them: school teaching, social work, library science, or, if they were exceptional, teaching on a women's college campus. The message of the curriculum was, in brief: men achieve and work; women love and marry.

In the forties, I thought nothing was wrong with this portrait of the world. And in the fifties, when I proved one of the exceptions and went on to graduate school, the curricular portrait extended itself without any changes. Though I moved from Hunter to Smith and then to the University of Wisconsin, where I taught and studied for the first time in an obviously male world, the garment of my studies, their cloth and design, never varied. When I began to teach in 1960 − as expected, at a women's college − I

---

*This essay is an edited version of Florence Howe's keynote address to the Wingspread Conference on "Liberal Education and the New Scholarship on Women: Issues and Constraints in Institutional Change" (October 1981). Slightly different versions have appeared in the April 1982 issue of *Change* and the Spring 1982 issue of *Women's Studies Quarterly*.

taught what I had been taught: the male-centered curriculum, male writers, male perspectives; about mainly male worlds – bear hunting and whales and priest-ridden young men, for example – not about birthing, mothering, or even school teaching. I was not only without consciousness of gender; I had accepted that male-centered world as "universal." The question of where I was located in that world, had anyone asked it of me, would have been puzzling or irrelevant.

At Goucher College, where I began teaching in 1960, I was not only not interested in gender, I was, from the first, regretful that it *was* a women's college. I supported those who wanted to see that campus become a coeducational one, arguing that it was not "healthy" for women to be isolated from men. If the "real" world, the "public" world, was male, women could only gain access to it through being at least in the presence of those who could enter it. I didn't know it then, but those arguments also reflected the homophobic, male-centered curriculum I had been studying and teaching without consciousness, understanding, or knowledge.

Something began to puzzle, then concern me. These students were bright; they came in with high scores and good skills; and yet their writing was bland, empty of conviction, opinion, idea. In conference, they were directionless, without ambition. They were without vocation. Even those who had arrived with a vocational goal had lost it within the first quarter of college life. They were at Goucher because their parents wanted them in a safe place between the years of high school and the years of marriage, and in a safe place that would allow them to marry well – they could choose from Annapolis or Johns Hopkins. Such women students expected to marry and to be cared for economically. Their privilege cost them their history and, of course, their future.

The single most important difference in 1981 is that regardless of social class, young women today know that they are likely to spend most, if not all, of their lives working outside the home. Older women are returning to the campus in large numbers and their urge is usually vocational. Many circumstances have contributed to this new social milieu: the economic belt-tightening amid rising expectations and a rising inflation around the globe; concern about the population explosion, about food shortages, and an awareness of the relationship between birthrates and the access of women to job markets; in some countries, the need for a new underclass of women workers; as well as the energy of a women's movement in several countries of the West, and the broad-based consciousness-raising experience of the late sixties that led to the women's studies movement.

Whatever the combination of circumstances, young women and young men see a different vision from the one that my generation viewed. Indeed, privileged women students on Ivy League campuses may be somewhat blinded by the rhetoric of "you can be anything you want to be." Such students do not want to hear about wage differentials between women and men, or about discriminatory hiring and promotion policies. They want to believe they can attain their vocational goals as easily as the young man in the chair next to them.

While the vocational curriculum has traditionally segregated female and male students openly, the liberal arts curriculum, similarly assigned to women and men, thrives upon and supports the assumptions beneath sex segregation. It is the liberal arts curriculum that defines the possibilities for boys and girls, tells them how they will become masculine and feminine beings, offers them a reading of history in which they do *not* all appear. It offers images of hundreds of vocations to boys; to girls, still only a few are presented – despite all the energy of the seventies. The liberal arts curriculum still tells college students about their fathers, not their mothers; teaches students not only how to think, but that men have been the only thinkers. The sex segregation of the workplace has, for the most part, not changed. In addition, even the small changes begun in the seventies will not continue unless educators press more urgently for curricular reform.

But it is also obvious that the liberal arts curriculum is currently in trouble, and for many reasons. Attacked as irrelevant by the vocationalists, it began to lose students, especially in the humanities, long before the women's studies movement gained its current position on campuses. By the mid seventies, such courses as "Women's History in the U.S." were compensating for low enrollments in other history courses. By the mid seventies also, campuses were gearing up for the next round in the battle to save the liberal arts. Through faculty development and the new push for a general education curriculum, the liberal arts were to reemerge as sovereign. I must add, of course, that this last development has occurred with little or no communication with, or acknowledgement of, the concurrently developing area of women's studies. In general, the reforms proposed return the campus to basic books in the white, elite Western male tradition, or add several Eastern male texts.

I suggest that that won't do, for many reasons, including the obvious fact that a male-centered curriculum that continues to forward a misogynist view of achieving men and domestic or invisible women will clash with or confuse the vision and aspirations of half, or a bit more than half, the student body now attending college. Perhaps more important even than that humane reason is another: a return to the old masters does not forward the search for truth which has traditionally been at least part of the liberal arts mission. St. Augustine, Aristotle, Erasmus – these men return us to the monstrous misogyny of the past, which we must of course understand, but which, as the mainstay of the curriculum, is hardly sufficient. In short, then, if the traditional liberal arts curriculum won't do, what will? Nothing short of transformation, the major resource for which is women's studies.

Women's studies hardly had a name when it began in 1968 and 1969. Faculty on less than two dozen campuses met to consider what, in addition to teaching single courses, they were attempting to do. If you read the early women's studies program manifestoes – and that is what they sound like – you find five goals listed: first, to raise the consciousness of students and faculty alike about the need to study women, about their absence from texts and from the concerns of scholarship, and about the need to raise consciousness about the subordinate status of women today, as well as in the past; second, to begin to compensate for the absence of women, or for the unsatisfactory manner in which they were present in some disciplines, through designing new courses in which to focus on women, thus providing for women in colleges and universities the compensatory education they needed and deserved; third, to build a body of research about women; fourth, with that body of research, to reenvision the lost culture and history of women. The fifth goal is the strategic one: using all four goals, the fifth presumed that women's studies would change the education of women and men through changing what we have come to call the "mainstream" curriculum. We know now even more clearly than we did a dozen years ago that it represents far less than half of human history, and only a small portion of human achievement.

Thus, from the first, there were two conscious goals in women's studies: to develop a body of scholarship and a new curriculum about women and the issue of gender; to use this knowledge to transform the mainstream curriculum, turning it into what it has never been – "coeducational." Until now, we have mainly worked at the first goal. We have tended our own gardens, fought for our own tiny budgets, and written grant proposals for the three dozen research institutes in women's studies that exist in the eighties. Both in curricular design and in research development, women's studies is on the edge of significant new breakthroughs: in women's history and in the ways in which we will begin to teach women's history with and without men's history; in economic theory and in the understanding of women's role in the economics of industrial and developing countries; in theories of women's moral and intellectual development; in sex differences and in the socialization of girls and boys. The scholarship of patriarchy will remain in question until it is corrected by this new surge of research. Whether or not you are in women's studies, its scholarship will affect your discipline.

Because I see this body of knowledge and this curriculum as being revolutionary for our century as the original body of scholarship that changed the theistic patterns of education in the United States a century ago, I want to list its major components. The list is both disciplinary and thematic. It is also meant to be interdisciplinary: whatever your discipline, if you are to teach about women, you will need at least a slight acquaintance with almost all the other elements on the list. This list also describes the basic curriculum in well-developed women's studies programs and serves as a design for evolving an interdisciplinary program of courses for those who would transform the liberal arts. Perhaps I should say, in anticipation, that this list and all the scholarship it represents is both our major resource for the future and – because it is formidable – one of the major barriers to the goals we seek. Someone recently said that to begin to gain an understanding of the new scholarship on women – whatever one's discipline – is comparable to beginning to earn a new doctorate. I don't think that is an exaggeration. Understanding the dimensions of our task may help us move forward.

Here is the list as I see it:

1. an understanding of patriarchy in historical perspective; philosophically and sociologically: its relationship to the

religions of the world, and to ideas of knowledge and power — hence, an understanding of what it means to be born "permanently" into a subordinate or dominant status; a knowledge of feminist theory.

2. an understanding of the complex, confusing, and still chaotic area of biological/psychological sex differences; the importance of null findings.

3. an understanding of socialization and sex roles, as well as of sex-role stereotyping: the relationships among gender, race, and class — all from a crosscultural perspective.

4. an understanding of women in history, not only in the United States but throughout the world: recognizing that such study includes legal as well as medical history — the history of birth control, for example, is essential to the study of women, even to the study of fiction about women.

5. an understanding of women as represented in the arts they have produced, some of which have been buried or ignored as arts — quilting, for example, or the pottery of North American Indian women; and as represented in the significant literature by women of all races and nationalities that was never included in the literary curriculum; as well as an awareness that the images of women portrayed by the male-created arts have helped control the dominant conceptions of women — hence, the importance of studying images of women on TV, in the film and the theatre, and in advertising.

6. an understanding of the ways in which postFreudian psychology has attempted to control women's destiny; an awareness that other male-centered psychological constructs like those of Erikson and Kohlberg are potentially damaging to women; an understanding of new women-centered theories of female development.

7. an understanding of female sexuality, including perspectives on both heterosexuality and lesbianism; special issues involved in birth control and reproduction.

8. an understanding of the history and function of education as support and codifier of sex-segregation and of limited opportunities for women; some perspectives on education as an agent for change in the past and present.

9. an understanding of the history and function of the family in the United States and crossculturally; of the current variety of family structures, and of the conflict between beliefs and

research findings with reference especially to issues surrounding childcare.

10. an understanding of women in the workforce through history, in the present, and crossculturally: the economy in relation to women; the relationship between money and power in personal interactions, in the family, and in society.

11. an understanding of the relationship between laws affecting women and social change; the history of women and social movements.

Each of the items noted above is meant to include women of all social classes, races, and nationalities, as well as ethnic, religious, and sexual identities. This approach distinguishes women's studies from "the men's curriculum," a term invented in the late nineteenth century by M. Carey Thomas (second president of Bryn Mawr College) to describe what she thought college women had a right to, and which, at the time, was considered too difficult for their allegedly tiny brains or allegedly harmful to their childbearing capacities. This attempt to include all women in the women's studies curriculum distinguishes it from the traditional male-centered curriculum.

Two methodological issues also need to be noted: first, the *comparative approach*. Since most, if not all, learning occurs through comparisons, it would be strange indeed if the study of women did not also illuminate the study of men. On the other hand, it is possible to study half the human race in their own context and on their own terms without reference to the other half – which is what male-centered social science has done for almost a century. Obviously, we need both the comparative data and the data for each sex separately, but it may take a couple of generations before we have sufficient data about women to move on to some of the comparative questions. In the meantime, of course, there are also scholars attempting to look at the male data anew from a feminist perspective.

Secondly, the *documentary base*. Though we could see the outlines only dimly in 1969, more than a decade later we have many full portraits of the lives of women both famous and obscure, public and private, singly and in groups, and we understand that we have only touched the surface of the material still to be collected, studied, sifted, made available. For several hundred years, women have been recorders, letter writers, diary keepers, secretaries of clubs and other women's groups, as well as professional writers. There are also many more women painters and composers than we had even been able to dream of. Beyond those documents still coming to light in attics, county museums, and private libraries, women speak mutely in statistics of births, marriages, employment, deaths. In addition, there are the millions who await the social scientists: subjects of research for the next century, at least, to compensate for their absence and to improve by their presence the body of knowledge on which public policy is based.

During the first five or so years of its existence, women's studies programs carried out their work on many campuses in a form Gayle Graham Yates of Minnesota has called "creative anarchy." Courses were described on flyers turned out on mimeograph machines and circulated "underground" on campuses. Faculty members risked when they taught a women's studies course, and many of them played musical chairs. They left one institution's English department where they had taught women's studies and had been therefore considered "not serious," to go to another where they tried similar courses.

By 1976, mature programs were well on their way to being institutionalized: they had modest budgets; a paid coordinator, often in a line administrative position; and a formal procedure for regularizing the curriculum that was increasingly leading to minors and B.A.s, if not to M.A.s, graduate minors, and Ph.D.s. But what was also clear was that the format of women's studies programs was not that of academic *departments*. The model, even in all its variant forms, was that of an interdisciplinary program, much like the initial form of American Studies.

Women's studies programs function as networks on campuses, not departments. That means that most faculty members who teach in a women's studies program do so from a location in a traditional department. That is the way in which 90 percent of all women's studies courses are taught. Few programs − fewer than the fingers on one hand − have tenured faculty or directors in women's studies itself. Almost all have to depend on departments that are willing to tenure faculty who teach one or two women's studies courses each year.

What distinguishes a women's studies course from a course on women taught in a department? In general, the major distinction may be no more than the existence or absence of a women's studies program. What, therefore, is the virtue of having a women's studies program? Programs offer introductory, inter-disciplinary courses and often a few additional core courses as well, and sometimes all of these under their own label, as well as senior integrative seminars. They also advise majors and minors and prepare a logical organized curriculum within an inter-disciplinary framework for those students wishing either to be majors and perhaps to become scholars in the area, or to enlarge their educational perspective to include the other half of the human race. We need women's studies programs because we need to prepare another generation of scholars able to contribute to the new scholarship on women.

During the last few years, some of the oldest women's studies programs have attempted to think strategically about their second mission: the transformation of the traditional curriculum. In addition, on more than a dozen campuses without women's studies programs, and in several cases funded generously through the U.S. Department of Education's Women's Educational Equity Act, projects were begun under the rubric of "mainstreaming" or "integrating" women into the curriculum.

Perhaps this is the place to pause for a few paragraphs on terminology. What does it mean to *mainstream* or to *integrate* women into the curriculum? Leaving to one side the unsatisfactory psychology of the idea of women as necessarily *out* of the mainstream, the term has been used to signify a process: that women's studies courses are, *ipso facto,* ghetto courses; thus, that taking a course on women in a "regular" department is mainstreaming. If you understand that most women's studies courses are, in fact, *in* departments, this idea adds little to what we already have in progress. It reminds me of the dean I interviewed who felt that women's studies at his institution had completed its job and should be congratulated and dismantled. Women's studies at this dean's institution had developed fifteen different courses in some twelve departments. The rest of the curriculum had not been altered one jot, but this large urban university now offered its students fifteen different courses on women. The revolution had arrived – indeed, was over. Could I tell him that, in my view, the work had not yet begun; that these courses were, in one sense, preliminary to the real job?

Integrating women into the curriculum or integrating women's studies has still a different meaning, or series of meanings. It is coming to signify, at its worst, what Charlotte Bunch has called the "add women and stir" method of curricular revision. In practice, it may mean a single lecture in a course of forty lectures; or the ubiquitous week on suffrage in the American history course; or the addition of a woman writer or two to the traditional literature course.

All of this mainstreaming or integrating — adding tokens even — may be better than nothing (at least one can argue that case). It is not what I mean, however, when I describe the task ahead as *transformational*. I am talking about "changing the form of" — that is what transformation means — changing the form of the teaching of the curriculum so as to include all the human race and not just a small segment of it. I am assuming, and there is much now on which to base that assumption, that research on women is changing the shape of the disciplines, and that the shape of courses based on such research will similarly be transformed.

One more word about mainstreaming, integrating, and transforming. The first two are reforms that all faculty can begin to work on. Like women's studies in its initial stages, mainstreaming projects and projects that call for the integration of women into the curriculum require, perhaps, a single summer institute with a few months of study. The more depth, of course, the more time to read; and the more adequate the provision for some other means of learning, the better. Whether one organizes seminars, or a lecture series for faculty just beginning to study women, or whether one devises a coherent process of team teaching, faculty need more organized support for these efforts now than they did a dozen years ago when the field was new. Then a handful of intrepid persons who saw each other during national professional association meetings developed the scholarly base on which much of their own teaching about women moved forward. Now the scholarship accumulated through the past decade is itself formidable, in some sense a barrier as well as an aid, for those who wish to begin to add women to the curriculum in some form. It is simply hard for many faculty to know where to begin — at least without a guide.

On the other hand, it is clear enough that the place to begin is to read and then to teach *about women*. It is, in my view, impossible to move directly from the male-centered curriculum to what I have described as transformation of that curriculum into a changed and coeducational one without passing through some form of women's studies. One might begin with the unit on women, or even the single lecture; one might get on to a week or two, or a month, but one will have to teach a whole course on women and will have to understand the interdisciplinary base before one can begin to work at that transformed curriculum.

There is, in short, no way around women's studies, if by that term we mean a deep and rich immersion in the scholarship on women. I am not being, in the manner of academics, territorial about my claims. There is no need to be, the goal is quite the opposite. But without a clear view of the dimensions of the task, we may never get to it. How do we face this problem in ways that are both realistic and productive, not discouraging but not falsely optimistic?

I will try to list the resources and the barriers we have as we move forward; the barriers first, so that I can end on an optimistic note. I know that despite retrenchment and the reactionary backlash, despite the state of the academy, the country, and the world, there is still a great deal of energy for this work, and I believe strongly in the relationship of this work to the daily fabric of life of millions of women and men around the globe.

I will be brief about the barriers. First, that the body of knowledge now is formidable may be seen as a barrier. Second, what Wheaton College president Alice Emerson recently called the "devaluation" of women by women and men alike, the trivialization of the work and lives of women, the assumption that women's history is less important than men's history. This leads directly to what two colleagues have described to me as the greatest barrier on their urban campus – the "indifference" of the mainly male-tenured faculty. Jessie Bernard, in *The Prisim of Sex,** combines these barriers in an interesting formulation and links them to still another – the rewards in academia are not, thus far at least, for scholarship on women: "Men find female scholarship dealing with women boring, dull, unimportant. It is not about them and hence not interesting. If it is critical of them, they find it painful. In any event, they look to one another for professional recognition, and mastery of the products of female scholarship will not win that recognition for them." At least one other internal barrier should be mentioned – the possible resistance of vocationally bound students who may unthinkingly judge that learning about women won't get them a job.

---

* University of Wisconsin Press, Wisconsin, 1979.

External barriers these days are deepening. There is the "Moralistic Minority," a force in some areas of the country and on some campuses. There is the elimination of certain federal programs that had just begun to serve this area of curricular reform and the cutting of others. There is also the strain on the private foundations who have, in fact, led the way in this area, and who may not be able to do all that they would wish.

But what of the resources? On every campus, we have a core of persons with whom to begin working. We have our organizing committee; we need only to recognize them and call them by that name. Where there is no women's studies program, there are at least a handful of courses, the faculty of which might be the core — perhaps along with some faculty development folk — all of whom would have to devise an appropriate strategy for a particular campus. Such work needs both time and space and the vision of change as an ongoing process.

In addition to the body of knowledge, which I am of course listing here as a very real resource, we also now have a coherent conceptual frame. The frame has two parts: (1) What is a feminist perspective? Do we need it to teach about women? (2) Is this feminist perspective political?

A woman in Montreal recently asked me, "How can you teach faculty — male or female — to teach about women, if they are not sensitive to women's perspective, to feminism? How can you teach them to be sensitive?" I had been lecturing about how I came to feminism and women's studies, and for me the two terms are interchangeable. The process involved experience, sharing that experience with others, and then making sense of it through reading, thinking, analysis, often with the tools of social science, history, literature, philosophy. In other words, it was a complex process and, of course, I had the advantage of a life as a woman. I even had the advantage of my previous lack of consciousness. And it is that lack of consciousness that can be viewed both as barrier and as aid — at least if one can pierce it.

Coming to a feminist consciousness meant coming to the painful understanding that the world was divided into male and female, and that these categories, like those of race, were not to be changed or exchanged. Unlike students who might become teachers, or children who often become parents, males and females do not change places in a sexist society any more than Blacks and whites. Can men come to this understanding? Of course. Though they may not be able to replicate female experience, men can understand and study its existence. Provided they are alert to the differences between their experiences and those of women, men can develop a feminist perspective. And perhaps I should not assume that being alert to women's experience, listening for it, also includes valuing it for its own sake. This is perhaps the most difficult element.

Still more complex, but also clearer than a decade ago, is the question of the political nature of what we are doing. Is this feminist perspective, this teaching about women, a political act? The associated question is just as complex: Is a feminist perspective "political"? Is research about women politically biased research rather than objective truth? For me, it is more dangerous either to ignore or to support openly the patriarchal assumptions that govern our society than to challenge them openly through the feminist lens, and to ask that questions be reopened, that female experience be viewed alongside male.

Teaching is a political act in the broadest context of that word: some person is choosing, for whatever reasons, to teach a set of values, ideas, assumptions, and pieces of information, and in so doing, to omit other values, ideas, assumptions, and pieces of information. If all those choices form a pattern excluding half the human race, that is a political act one can hardly help noticing. To omit women entirely makes one kind of political statement; to include women as a target for humor makes another. To include women with seriousness and vision and with some attention to the perspective of women as a hitherto subordinate group is simply another kind of political act. Education is the kind of political act that controls destinies, gives some persons hope for a particular kind of future, and deprives others even of ordinary expectations for work and achievement. And the study of half the human race — the political act we call women's studies — cannot be excluded without obvious consequences to the search for truth.

Women's studies is a world-wide movement. We know that educational programs send people out to the world they must live in and guide them to think about themselves and others in human or inhuman ways. Everywhere in the world, education for women is a new frontier. In some European countries, very few women go to college at all. In Italy, women's studies courses are part of trade union activity for women who are learning that they have a right to read, and a right to the pleasures of cultural heritage, as well as to the eight-hour day. In most of the so-called developing countries, women are the majority of illiterates. Some of those in charge of women's education are learning that access to education is not enough if what women gain are, first, instruction in maintaining their subordinate status, and second, access only to the worst-paying jobs.

In developing countries, the need for accurate information on which to base decisions that affect millions of persons, half of whom are inevitably women, makes women's studies – meaning at least research on women – hardly a luxury. Thus, a pan-African women's research organization claims research on women as an essential activity for survival of the nation's economy and heritage, as well as the lives of women. In India, research on women at the beginning of the seventies turned up a striking demographic pattern: the declining percentages of women in the adult population despite the higher rate of female births. This is a singular phenomenon world wide, the changing of which – through education, among other means – might mean life rather than death to millions of women and female children over a single decade.

The study of women in the curriculum and in research institutes is not only an academic question; it is not only a question of the right of women to a place in the curriculum that will allow them images of achievement and aspiration comparable to those the curriculum has generally afforded to white middle-class males. It is also essential if the university is to continue to be able to stake its claim to truth. Because of the increasingly significant way in which knowledge is used in our shrinking world, it is also of ultimate importance to the present and future lives of women all over the world.

PART II

Alternative Structures for Feminist Education

Sagaris: A Feminist Institute

A Note on Sagaris

by Charlotte Bunch

IN THE SUMMER of 1975, Sagaris, an independent feminist institute, opened for two five-week sessions on a small college campus in Lyndonville, Vermont. Plans for Sagaris had begun some two years earlier among women dissatisfied with feminist studies at Goddard College in Vermont. The collective that formed Sagaris hoped to create an environment for studying feminist thought without the constraints of an existing institution. Operating out of New York City and Vermont, they sought funding for the idea from both foundations and individuals.

From the moment that the first announcement was sent out, Sagaris was surrounded by controversy. How much should a feminist school cost? Where should the money come from? How should the school be governed? Who should teach and how should they be paid? What should be taught? What should be the structure of such a school? The same questions have been encountered by every women's studies program and feminist community school before and since. But the Sagaris collective faced these questions more critically because they saw themselves as a model created without any givens from an outside institution, yet in a form and on a national scale that required that they have more formal structure than most community-based women's schools. The collective was ambitious in its goal of creating an independent national feminist institute. Unfortunately, it was not able to provide enough clarity and direction for Sagaris to survive.

The following articles were written out of the two sessions held that first summer. The original structure for both sessions was similar, with different feminists brought in as teachers. Jackie St. Joan, a student at Session I, wrote about that structure and how it functioned in a two-part article, originally published in *Big Mama Rag*. As St. Joan describes, the first session operated along the lines that the collective had planned but ultimately erupted in controversy over what should be the content and structure of a feminist school, indeed of feminism itself. Session II experienced a more dramatic schism centering on the question of funding for Sagaris, which led one group of students and faculty to form a separate structure, the August 7th Survival Community. Susan Sherman, one of the faculty who joined the separate group, discusses what she saw as underlying issues of feminism involved in that split.

Sagaris never fully recovered from the controversies of 1975. Partially in response to some of its critics, it joined with the National Black Feminist Organization in the summer of 1976 to cosponsor an intensive, three-day conference of workshops, lectures, and discussions to explore the links between racism and sexism. Although that conference was productive, the effort to revive the institute in the summer of 1977 with two-week sessions failed. Sagaris came to an end.

Although Sagaris received considerable national attention, there are other independent feminist educational ventures – many begun since 1975 and mostly regional rather than national in focus. The two articles printed here are, therefore, not meant to be definitive statements on Sagaris, or on feminist institutes. They describe some of what happened at this particular school, but more importantly, they reflect the issues facing any effort to develop structures for feminist education, especially apart from existing institutions.

The Ideas and the Realities: Sagaris, Session I*

by Jackie St. Joan

WOMEN CAME to Sagaris for a variety of reasons: to alleviate isolation in small communities, to study with specific teachers in a systematic way with a strong support group, to establish a unifying force of political organization in this country. Few participants came from big cities; the largest representation was from the Midwest. Well over half identified themselves as lesbian-feminists. Most were in their twenties and early thirties, although there were older and more politically experienced women present. Most came from women's studies programs, although grassroots organizers were very vocal. Most were from middle-class backgrounds, although a strong working-class caucus developed. All but five women were white. Seven women brought nine children with them. A few women left early; most stayed the duration of the session.

The days at Sagaris were tightly structured – breakfast at 8:00, political theory until 10:30, body development for one hour, lunch at the cafeteria, political theory for one hour, electives for one and one-half hours, back to the cafeteria for supper, some classes in the evening – with workshops, special events, and small-group meetings scheduled around, under, and in-between. With the tempo of a beehive and the intensity of a love affair, the session was exciting and exhausting, cramping together personal time/space, hard work, meetings, conflicts, and learning.

The ideas explored at Sagaris, both in and out of the formal classes, are important to the women's movement. I would like

---

* This is a somewhat revised version of an article originally appearing as "First Session Sagaris: What Happened" and "Sagaris: The End of A Love Affair," in *Big Mama Rag.*, vol. IIIA, no. 7 (1975).

116

first to outline the main points presented in the classes I sat in on (I did not attend all the courses), and then to discuss the context in which the classes took place. Finally, I want to try to explain what happened to the Sagaris community that was so unsettling to us all.

RITA MAE BROWN ON LEADERSHIP

The concept of leadership, as it affects an individual and as a set of shared but unexpressed assumptions, was explored historically, both inside and outside the women's movement. Brown pointed out that we are all potential leaders, and that in the past we have borne the scars of woman-hatred for trying to exercise our leadership and organizational skills. The women's movement needs leaders who are responsible and accountable to the movement in order to accomplish the tasks necessary for building a women's revolution. Women must make these leaders legitimate so that their energy is not dissipated in constant struggles to consolidate their power.

The women's movement has come out of small-group experiences, but we must take responsibility for learning large-group skills. Different kinds of leaders are needed – task leaders who can guide the group toward its goals and maintenance leaders who can deal with the group's immediate internal needs.

Women must be willing to deal with conflict directly and openly as a way of distinguishing our differences and moving ahead. Too much energy is spent trying to avoid the very conflicts we *need* to experience politically. Our political reality is patriarchal and, as such, responds only to power and to money. To our generation has fallen the task of facing that very real power and of making plans to overcome it. We cannot live as postpatriarchal women in a patriarchal society. We must face the question of morality and ethics. Is private morality applicable to the public arena? Isn't all morality male morality? Is morality useful in gaining power for women? What is feminist morality anyway?

CHARLOTTE BUNCH ON ORGANIZATION

The idea of political theory must be demythologized. Actually working with theory means looking at what we've done and planning structures, organizations, and strategies from what we've learned; analyzing the whys of our existence as women; deciding what our values are; and acting on our decisions and analyses – making theory practical.

The women's movement needs a clearer political framework – theories to guide long- and short-run plans for winning and to give us flexibility for the changes we need while we are in process. What are our *political* goals? How is women's fear of power related to our fear of responsibility? What do we want power for? What are our *economic* goals? We must deal with class issues so that we understand individuals' real differences in style and experience and can use those differences to our mutual advantage, to advance the movement as a whole. What are our *cultural* goals? What builds women's sense of self and sense of community? We must depersonalize criticism so that we can examine just how the personal and the political interact. The crucial question is: What are the politics of feminist culture? It is not: Which is more important, politics or community?

One of the steps necessary for effective action is to stop concentrating on everything that is wrong with what we consider doing and to admit to ourselves, as revolutionaries, that all activities are reform – only a partial strategy working toward a larger goal. Then we will be able to risk change, experimentation, making mistakes, creating hope and a vision. In so doing we must examine movement rhetoric, language, and thinking. Is a collective structure applicable to all situations? Why are we often so focused on our process that we are unable to complete our tasks? Do we, individually and as groups, take our own power over our lives? Why aren't we doing what we think we want to do? Is the approval of other feminists so important that we are unable to break any feminist "ideal" to think independently about a situation?

MARY DALY ON KNOWLEDGE

Mary Daly's lectures were a synthesis of her thoughts since the publication of *Beyond God the Father* and of the ideas expressed in her article, "Women and Spirituality" in *Quest,* vol. I, no. 4. Daly focused on the importance of women recapturing the *knowledge* which the patriarchy has stolen from us. She sees language as "semantic pollution" which controls our thought processes and, therefore, our thoughts themselves. For example, thinking of courage, or being, or God as nouns rather than as verbs – being, couraging, the power of being present – limits what we can think about these concepts. Categories are a substitute for thinking, and although we end up using them anyway, categories are more likely to enclose thought than to disclose one's being.

Feminists must continue questioning in order to keep from being possessed by men who, especially in their absence, have power over our minds. In trying to get through the mind-binding, Daly suggests four kinds of perception we must be especially aware of: (1) Erasure — vague thinking which does not answer the question, who is doing what and to whom? (2) False polarization — creating male-identified polarizations by forgetting we are in process; (3) False inclusion — imagining that women are included in "human" liberation or other broad male-defined categories; (4) Divide and conquer — falling victim to men who turn us against ourselves.

One of the strongest threads running through Daly's lectures was the idea of individuation (the ability to stand alone) and participation (the depth of our bonding with other women). Daly believes that communication can happen best when you are alone and that women subject themselves to a kind of "insectitude," acting in unity from instinct and group pressure, appealing to the lowest common denominator among us, and producing mediocre results. We subject each other to "spiritshed" and "timeshed" (like bloodshed) by demanding group participation and psychically sapping one another of our creativity. We need to have the strength to be alone. The fear of being alone drives women to male presence and male identification.

EMILY MEDVEC ON ECONOMICS

Emily Medvec's lectures focused on what is political about women and the economy. In order to make a revolution, women must understand how work, as our basis of survival, is organized. Each class began with everyone closing her eyes while Medvec gave us a word which we then had to define in one sentence without using that word again in the sentence. For example: Capitalism is ---; Economy means ---; Socialism is ---; Money is ---; A bum is ---.

Medvec discussed issues such as how we spend our money, the food industry, unemployment, housing, the consumer price index, the banking system, oil, scientific labor management, and multinational corporations.

She demonstrated how our lives have been fragmented by the capitalist system. We all exist as producers, consumers, and citizens; we are creative, receptive, and political beings. But when one group is pitted against another, our consciousness about economics becomes blurred. For example, citizens blame the workers (the producers) for inflation without looking at themselves as workers (and consumers) also. Women must create new ways to organize work as the basis of our survival and as the basis of change.

PROJECTS AND POLITICS

In addition to the lectures given by Brown, Bunch, Daly, and Medvec, the courses offered specific projects. Classes were divided into small groups to work on tasks and prepare presentations. Theoretically, for two weeks we were in groups of ten, the third week in groups of twenty, and the fourth week in groups of sixty. Each week we had a task to work on, and we experienced working on different kinds of tasks in different-sized groups.

The first task was to assume our group wants to develop a project which will help others as well as ourselves. What will we develop? A low-priced food store? A newspaper? An employment agency? A credit union? Which one, and why? What are the goals of the project? How will we structure it internally? What criteria will we establish to determine if we have been successful or not?

The second week the task was to deal with a political split — lesbian/straight, working class/middle class, or with a disruptive member who was taking too much time away from the group's focus on the task. Ironically, by the second week most of the groups had themselves dissolved.

The third week the groups combined to work on a question of political strategy in a hypothetical situation: You are a well-organized feminist group which is powerful in the community. A new factory that has agreed to a strong affirmative action program comes to town. But the factory is polluting and has threatened to discontinue the affirmative action program if your group pushes for environmental action. What strategy does your group use in this situation?

The fourth week the class was to work as a whole on the problem of choosing whether to form a third party, to take over the Democratic Party, to form a National Feminist Union, or to develop an alternative form of government. Which of these alternatives is best at this time in history? With whom will you make coalitions and under what conditions? How do you challenge the present system while taking care of your own people?

In addition to the above tasks developed by Rita Mae Brown, Medvec gave the small groups the task of developing a woman-defined economy, with the goal of feeding the largest number of women the best possible food with the least consumption of energy.

For some women the small groups provided the space within which to work out the practicalities of the theories they were studying. Many of the small groups, however, were unable to complete their tasks; others refused to do certain tasks because of the energy required. Several groups were successful in completing their tasks and presented oral and written reports to the class on what they had done. A couple of groups even began to plan concrete structures that would go beyond Sagaris.

There were four elective courses at Sagaris: Educational Alternatives, organized by Margaret Fiedler; The Psychodynamics of Minority Group Membership, taught by E. Kitch Childs; Journalism, taught by Blanche Boyd and Joan Peters; and Creative Writing, taught by Bertha Harris. Since I participated in only one of these courses, Creative Writing, I will describe what happened there.

BERTHA HARRIS ON "GOOD GIRLS"

Bertha Harris, head of the Women's Studies Program at Richmond College, Staten Island, New York, organized a class of forty-five women, most of whom were new writers or women who had never written before. The class met once a week for a lecture and twice a week for small group readings and discussions of individual work. By the third week the class was down to twenty women.

Harris's lectures focused on the connections between political ideology and who we are as lesbian artists. Our delight in our differentness as lesbians, our erotic sense of specialness, is the impulse of the lesbian imagination. Literature is not made by good girls; we need to clean up the sweetness and light in the women's movement. We must bring out our differences and be direct in our conflicts, or we will inevitably settle down into a banal mentality. Harris believes we must identify with the badness men have bestowed on lesbians, for it is the source of our energy. It is dangerous and taboo to be both smart and sexy, and lesbians are both. She pointed out the political reason for literary taboos: the taboo serves patriarchal interests. Harris discussed the idea of the lesbian brain, of the connections between sexuality and our think-ing. She believes that the lesbian's sexual organ is the brain – that we fall in love with each other's minds. Writers must demystify romantic love and in so doing will bring reality to our lives and to our art.

The class created works on the forbidden subjects of going down on a woman, mother/daughter relationships, incest, cannibalism, our sexuality as children and with children. The work was presented to the Sagaris community later in the session.

BODY DEVELOPMENT

Many women at Sagaris felt that their sanest moments and least energy-draining experiences occurred in the body development courses. Karate, taught by Thomasina Robinson, and T'ai Chi, taught by Harmony Hammond, provided a structure within which women could feel their own body/mind power. Thomasina and Harmony, both experienced in the meditative as well as the phy-sical aspects of their arts, encouraged us to relax, to keep centered amidst the turmoil, and to understand the political importance of being physically strong.

SOMETHING TO WRITE HOME ABOUT

Sometime during the first week, most of us gave up trying to write home to explain what was happening at Sagaris. Caught in a web of friendliness and disorientation, we were minding our man-ners and making connections with each other. Charlotte Bunch noticed and told us to relax: "There's an atmosphere here of everyone trying to be the perfect feminist. Take some risks. Ex-periment. You need not stand by every word you say forever." But we passed over many of our differences, bathed in the glow of sisterhood and assumed commonality. The conflicts that did arise in the community were spoken softly one-to-one or in small groups. No one wanted to make waves that would disrupt this wonderful gathering.

Underneath the sweetness and light, however, there were re-sentments building. Some had appeared even before women had left their own communities. One woman from California told me she had been labeled an "elitist" for coming to Sagaris in the first place, since many of the activists back home couldn't afford the time or the price of attending ($700 per session), and she could. Others wondered why students weren't allowed to have their dogs in the dorms when the Sagaris collective and one of the faculty members had *their* dogs with *them* in the dorms. The childcare workers (who were working for their tuition, room, and board) were angry at having to work thirty hours a week and take classes too. And at dinner the first night, one long-haired dyke called for a community meeting that evening to discuss lesbian invisibility at Sagaris.

So lesbianism was the first issue out of the closet. Some women felt that the collective's announcement at dinner that foundation people and evaluation teams were on campus was an unspoken instruction to "be cool" and not to act like dykes. When the collective was asked how they explained a lesbian presence to foundation and press people, they answered, "We tell them we don't question sexual preference. Who the women sleep with is their own business. Or we tell them that lesbians represent a large part of the women's movement, so naturally a lot of lesbians would come to Sagaris." Some women complained that this was a closety approach to the issue. Others said no foundation is going to fund a dyke school. Or, we don't need the man's money anyway. Or, let's not be purists.

Women were straining to be reasonable and not to indulge in conflicts. The students were looking to the collective or to the faculty for leadership and had not yet accepted responsibility for being leaders themselves. It seemed important to them to know if the collective members were lesbians. "They give off straight vibes," one woman told me. "They may sleep with women, but they sure don't act like dykes." Feeling protective of their straight members, the collective didn't want to discuss the issue publicly. Eventually, we knew four women were lesbians, one was bisexual, and two were straight. So what? The underlying issue of whether Sagaris represented the interests of lesbian-feminists went unresolved and continued to fester.

Since lesbianism had been pegged a nonissue (although many women labored over that particular "nonissue" quite a bit), the problem of class was brought out of the closet. In lectures we were told that guilt about class is irrelevant and destructive; that we should look at how our class backgrounds affect us and use the advantages that our different backgrounds give us. So we began to examine our class backgrounds to try to understand and to identify with them.

The working-class caucus was getting more vocal and kept asking for money. Emily Medvec arrived to teach economics and the politics of money became even more real. In one class she asked seventy of us to write two items on a slip of paper: our annual salary total and our annual surplus total. We began to understand how our movement need not depend on outside grants for its survival — that if the class privileges were really broken down in the movement, we could support our own institutions and each other.

At one point the Sagaris collective was asked how it represents the interest of working-class women. The collective noted that everyone who had applied for a scholarship had been given one; that they had tried to recruit minority and working-class women; and that two members of the collective had working-class backgrounds. To many of us it became clear that one member of the collective identified with working-class women. She participated actively in the working-class caucus and formed relationships easily with the working-class women. The rest was not clear at all, and the issue was not resolved.

Meanwhile, the six childcare workers met with the collective to find a solution to being overworked. They were angry that they were earning about $2.50 per hour while faculty members each earned $300 per week (except those who had voluntarily lowered their salaries). The workers said they had been told that the collective didn't want to deal with childcare, that they had hired a childcare coordinator from the community to deal with childcare problems. A "working solution" was found by hiring one more worker, which cut the hours back to twenty per week, but the question of the pay difference between childcare workers and faculty was never resolved.

The mothers never became very militant, except for a fly-by-night "Sagaris Mothers' Union" which put up signs urging child-free women to awaken and relate to the children. Another group, most of whom were mothers who had left their children at home, did insist that Sagaris provide childcare in the evenings and on Sundays, since the childcare program functioned from 9:00 A.M. to 6:00 P.M. only. The childcare workers were not about to extend their hours to operate a twenty-four-hour program, and the collective said there was no more money in the budget for childcare. They complained that it cost more money to put a child in childcare than for tuition for one student. One of them asked me if twenty-four-hour care was really desirable anyway. They thought they had discharged their obligation by providing free childcare and by hiring a coordinator to deal with childcare problems. There were no mothers in the collective.

The "working solution" was that the group was to raise money to pay women $2.00 per hour to babysit. A dance was held; some Florida women silkscreened T-shirts; almost $200 was raised. However, after about ten days very few Sagaris women had signed up to babysit, and the job fell mostly to a fifteen-year-old from the Lyndonville community who thought that $2.00 per hour looked pretty good. The question of whether Sagaris represented the interests of mothers and children was never resolved.

By the third week many women were tired of the cafeteria, its food, its bustling atmosphere, and the constant shouting of announcements during meals. Some women felt we had no control over our physical environment and wondered if the $42,000 ($300 per person) paid to Lyndon State College for room and board was really worth it. One woman told me she thought we could have created something better ourselves – building tipis, cooking communally. The collective felt there would have been no time in the class schedule for such tasks. One student said it was strange to have others doing our day-to-day maintenance for us – cleaning bathrooms, cooking meals, washing dishes. This issue also went unresolved.

During the middle of the session, the Sagaris collective held a community meeting to discuss its own history, structure, and conflicts. They talked of meeting for over two years, of the tyranny of structurelessness that besieged them in the beginning, of learning new skills and strengths. They also talked about their past internal conflicts. Some six months before, they had decided to ask one collective member to leave, and two other members had left with her in protest. They explained the disagreement: "We found out one and one-half years down the road that we had different goals. They wanted to do something less structured and less expensive. They stopped doing their part of the work, which sabotaged what we were trying to accomplish. They attacked two of us personally. It became clear that we could not continue this way."

The ousted women were not there to give their side of the story, and I asked them about it when I met them in Plainfield some days later. Samm Stockwell told me: "I wouldn't say or do anything to hurt Sagaris. But it's not true that I wanted a structureless situation. I was one of the originators of the idea of Sagaris and believed structure to be important. My concerns were more with the internal workings of the collective and the cost of attending. Two of the collective members were in New York and were making contacts for money and for public relations. They were also making decisions, based on those contacts, about who was being hired to teach. Those of us here in Vermont were left with other work to do. I also think they could have found a cheaper place to hold Sagaris. It was not a personal attack but a demand that they be accountable to all of us. To me it was a class issue. I knew the price would exclude many working-class and minority feminists."

During the community meeting at which the collective discussed its process, students at Sagaris didn't confront them with questions about the politics of their organization. One woman told me later that it was clear to her that students could express their ideas, but that they had no power to change the collective's decisions. Another woman said that the evening had reminded her of a new mother cooing over her baby, and that she felt that any political questioning would be taken personally, as an attack. Others said they were very impressed with what these women had actually accomplished and felt a personal obligation to support them. Another woman disagreed. She said support doesn't mean propping them up − it's not nonsupportive to express your disagreements.

During the last week at Sagaris, one or two women had taken it upon themselves to pass around a form requesting women to pledge money to Sagaris. At a community meeting, several women said that they weren't sure if they wanted to pledge money since they didn't know what direction Sagaris was going to take. They wanted to know where the collective members were coming from politically within feminism and in what way the collective felt accountable to the women's movement. A hot discussion began, and the "working solution" in this case was to submit written questions for the collective to answer at a later meeting, since this particular one had been called to discuss socialism.

A group of about twenty faculty members and students met to draw up the questions, which were given to the collective the day before the next community meeting. The questions asked each member to discuss her position politically within feminism and her goals and motivations for working at Sagaris; to describe the existing hidden and open power structures within the collective; and to consider whether the collective was willing to share responsibility and power at Sagaris with students.

This was Wednesday of the last week. Some women feared a huge confrontation, others had already left, and many were packing up to leave. The group which had drawn up the questions met before the community meeting to reaffirm its commitment not to let the issues slide by again and to try to focus on a discussion of the political issues and not on personalities.

About sixty women gathered in a circle in the Academic Center. The collective arrived and distributed written answers to the questions and a statement of goals. Two members read the written answers. Some women protested during the reading that they wanted to talk, not be read to. The two collective members read their statements through. They then said they were all going to leave, and they wanted us as a group to take a vote on whether or not Sagaris should continue. They would take a vote of second session students, and if we decided Sagaris should not continue, they would shut down. They said they hadn't had enough time to respond, and that they were very tired. Then they all got up and left.

The vote never took place. A fierce, then more and more moderate discussion followed. Some women wanted to know what was happening. Others said it was useless for us to sit there since the collective had said in their statement that student participation was not a priority at this time, and they had the power, and the power had just walked out the door. Some said that they are organized, we are not. We should get organized and do something. Others said that they didn't like confrontation politics, and if the collective hadn't walked out, Sagaris would have fallen apart. Others said that Sagaris must not be important to their survival if they were so willing to let it go without a fight. Others said that the "powers-that-be" may have planted an agent in our midst to disrupt us. Others said, "fuck you."

One thing was clear – the honeymoon was over. They had walked out the door and we were left, like abandoned lovers, to beg them to return or to get ourselves together and face the future. Some of the thirty women who stayed to discuss what happened told me later that they saw the episode as a lesson in what we had been learning at Sagaris all along: control over our institutions, power, being direct about criticism, getting organized.

Many women were up late that night. There were group meetings in the dorms, long talks, tears, talk of going home, wanting to get away from it to think about it. A couple of women decided not to stay for the second session. There was talk of finding a community to work in. There were no more classes, no more mealtime announcements, no more meetings.

By the time I left three days later, the collective seemed to be standing by its decision of Wednesday night. I told one of them I thought they had made a big mistake in walking out on a group of politicized feminists. Many of these women had been through this struggle before in the movement or in student power days, or they were women who had been in the collective's shoes — held accountable for their leadership. These were women who understood the struggle of sharing power and responsibility, and who also recognized that it is politically necessary for institutions to do so.

Some feminists wanted more control over Sagaris than is possible through personal expressions on an evaluation form or the consumer's choice of whether or not to attend. I, for one, wanted Sagaris to be structured in such a way that students would have equal power and responsibility with the administration in influencing the direction of the institution. I didn't want "working solutions" which bypassed the political decisions Sagaris needed to face.

The collective stated that it wanted Sagaris to be the "most valuable and relevant program possible." Valuable to whom? Relevant to what? It wanted Sagaris to be a "forum within which the major issues and theories of feminism can be analyzed from different radical feminist perspectives." Who decides which are the major issues? And who is a radical feminist?

To me, these statements are meaningless. Running any institution requires making choices every day. An institution like Sagaris has to face the issues of lesbianism, class, minority women, mothers, hidden leadership and accountability, and students' demands for power. It also has to face harder questions: Who will teach? Who will be accepted as students? How much will it cost? What is a feminist institute like Sagaris for? An alternative to women's studies programs? A training ground for organizers? We need to know by what criteria these choices will be made. Choosing criteria requires taking a political stand, and those criteria must be developed so that the politics of radical feminist education relate to the survival of us all.

Sagaris: A Feminist Institute

Women and Process:
The Sagaris Split, Session II

by Susan Sherman

THE SAGARIS INSTITUTE was intended to provide an alternative educational situation for women and to develop the basis of a new feminist curriculum. The first session ended on the verge of chaos, and two and one-half weeks into the second session, approximately twenty-five women (almost one-third of those present) including students, faculty members, and children left the main group to form a separate community, the August 7th Survival Community.

To understand what happened that summer at Sagaris is to understand how Sagaris mirrored the contradictions of our society as a whole. The United States is a white patriarchial (paternalistic) capitalist system, a system grounded in dualism and conflict, a system based on exploitation and competition and balanced on the twin pillars of racism and sexism. To fail to understand the values of this society and how they consciously and unconsciously affect our actions and attitudes, individually and collectively, both when we accept and when we reject them, is to leave ourselves open to and at the mercy of the very forces we are trying to destroy. To be political is to understand yourself in relation to other people, in the context of a community. To be political is to understand your position in the midst of that process which is history.

The failure of Sagaris as an "institute" was precisely its lack of self-definition, its inability to understand and deal with social forces, to see itself as part of a continuing process. The irony was that Sagaris finally did provide a setting in which a real political process worked itself out. In fact, *because of* the struggle which culminated in some women formally separating from the original structure, Sagaris accomplished what it had set out to do – provide a place where feminist political theory could evolve, where the separation between thought and action could be resolved.

THE CRISIS AT SAGARIS

It is in the interest of any establishment, any system in power, to maintain the status quo. The present structure of a community, if not represented as a law of nature, must be represented as the best possible structure given the circumstances. While you are allowed, even encouraged in some cases, to reform the system, to change individual elements (even alter the balance somewhat as long as you don't tip it), you must never threaten the structure itself or question the premises on which the structure is built. In this way, structure is defined as a static order, a form like a house into which things fit. But societies are not made up of things; communities are not made up of objects. They are composed of people – people in growing and changing relationships with each other. The society we live in, that means by which we order our ways of being with each other, has to be seen as a process, a sense of order (a structure) that grows and changes.

The crisis that occurred at Sagaris resulted directly from the fact that the Sagaris collective, the eight women who then constituted the final decision-making body of Sagaris, were themselves trapped by the very attitudes they were attempting to combat. They saw Sagaris primarily as an institution and were concerned with the perpetuation of that institution. They were concerned with Sagaris as a thing, a producer of a product, and not as a network of intricate relationships – women engaged in thinking and sharing and learning in a specific place at a specific time.

Sagaris became a concrete example of the primary contradiction facing the women's movement. Either the women's movement represents political activity (both theoretical and practical) directed toward a radical change in the structure and the basic premises of the present system, or it represents the self-interest of some women who wish to obtain power in what remains a traditional patriarchal system – power which can only be obtained at the expense of other oppressed groups or other women.

It is impossible for women to have power as a group operating within a system whose foundation is the oppression of women. To believe the contrary is to engage in a process of self-contradiction which must inevitably lead to conflict and pain. The Sagaris collective effectively put students and faculty in a position of powerlessness, the position of women in our society.

The eight women who made up the Sagaris collective claimed that Sagaris had no partisan politics, that its purpose was to provide an educational forum for many radical feminist points of view, "to provide a framework, for women with prior involvement in women's issues, to study with some of the important feminist thinkers" (from a Sagaris brochure). The position of the Sagaris collective would not be that of a "governing" body per se, but of "administrators." In other words, within the general terminology "radical feminist," the position of the collective was to remain objective.

But is it possible for an institute designed to study political theory to be apolitical? Is it possible for an administrative body to be objective? What exactly does that mean? Implicit in the structure and functioning of any organization is a value system. Since the final decision-making power at Sagaris lay with the collective, Sagaris as an institution had to reflect the values and politics of the collective. And if, in fact, one has no specific commitment or set of values, one *must* work from expediency or self-interest, since decisions are always based on something. A choice presupposes both a method of choosing and a set of criteria by which to select.

Sagaris was presented as a broadly based theoretical think tank, and yet the choice that precipitated the second session split – not just to accept but to solicit money from the Ms. foundation – was, given the controversy surrounding *Ms.* at the time the funds were solicited, a highly charged, highly partisan political decision. If they had been consistent with their own stated policy, the collective could never have made such a decision; particularly since they must have known that some members of the faculty, because of their own political commitments and the stands they had taken against *Ms.* politics in the past, could not, under any circumstances, have accepted part of their salaries from *Ms.* This is to say nothing of the students and faculty who felt that identification with *Ms.*, at that specific time, was totally unacceptable. Representing all views within the radical feminist community means respecting those views. Respect is not open to debate or majority decision.

The end result of trying to play it both ways is that you wind up, at some point, hurting everyone. The collective wanted it both ways: they wanted the money and they wanted to avoid partisan politics. But you can't simultaneously act out both sides of a contradiction. Not, at least, when someone is aware of it and speaks out. The only way you can possibly balance opposing views is to refuse to act on anything that will prove totally unacceptable to either side, a position that at some point has to lead to a crisis. The collective put themselves into a difficult situation and then, instead of analyzing what internal contradictions in the structure of Sagaris itself had brought them to this impasse, they threw the responsibility onto the dissenting faction.

Once the collective solicited and accepted *Ms.* money, putting the faculty and students who didn't agree with them in the position of changing their own political beliefs or leaving, it was inevitable that the session would be divided. The women disagreeing with the decision of the collective were put in the situation of having their loyalty to the women's movement called into question by their dissent – the classic double-bind situation. If you said yes, you compromised what you believed in and were committed to politically and were disloyal to yourself and your sisters. If you said no, you were causing a split in the movement and were accused of being disloyal to your sisters.

It was no accident that the final crisis that split Sagaris was prcipitated by an argument over funding, an argument the collective kept insisting was financial and not political. It should be clear to anyone with political experience that it is the person controlling the money who holds political power. This is political reality.

The collective as an *administrative* body controlling the budget was, in actuality a *governing* body controlling the politics, the value system, of Sagaris. The fight over the *Ms.* money was a catalyst that brought the internal contradictions plaguing Sagaris since its inception to the surface: the stratification that permeated every level of the Sagaris community; the fact that Sagaris, rather than being an alternative situation, was a caricature of the traditional educational system.

THE ALTERNATIVE COMMUNITY

Given the increasing hostility at Sagaris directed against those who opposed taking the *Ms.* money, the women who voted no to the *Ms.* funding decided to band together to discuss further action. Two alternatives were presented: (1) to seize power (take over the original structure), or (2) separate in some way and use the time remaining in the session to analyze what had happened and to set up a real alternative community.

After much discussion, it was decided to separate from the Sagaris structure, to set up an alternative community, and to remain at Lyndonville State College — at least for room and board, since those expenses were already paid and were nonrefundable. It was also felt that a move to another location in the amount of time left was unrealistic. Some of the women argued that in order to make the most effective political statement, it was necessary to remain at the Lyndonville campus in plain view of the Sagaris structure. This meant having to develop an alternative community in a hostile situation constantly aggravated by forces both outside (which also served as an artificial unifying factor) and within the community — a difficulty which had to be dealt with since it is true of any *real* political struggle.

With the birth of the August 7th Survival Community, the crucial step had been made from an educational *institution* run by a collective of eight women to the formation of an alternative educational *community* run collectively by all the members of the community. The August 7th Survival Community was searching for a new structure and consequently for new content. It was a struggle complicated by the pressures of the situation, the attitudes and prejudices of the community members, and the overwhelming fact of there being so little time.

As Sagaris caricatured the larger society, the August 7th Community in many ways reflected the difficulties of the movement. While the collective for all intents and purposes ignored process, the August 7th Community got so involved in the exploration of process that there was a danger of ignoring everything else.

But the alternative community was in many ways a human miracle. In the space of two and one-half weeks, twenty-seven women — who, with few exceptions, hadn't even known each other three weeks before — working under incredible pressure, managed to put out a preliminary statement and later a full analysis of the Sagaris rebellion, print a newsletter, get a place in Lyndonville to hold meetings and classes, arrange collective childcare, set up some classes and workshops, and stay together through it all. But perhaps the most important validation of the struggle was the fact that basic questions, rather than being simply the content of lectures and intellectual abstractions, became a part of daily life.

Underlying all the questions faced by the alternative community was the fundamental fact that a change in structure, in outward form, is meaningless unless it grows from and is accompanied by a change in attitude. It is easy to feel you have constructed a new form when what you are really doing is substituting the opposite of what you're reacting against – the elements and even the external structure might be somewhat different, but the basic premises remain the same.

In a capitalist society, everything is based on commodity value and commodity production. Things are valuable in so far as they can be used to procure material advantage. Even relationships are seen as investments. Love is exploited and permitted only in so far as it has a "future" – it ends in marriage and the *production* of children, or it in some way makes life easier for the person who produces labor or services for the society.

How these values actually work themselves out unconsciously in our attitudes toward ourselves and other people, particularly in a situation of struggle, is not always so clear. Consequently, we often exhibit the same prejudices, in a different framework, that we are working to destroy. For example, conventional attitudes functioned to an extent in the alternative community over the question of status. In a conventional educational community, status is determined by college degrees and a certain amount of experience and/or expertise. This subgrouping status obscures the fact that while in our society *education* is mandatory, *learning* is considered valuable only in so far as it maintains and supports the establishment and is useful pragmatically "to get ahead." Apart from its utilitarian dollars-and-cents value, learning – knowledge itself – is considered a luxury and discouraged. *Learning* (an active verb) becomes synonymous in our minds with *being taught* (a passive verb). Education is then a concept so repulsive, so representative of oppressive authority, that we construct a block against acquiring the very skills we most need to make a successful revolution.

The need for proper credentials is no less a fact in most alternative structures. These credentials, if not merely identical to those of the establishment (or their exact opposite), are often also based on generalities and appearances. In one meeting of the August 7th Survival Community, a woman who was totally new to the Sagaris situation was allowed in five minutes to change a decision that had taken hours to set up. She was emotional and eloquent, over forty-five and conventional looking. In that situation, she had the proper credentials.

There are real differences between women that have to be dealt with and not obscured. It is precisely because there is rampant racism and class bias in this country and in the women's movement that it is absolutely essential to move beyond labels and rhetoric and deal with the reality of what class and race differences are about. It is precisely because there is a lack of understanding of age, of the problems of mothers, of children, of what it is that separates us, that we cannot afford to be sidetracked by superficial distinctions. One way these attitudes expressed themselves in the alternative community was in the tension between former students and former faculty members – since that was one of the most obvious distinctions in an otherwise rather homogenous group.

Defining problems in terms of a student/faculty hierarchy in the specific situation of Sagaris obscured two things. First, it blurred the differences between individual faculty members (and, consequently, between the students) and, most important, it made it harder to deal with the really essential question – when we start off with an unequal situation, how do we correct it? Certainly not by wasting energy and experience and pretending that differences that are quite real don't exist. Teaching and learning are equivalent responsibilities. But how does one share experience? How does one get past the defensiveness and mistrust and fear *purposely* embedded in us? That is the heart of the struggle.

In mechanistic theory (in which stasis is the measure), the whole is equal to the sum of its parts. In a theory which takes the relationship of human beings into account, the whole must equal *more than* the sum of its parts because the interaction of discrete unique individuals forms a vital part of the equation.

But while approaching a situation from the point of view of the philosophy of stasis can cause one to err by not taking relationships into account, attention to process sometimes results in the opposite problem − a relationship loses meaning because it is cut off from its context, from the individuals interacting. A group is not an entity unto itself; it is the living relationships of the individuals who comprise it. To take all emotional, intellectual functions and put them into the primacy of the group is to change the group (society) from a collaborative of people into an artificial individual with a multiple personality of its own, an abstraction. The relation of the individual to the group, to other people, is the core question when one discusses politics, revolution, social change. One person cannot change a system. A human being cannot live in isolation. Our community is the context in which we move, the background that brings our life into focus. Our choice of what community of people we move in is the most important choice of our life. It determines what we are, how we exist.

In order to arrive at a solution, you must begin by formulating the proper questions. That is what the alternative community began to do − what the original Sagaris could not do. But alternative community is really the wrong term. The name the community chose for itself was finally the most appropriate − the August 7th Survival Community. Because the issue is more than finding an alternative structure, an alternative means of education; it is, in every sense, a question of survival.

A NEW BEGINNING

The Sagaris split was not about two groups with differing politics engaged in a battle for control of an archaic structure. The struggle of the August 7th Survival Community was against an oppressive act by a rigid system. It was a rebellion against constituted authority.

A new vision supercedes the old because it encompasses more, gives more, takes in new territory, leads us into new places. It is precisely about change, about growth, about the breaking of oppressive structures and reordering them, that creativity, that politics is all about. It is a revolutionary act to feel something, to open yourself and remain open to experience. It is an act of sedition to ask other people to do the same thing − because if people feel and question and think, they eventually act.

The only reason for the status quo is to maintain power for those in control. It is in direct opposition to the reality of existence − of change − and that is why at some point it begins to fail. Change is a fact of life. Growth is an expansion, a gathering

in, an assimilation of experience. When something stops growing, it begins to decay. Chaos results when the disintegration of a
system is not accompanied by the birth of a new vision. Chaos is
not brought about by rebellion; it is brought about by the absence
of political struggle.

No struggle is unimportant when people say no to a situation
that oppresses them. The question is whether, once having faced
the consequences of struggle, you continue to risk, continue to
fight. The real import of Sagaris is what we as women brought
away with us — what it meant in our everyday lives.

We carry our history, our values with us. Whether they are a
burden or a source of energy depends on us. How long the struggle lasts will depend on how many times we have to go through
the same thing before we begin to learn and change.

Califia Community

by Marilyn Murphy

A MEMBER of the Califia Community was talking with a young, very politically active Los Angeles lesbian-feminist. She mentioned that our collective makes all decisions by consensus. The young woman was shocked. "Consensus. I can hardly believe it. I didn't think *anyone* bothered with consensus nowadays."

This incident is a good introduction to the Califia Community. We are considered an anachronism by some 1980s feminists. To most of the more than two thousand women who have attended Califia Community sessions during our seven-year history, however, Califia is a dynamic experience which changed their lives, or renewed their political fervor, or gave them a focus for political action, or enlarged their world view, or taught them hard truths about themselves. At Califia Community sessions, the women's liberation movement is alive and working its magic in women's lives as powerfully in the 1980s as it did in the 1960s.

I credit the idea for a feminist education "something" on the West Coast to Betty Brooks. She had been talking about it at least since she and I became friends in 1971. In 1975 I convinced her to go with me to Sagaris, a feminist educational institute in Vermont, by telling her over and over again that she might learn how to start her own if she went. At Sagaris, Betty talked to other California women about a West Coast institute, and back home again, she practically forced me to attend planning meetings. I was hooked on the idea by the time she called a large public meeting, which forty-four women attended. Although most of the initial collective members had not been at Sagaris, the Sagaris experience was the informing spirit of many of our decisions. We wanted to recreate the magic of Sagaris while correcting what we perceived to be its problems. Califia Community is the daughter of Sagaris and, like most daughters, is both similar to and different from her mother.

WHAT IS CALIFIA?

Eleven months of discussions preceded the first Califia Community session of July 1976. Collective members belonged to the "Sisterhood is Powerful," the "Personal is Political," and the "Free Our Sisters; Free Ourselves" radical feminist persuasion. The transformation of radical feminist ideology into an educational program was an exciting and challenging experience, as it still is for each new collective as we plan our yearly program. We began this transformation with our name. We call ourselves *Califia* because she is the legendary Black Amazon/Goddess for whom California was originally named. We call our organization *Community* to express our commitment to the development of an *informed* community spirit among Califia women which recognizes and affirms our differences as we celebrate our sisterhood. Califia Community is committed to the development of a multicultural community of the spirit of women through feminist education.

Once we decided to make Califia Community our goal, the decision to conduct live-in sessions followed. ". . . An opportunity for women to participate in a dynamic process of creating and living feminist theory" reads our brochure. Also, we wanted Califia women to experience what Sagaris women had, "a glimpse of freedom in a feminist environment." We rent California forest camps for our sessions. They provide natural beauty, privacy, facilities for work and play, and the opportunity for groups to do their own cooking. Unhappily, a camp setting and limited wheelchair accessibility often create additional barriers for physically disabled women. We hire ASL signers and charge no fees for the attendants of disabled women, but the fact remains that, at present, we often trade the comfort of disabled women for the advantages a camp setting provides for other women.

Sessions are of one week and long-weekend duration. We would like them to be longer, but most working women could not attend longer sessions. Our children's community provides twenty-four-hour childcare for children three and over, and partial childcare for younger ones. Approximately 150 women and 25 children attend each Califia session. About 25 percent are women of color, 25 percent are Jewish women, 20 percent are women who lead heterosexual lives and 10 percent are disabled women. Women with working-class origins make up 40 to 50 percent of the community. At present, women over forty comprise almost half of the Califia population.

We charge a regular-income fee and a low-income fee and encourage women to contact us if they cannot pay all of the fee. We then charge them only for food and their share of the rent and arrange for later payments if they wish. Fees for children are on a sliding scale. Califia women themselves, not the collective, decide which fee they should pay. We do not have work exchanges. We hire women to cook, coordinate childcare, sign, and lifeguard. All other work is done by all the women in the community. At least one-fourth of Califia women pay less than the low-income fee. The rest are divided more or less evenly between those who pay the low and regular-income fees. To keep costs down, the collective members get no salary for our work.

Califia attracts women with a varied history of political activism and awareness. Some Califia women have been involved in Communist Party politics in the 30s, and some come to Califia thinking "political" means Democrat or Republican. Young Amazons and original Daughters of Bilitis members come to Califia. Women who believe in "working within the system" and women who founded and/or work in alternative feminist programs meet and exchange ideas. Feminist activists in despair and newly politicized women attend. Socialist feminists and country dykes scrub pots together. NOW members and lesbian-separatist anarchists learn to respect at least part of the work the other is doing. From this diversity, Califia women experience the breadth of the women's liberation movement. Newcomers see the variety of ways they can participate in our struggle, and overworked activists realize that they are not the "only feminists in the world."

STRUCTURE AND ACTIVITIES

We believe the success of the Califia Community experiment lies in our adherence to a preplanned structure. Specific workshops are given at specific times. Time is structured so we may teach and counsel each other. We can meditate, exercise, and learn to defend ourselves. We can entertain each other and meet in affinity groups. We can experience the power of sisterhood that does not assume we are all alike. We can solve the problems and disputes of community living in a sisterly way. No woman is made to do any of these things, but the structure of the week makes them all possible. Our structure enables a group of strangers to become a real community.

Because the collective takes responsibility for structuring each session, we have enormous power. At a collective meeting the day before the opening of the third session of 1977, some collective members suggested that we divest ourselves of that power. They believed we had no right to choose the issues to be presented, and that it was elitist to present any organized programs. Feelings on this issue were so strong that after ten hours of argument, consensus was impossible. We decided to vote, and the "no structure" side won. The following morning, two hundred women, new to Califia, were met by exhausted collective members and a schedule consisting only of meals for the week. From the chaos of the next few days, after which the original schedule was followed, several Califia policies were determined:

1. A time and program structure for at least the first two days of a session is essential because it gives women a chance to become acclimated to their new environment and to realize that they have the power to make the session whatever they choose it to be.

2. Califia collective members have the right to have some of our political needs met – in this instance, a structure that makes possible the examination of the issues of sexual preference, white racism, and class.

3. No structural or content changes will be considered at the last planning meeting before a session.

4. All collective decisions will be reached by consensus.

5. Collective meetings will end on time.

The collective power inherent in scheduling has not been seriously criticized since these events.

Practically every aspect of the Califia day-to-day activities has been questioned and reviewed, including the way we handle food preparation. We serve a primarily vegetarian menu, planned and carried out by two women hired as cooks. Each Califia woman signs up for four to six hours of food preparation and cleanup a week. Some of us were initially opposed to putting women in the kitchen at Califia since we spend so much of our lives in the kitchen at home. We were persuaded to give up our position not by the political reasoning of the rest of the group, but because of the practical truth that doing it ourselves was cheaper. However, even the pro-kitchen-duty members were surprised to see how women enjoyed the camaraderie of working in the kitchen with a group. The kitchen also became a refuge for women in distress. We now know to look in the kitchen for women upset by a presentation, a program, or the overall Califia experience.

The Califia experience is much more intense than we anticipated. None of us know when another barrier to consciousness will dissolve and leave us reeling with new awareness. Needing a structure to work out our distress, we developed Woman Care as the Califia version of peer counseling.[1] We supply peer counseling guidelines in the registration packet, a signup schedule, and lots of encouragement. Women sign up for an hour or two at a time to sit in a quiet, secluded place, usually under a tree, available to talk with other women. This demonstration of women helping each other has become a valuable part of the Califia experience.

For the Califia children's community, we hire a childcare coordinator and three to five assistants a session. They are responsible for scheduling activities for the children and for assisting, organizing, or supervising community members who do childcare shifts of two hours each, two to three times a week. Since many women do not like to do childcare, or do not feel comfortable around children, we suggest they either trade for kitchen shifts with women who welcome the opportunity to interact with children, or do other services for the children's community like preparing their snacks or packing picnic lunches.

We have been criticized for not providing comprehensive educational programs for the children at each session. One year, the collective included Liz Bernstein, an early childhood educator, who developed a program which complemented the issues presentations of the adult community. Since her resignation, however, the collective has not included a member interested in doing such a program. We have tried to organize a task force of community women to develop an educational program that could be implemented at each session, but that has not happened yet.

At a 1980 Califia session, the children's community became an explosive issue. It started with the sexism presentation prepared by collective members Diane Germain and Betty Brooks about the patriarchal control of women's bodies. The program was to start with the film "Killing Us Softly." Then Diane, whose art work had earlier been defaced during its exhibition at California State University, San Diego, planned to show her work and lead a discussion about woman-hating, demonstrated by the defamation. Next, Betty was to show slides from her "Women and Their Bodies" course, followed by a self-examination program by Califia woman, Wendy Votroubek. As we were introducing the program, some women said they felt uncomfortable talking about such personal things around children. Others thought the children could not be trusted to keep confidential what they heard at the group. A heated discussion erupted. In the interest of time, we decided to discuss the issue at the community meeting that evening, to exclude the children from this program, and to do the program for interested children and their mothers after lunch.

At the evening community meeting, several important questions were raised:

1. Does the collective have the right to exclude children from a Califia program, especially when their mothers want them to attend?

2. Is it an infringement of children's rights to give only young women, twelve and older, the right to attend programs they choose?

3. Who has the right to make a judgment about what is suitable material for children?

4. When does "providing a safe place for women" become the female version of "protecting women for our own good?"

Because we could not reach consensus on these complex issues at the community meeting, the collective promised to discuss the issue fully and to put it on the agenda for the next Los Angeles meeting. (These meetings are called by the Califia collective for community input into the next year's programs.) At that later meeting, after much discussion, we finally resolved this issue. We admitted to ourselves that we were not specifically interested in planning programs for children. We agreed, though, that whenever possible, we would seek a coordinator of the children's community who could provide educational programs. We would also encourage community women to bring their programs to the children's community as well as to the adult community. However, the most we would promise was childcare in a safe environment with a feminist perspective.

That decision cleared the way for us to state that the children's community existed for the convenience of the mothers, not for its own sake. Califia Community is designed to be a place for women. At Califia, women should not have to sacrifice their needs for privacy and comfort to further the education of children, no matter how worthy the cause of children's education is. We made one of our few policy decisions. At Califia, women come first. Anytime a conflict arises between the rights and needs of women and those of children, women take precedence.

A vital part of the process of turning a group of strangers into a community is the nightly Community Meeting. Facilitated by two community members, it is scheduled for one hour – after dinner and before the evening program. An agenda sheet is posted every morning, and women write their agenda items on it. Collective members attend but do not participate unless asked specific questions. The Community Meeting may become a forum to continue discussing presentations that took place in the morning, or it may be the place where the collective is criticized. Often the concerns of the community are aired: children's rights, picture taking that might jeopardize a job or a child-custody case, smoking, drinking, vegetarian meals, marijuana, man-hating, loud music and partying in the cabins, insensitivity to the needs of disabled women, the age at which boys become young men, and so on. By the time the meetings end, we are a most grateful and noisily appreciative audience for the evening poetry, music, theatre, and film programs. The Califia Talent Show at the end of the week is always a high spot. After a heated Community Meeting, it is a joy to experience the loving, humorous skits that poke fun at the week we have just spent with each other.

A relatively new Califia tradition is the Late Night Conversation designed as an alternative to the nightly dancing which takes place after the evening entertainment. The Late Night Conversation provides another structured opportunity for women to continue dealing with unfinished business raised in the day's programs. Often women who have not spoken out strongly about the issues during the day come to share their views. For example, in our first Late Night Conversation, we met the women for whom our "women come first" policy was necessary. Fat women, women our society describes as ugly, women terrorized when they were children, and women who were physically abused as children came to say the things they feared to say in the large group: they hated or feared children after years of their own teasing and ridicule; they were afraid of the rage they felt around children; they were afraid they might hurt a child they were supposed to care for during childcare shifts. The women were expressing feelings they knew were "politically incorrect." It was a freeing experience for them and a humbling one for the rest of the group, and Late Night Conversations became a regular part of our schedule.

Another program created for Califia is the Feminist Primer. Those of us who have been immersed in feminism a long time tend to forget how different our vocabulary is from the world around us and how differently we relate to each other. Words like "matriarchy," "patriarchy," "privilege," "process," and "separatism" roll off our tongues with an assumption of shared definitions. Consciousness-raising techniques (CR) of speaking one at a time and not interrupting with comments of sympathy, support, or disagreement are not familiar to many women. For women new to feminism, this lack of knowledge greatly increases their feeling of alienation. To overcome this isolation, we hold breakfast Feminist Primers where we can discuss a variety of feminist issues. As each woman realizes she is one of many, she begins to feel less estranged.

In Califia's seven-year history, the hour before dinner has been set aside for small groups. We see this as a way of building smaller support systems within the larger community. In spite of the collective's commitment to the small group, we have had to experiment and learn about an appropriate structure for the groups. Initially we randomly assigned women to CR groups. Now we organize on the basis of geography or special interests so that women have a support group for work that they can continue after the Califia session.

COLLECTIVE PRESENTATIONS: SEXUAL PREFERENCE, CLASS, WHITE RACISM

The original collective decided that the issues of sexual preference, white racism, and class – issues which often divide and separate us from each other – should be highlighted by specific collective presentations. Since that time we have discussed making other issues such as anti-Semitism, body image, ageism, disabilities, and motherhood additional collective presentations. While it is tempting to add them to our presentation, especially for those of us who are members of those groups, we have decided that to do additional presentations would leave little time for community workshops, and Califia would become a conference rather than an educational community. We depend on community women to see that these issues are addressed during the sessions.

In our issues presentations, we begin with the assumption that as feminist women, we want to rid ourselves of beliefs, attitudes, and behaviors that oppress others. We use the term privilege — white privilege, class privilege, heterosexual privilege — to inform each other of the profit accruing to members of oppressor groups, with and without our consent. We attempt to bring to consciousness the ways we have personally both actively and passively cooperated and still cooperate in the oppression of others.

The collective presentations begin on the first morning with an examination of the systematic oppression of women's bodies. We remind ourselves of the oppression we share regardless of our race, class, sexual preference, religion, appearance, age, or bodily health. This first presentation is the easiest one for us to organize. We have more ideas and material than we can possibly use. The program which is called "Misogyny" has been criticized as "man-hating." We explore with the community what it means that a program on the woman-hating behavior of men becomes a program on man-hating in the minds of some women.

At present, the introduction to the sexual preference issue on the afternoon of the first day consists of a slideshow illustrating the relationship of lesbianism to the liberation of all women. By delineating the nature of compulsory heterosexuality, we show its oppression of all women regardless of sexual preference. After this introduction, we meet in small groups to discuss several questions we have formulated. All of the women discuss the same set of questions, but lesbians and nonlesbians meet and talk in groups separately. The discussion questions include: What was your reaction when you first realized that lesbianism had some relationship to your life? What myths and stereotypes about lesbians do you know, and what effect did they have upon that realization? After this exercise, we all view a slideshow, "Women

Loving Women" by Lavender Horizons. We then share a brief summing up and a reading of "Applesource," a short, humorous retelling of the Adam and Eve story which ends with Eve and Lilith walking hand in hand in the Garden of Eden while an apprehensive god and Adam watch.[2]

An important dynamic develops around the sexual preference issue at Califia. Women who are members of the oppressor group in the world are the twenty percent minority in the camp. This creates a wonderful opportunity for women who are not lesbians to experience some of the feelings lesbians experience in the real world and, as a result, to become firm allies of lesbians in the struggle for lesbian rights.

For this to happen, however, heterosexual women must learn to deal with the discomfort they feel during the first few days of the session. Lesbians new to Califia attribute this obvious discomfort to the women's homophobia and, in some instances, this is true. Usually one or two heterosexuals leave each session by the afternoon of the first day. But homophobia is not a satisfactory explanation for the discomfort of many heterosexual women who attend Califia. These women often work in organizations with lesbians and/or have lesbian daughters, sisters, mothers. Their discomfort is a shock to them, and suspecting that undiscovered pockets of homophobia are causing their reaction, they become even more distressed. Lesbian and heterosexual collective members help them understand that what they are experiencing is a temporary loss of heterosexual privilege. In the world, they do not emotionally experience that privilege, though they may recognize it intellectually. Because heterosexuality is the dominant mode of affectional/sexual bonding, its privilege goes unnoticed. But when a woman "feels funny" mentioning her husband's name in conversation with her cabinmates at Califia, she is experiencing loss of privilege. When she connects that funny feeling with the everyday reality of lesbians, she can make the quantum leap of identification and solidarity with lesbians. She understands in her emotions and body the feelings minority groups have as they try to live in a world not designed for them.

To facilitate this movement from discomfort to political awareness, we have developed some first-night get-acquainted exercises which enable women who are not lesbians to see that they are not the "minority of one" they sometimes think they are. We make sure that community members know which collective members are not lesbians. A heterosexual collective member is one of the facilitators of the Late Night Conversations on the first evening so tht the subject of loss of privilege can be introduced. The sexual preference issue presentation the following day begins with the recognition and explanation of the difficulty heterosexual women experience coming to Califia for the first time.

The decision to examine class as an issue which divides women came out of the experience of collective members who had participated in the working-class caucus at Sagaris. Because class is such a hidden issue, we had to discover a method which would demonstrate that class, indeed, was a significant issue, and that most of us are unaware that a working-class upbringing fosters attitudes, values, and behavior different from those of the dominant culture. We needed to learn how to show that these hidden differences cause difficulty in the personal and political relationships among women, and that frequently women who think of themselves as middle class are from working-class backgrounds.

To accomplish these goals, we begin with an informal lecture on value, attitude, and behavior developmental theories as they relate to socio-economic class. We illustrate these theories with examples from the lives of working-class women and from the class conflicts we have experienced. The original lecture was written by Ahshe Green, from our first collective. It has been revised each year since then as we learn more about the subject and learn more effective ways to present the material.

After the lecture, we read aloud a list of twenty-five questions developed by the working-class members of the first collective. The list includes such questions as: When you were a child, did you have enough underwear and socks? Did you get regular medical, dental, and eye check-ups? Did you get a regular allowance? We ask about parents' job histories, about parents' aspirations for their children, and about use of leisure time. These questions are meant to be an experiential translation of some of the socio-economic indices of class. The women are not to answer these questions, just to think about them. The questions are designed to unlock the years of painful memories "forgotten" by many working-class women, especially upwardly mobile ones like ourselves. Unless we bring those memories to consciousness, we cannot use our past to inform our present, to change ourselves or the women's liberation movement.

The immediate goal of the questions, however, is to prepare the women for The Passing Game developed by Mary Glavin.[3] As a working-class woman for whom scholarships to prestige schools were the ladder to a Ph.D. and university teaching, she was acutely conscious of her personal passing game. She thought that the concept of passing might be the way to break the silence of working-class women. So we had all the women sit in a large circle and answer, in turn, two questions: How did you pass as middle class? and, What price did you pay for passing? We explained that middle-class women were to be silent and listen nondefensively. We had no idea what we were unleashing as we sat in the circle at the first Califia. We expected women to talk as we had in the working-class caucus at Sagaris. But by bringing up passing, we had inadvertently caused women to remember not only the facts of their youthful deprivations but also the feeling of shame and humiliation they suffered lacking the "right" clothes, parents, accent, and vocabulary. It brought up their feelings of resentment toward and alienation from their middle-class friends, lovers and coworkers. The working-class women, including the collective women, were distraught; the middle-class women felt guilt and resentment; the class-confused women were even more confused. It took the rest of the week to heal the class split that resulted.

We have not had a class split since. Now we know to tell women what to expect. Many women now come to Califia because they have heard about the class presentation and want to experience its freeing results. Others, who have participated in previous years, come to continue their healing process; they give grounding to the large group. In addition, when the exercise is over, working-class and middle-class women meet separately to process the experience, allowing both groups time to relieve their feelings in safety.

The class presentation works well for working-class women, freeing us from our past and helping us to recognize behavior developed in the scarcity of our youth that is inappropriate for our adult lives. It has made us more aware of middle-class assumptions and of ways organizations structure out participation by working-class women. We have not been as successful in making the class presentation work for middle-class women. In 1982, Jan Hines and Suzanne Beford, middle-class collective members, devised a format for the middle-class group which enables the participants to move from guilt and resentment to understanding and positive action. This is an important breakthrough for us and should make the class presentation even more powerful.

Califia's white racism presentation has also had a stormy history. Each collective has renewed our commitment to examine racism as an issue which divides women. In the early years of Califia we made up programs by sharing ideas and theories that had moved us individually to take an antiracist stance. We read poetry by women of color. We organized white women into small groups to talk about their initial awareness of racism. We talked about the connections between racism and sexism, but the presentations lacked emotional intensity. We could disperse information about racism better than we could move women's hearts.

Everything began to change when Maria Diaz and Gloria Rodriquez came to Califia in 1978 and saw its possibilities for women of color. Before the week was out, they had organized the women of color and some white women into a caucus and issued a statement of demands. These included having a Califia outreach to women of color task force by September of 1978 and three women of color on the collective by July 1979. Maria and Gloria took the responsibility for encouraging women of color to respond to our call for members on the outreach task force. The task force, composed of women of color and white women, worked to familiarize area women about Califia, to raise money to assist women of color to come to Califia, and to find women of color willing to risk becoming members of the all-white collective.

In 1978 and 1979, the collective was asked to do racism workshops for a number of Los Angeles women's organizations. In June 1979, Califia and the Los Angeles Lesbians of Color cosponsored a successful Racism/Sexism Conference at the Los Angeles Woman's Building. The collective members became more skilled in presenting antiracist workshops as a result of these programs. The 1979 and 1980 Califia white racism presentations were a joint effort of white women and women of color. They were more effective than our original presentations, but it was apparent that the emotion and energy expended by women of color participating in these programs took its toll. Once again we learned that women of color should not have to do white women's work in the struggle against racism.

Irene Weiss has coordinated our white racism presentation since 1979. She and the other presenters experiment with exercises we have used before as well as with materials and ideas from several additional excellent sources.[4] Irene introduces and explains the ideas and concepts that are particularly hard for well-intentioned white women to hear: that all white people are racist; that we have white privilege and the responsibility to use our privilege against racism; that the good intentions of white people often result in unintentional racism, and so on. She talks about the difference between racism and prejudice and presents the statistics of the physical, economic, and social costs of racism for people of color. Other collective members facilitate the exercises which follow the introduction. We use a guided fantasy which opens white women to the realization of their hidden, and not so hidden, pockets of racism. We use a variety of small-group techniques to facilitate the movement of women from guilty awareness to positive action.

At the four 1981 Califia sessions, collective members Carmen Silva and Anna Maria Soto began meeting daily with women of color. At those meetings the Califia Women of Color Network was founded. The Network inspired more women of color to join the collective. Also, the Network proposed that Califia sponsor a women of color only weekend, and over the 1982 Memorial Day weekend, one hundred women and their children attended the first Women of Color Califia.

ADDITIONAL PROGRAMMING

Except for the issues presentations conducted by the collective, all educational programs are in the form of workshops facilitated by community women. We do not permit women to come to Califia for a few hours, present a program, and leave. We say that at Califia all women are the teachers and the taught, that no woman comes to Califia empty-handed, with nothing to share. To have an "expert" come in, do a program, and leave, implies there is nothing important that she can learn from the women she taught. We find it a powerful experience for women to exchange educational roles with each other.

Some women come to Califia prepared to do a program and others call an impromptu group together after they arrive. It is in workshops that women who are experienced organizers share their expertise with others, where new women learn that their personal experience is important, where burned-out feminists are sparked by the vitality of newcomers to the women's liberation movement, and where new groups and programs emerge.

All of us see Califia sessions as a time for women, including collective members, to become more conscious, better educated, politicized, and radicalized. Out of these desires have come the SEA groups (Support, Education, and Action). These small groups, organized on the basis of geography or special interest, have generated specific actions outside of the Califia session. The 1979 Northern California SEA group became the organizing group for our first Northern California Califia in 1980; and the 1980 Sacramento area SEA group organized our second Northern California Califia in 1981. Members of the 1979 San Fernando Valley SEA group began plans for a rape crisis service which was founded in 1980. The San Diego SEA group in 1981 resolved some serious problems plaguing a San Diego lesbian organization. Several 1981 Califia sessions have been educated by presentations organized by Jewish women's SEA groups and by SEA groups of disabled women. White Women Against Racism groups in the San Francisco Bay and Los Angeles area were founded during Califia 1980 and 1981, and the women of color SEA groups in 1981 developed the Califia Women of Color Network which organized and conducted the first annual Women of Color Califia Community in May 1982.

There are many smaller events which have become an important part of our program: our opening circle, where each woman calls out her name and the name of the women in her family; our closing circle, when we build an imaginary dome to house our Califia experience; the storytelling around the fire late at night – informal, essential telling of our histories; our group photographs; the smoker's caucus, banished to a table under the trees; the obligatory popcorn during movies; the last night procession to the dining hall; the dining room, festively decorated by the children for our banquet.

It is almost impossible to recount the seven years of Califia collective meetings (approximately thirty a year), seventeen Califia Community sessions, the formal meetings between the collective and community members, the written and oral community evaluations of each session, the Califia outreach to women of color meetings, Califia Women of Color Network meetings, the programs on racism and class we have conducted for women's organizations, and all the informal exchanges between collective members and women who attend Califia sessions – which produced the present Califia Community, its structure, content, and methodology. We call ourselves an experiment in feminist education so that we can feel free to change as we learn, so that we will be open to new ideas, so that we can welcome criticism and suggestions. The process by which women attending Califia sessions become responsible for each session has produced Califia members and collective members who are devoted to Califia. We all find satisfaction in the changes Califia has made in our lives, in the organizations we work in, and eventually we hope, in the world we all inhabit.*

NOTES

1. This program was started by Mary Glavin in 1978 and then formalized by Carol Rabaut in 1978 and refined in 1981 by Yvonne King.

2. See "The Jewish Woman," edited by Liz Koltun, in *Response: A Contemporary Jewish Review,* no.18 (Summer 1973).

3. Since Califia introduced The Passing Game, other groups have used this concept very successfully when doing consciousness raising about anti-Semitism and lesbianism.

4. *Teaching About Racism in the Classroom and in the Community* by Linda Shaw and Diane Wicker. (Write the authors at The Center for Women's Studies, California State University, 1240 N. Bellflower Blvd., Long Beach, California 90840). *Rooting Out Racism* by Sara Winter and *White Awareness* by Judy Katz. (Send $1 for copying and postage to Califia.)

---

* 1983 Califia Community Collective members are: Suzanne Beford, Betty W. Brooks, Ann Carino, Paula Fisher, Diane F. Germain, Jan Hines, Betty Jetter, Mary Lorang, Marilyn Murphy, Rosalie Ortega, Kate Rosenblatt, Carmen Silva, Anna Maria Soto, Janet Stambolian, Sarah Stroud, Marj Suarez, Irene Weiss, Lillian West.

Former Califia Community Collective Members include: Dani Adams, Christina M. Alvarez, Margaret Barker, Liz Bernstein, Josie Catoggio, Dawn Darington, Sue Donne (Cybelle), Barbara F. Forrest, Norma Fragosa, Mary Glavin, Ahshe Green, Rose Green, Gail Harris, Kari Hildebrand, Donna Hill, Yvonne King, Cecilia Lami, Sidra Moore, Alice Myers, Carol Nelson, Lois Nevius, Glenda Osborne, Marilyn Pearsol, Anne Perna, Kathy Plowman, Carol Rabaut, Wanda Ross, Shari Schulz, Jody Timms, Shirley Virgil, Karen Williams, Sue Williams, and Denise Woods.

Califia Community can be reached by writing P.O. Box 1034, Studio City, California 91604.

Feminist Art And
Education At Califia:
My Personal Experience

by Diane F. Germain

FEMINIST EDUCATION at Califia is a process of contact, discovery, healing, release, mobilization, creation, sharing, growth, and action on spiritual, social, and intellectual levels. Under these unusual circumstances, I was able to throw off the effects of certain oppressions and become a feminist-artist-educator myself.

I began at Califia in the summer of 1978. I was angry, impatient, and critical. I graduated from U.C.L.A. in 1975 with a psychiatric M.S.W. degree only to discover that I couldn't tolerate the traditional (read "white male") idea of what was good mental health for women, much less lesbians. My favorite phrase while at camp was "this is the pits."

In spite of my multiple complaints about Califia, I came back each year for "a week in the woods with 150 women," as I characterize it in lighter moments. The expression of all my feelings was tolerated, my own way of communicating understood, and my ideas and fantasies appreciated. Sounds more like therapy than education, you say. Well, I'm convinced that many frustrated and crabby women are merely feminists in restraints. They need a bit of therapy, a bit of healing, a bit of validation before they can throw off the restraints and concentrate on the education. Califia is a very necessary, very special education for the total adult woman.

My involvement with Califia from those first days to my joining the collective in 1981 was a dramatic series of exchanges for me as a learner and increasingly as a teacher.

One of the prominent mottoes on education at Califia is: "the teachers are the taught and the students do the teaching." In concert with that is the feminist directive, "woman, take your power." Now, I take sentiments like that earnestly to heart with goose-bumps-a-tremble. So even in those early days of confusion and anger, I did a bit of teaching as I was gobbling up the learning.

At my first camp experience in 1978, several women began to develop a guerrilla theatre piece. I had to learn the meaning of the word "guerrilla" from a few young Berkeley amazons, but to tell the truth, I loved the way it sounded right from the beginning. At the L.A. County Welfare Office where I had been coordinator, I was known as a "troublemaker"; at Califia I was "Amazon guerrilla." Given that choice, what camp would get your allegiance? In any case, we developed a theatre piece that ruffled not a few feathers of the collective members as we told them in a dramatic way that the structure was too pressing, immediate concerns needed to be addressed, and "damn the next event planned on the schedule."

Another time, being fed up with participation at workshops, I decided to give up my fastidiousness and take a morning hike with a group of women. I had on my shorts, daypack, and big hiking boots and was pacing around the lodge waiting for the others to congregate. I heard they would be a half hour later than planned. I also heard that Alice Eldred was giving an anger workshop nearby. Now, I could sit around for a half hour working up an aggravation toward less punctual women, or I could divert my attention with Alice and not spoil the hike with a case of "attitude." Light bulb!

At first when I joined the circle, I was pretty skeptical of how this event would even scratch the surface of my voluminous anger. We were asked to march around in a circle saying "no! no! no!" and "do it *my* way." Being 5'4" most of my life, I rather liked that, especially with my big boots on the hardwood floor.

Then, we were asked to tear up newspapers lying around inside the circle. "Silly," I thought, but obediently I began the task. I happened upon a page of wedding photographs and said, "there'll be no wedding pictures for me." Rip! Rip! Rip! "No *L.A. Times* wants pictures of a lesbian wedding." Rip! Rip! Rip! We all really got into it, as they say. Before long there were no pieces bigger than postcards anywhere. What a proud job we had done and how we laughed.

I saw a woman beat a towel on the floor and scream her agony over her two strong beautiful daughters who would not get a chance to play out their full destiny in a racist-misogynist system. I was angry for her and with her. I began to walk around her as she cried. Just before that, I had heard from a woman who was angry over the loss of connection with her original Black culture through the white male whitewashing of history and literature in traditional education and mass media. Her words were still bumping around in my head as I watched the other beat the ground.

I began to stomp around and talk out my own feelings about being thirty-eight without knowing but a few of the names of the many women poets, women painters, women inventors. "I want my culture back. I want my history back." I was determined to find out who the silenced women were, uncover the hidden women, recover any clue to women's destroyed creations. ". . . and I will know!"

One year later at Califia I did an art performance about this experience, about the joy and strength attained in uncovering creative women, achieving women, lesbian women through reading, talking with older feminists, and seeing visual and performance art by women.

So what does all of this have to do with education? I learned and am learning to release myself from racism; I learned and am learning to release myself from class oppression, with its shame, self-hatred, and never-quite-good-enough syndrome. I have the energy to seek out the history and literature. Finding truth in all the distortion is a feminist miracle.

In the performances, we re/create an education that fosters an increase in power, a validation through woman-positive stories, an encouragement to create on one's own, and a joyfulness so often missing from public and competitive "higher" education. Some of the art performances originate at Califia; others come from our home communities and are integrated into Califia programs.

I produced a Gertrude Stein Triptych for the San Diego Lesbian Organization out of three women's poems. We do it often for

Califia now. Women tell me that they previously never touched Gertrude's writing because they were intimidated by the complexity and lack of "normal" syntax. Now it becomes understandable and fun. Lesbians say they didn't know her poems were meant for them.

I also do a mock interview with lesbian painter Romaine Brooks. Muriel Fisher, a San Diego weaver and artist, does a delightful interview as Eleanor Roosevelt. In both interviews, we talk about the lifestyle of the women. We allow the lesbian relationship in each to flow out lovingly and with approval. Our audiences often cheer or sigh throughout. We make time at the end of the interview for questions from the audience, with predictable hilarity.

Besides performances, other forms of visual art educate at Califia. In 1978 for the San Diego Women's Art Show, I created a photographic display. It consists of three 3-by-2½-feet white panels on which are pasted large black letters spelling out the words commonly used to describe women's genitals – slang, medical, and literary. Alongside the words are 2-by-2-inch photographs – all identical – of the triangle of a woman's pubic hair. Care has been taken to de-eroticize the image by allowing no curve of hip, nor navel, nor dimple to show. One woman said they looked like little furry wine glasses, as the only line apparent is where the legs come together. The panels were defaced by hateful graffiti, and in the third week of hanging at California State University in San Diego, they were ripped from the walls and thrown to the ground. One letter from a university leader speaking for the acting president said, "We do not wish to censor or inhibit creativity. Neither do we wish to provide an outlet for statements that may be *political* rather than artistic in nature." With the verbal support of only one woman librarian, I went alone to the library and rehung the piece for its final week.

Much of the graffiti revealed misogyny around fatness, too much hair, and nonblondness of the model. Other remarks were racist and anti-semitic. The worst were references to violence against women and destruction of female bodies. I have covered over the repaired panels with plastic sheeting and now use them to begin discussions with women-only groups about misogyny and self-hatred around body image, sexual practice, and female genitals.

In 1979 when I took it to Califia, a controversy began about whether the children should sit in on all aspects of the presentation. I was opposed to including the children as I was fearful of the effect of the violent comments on young minds. After much agonizing debate, the women decided to have a separate showing of the panels for a children's group. I agreed, with reservations. As it turned out, almost all the girls and boys were there and a half dozen interested adults as well. The children were serious, full of questions, and seemed anxious to have a time to discuss the everyday experiences of sex in their immediate lives. As for my fear of bringing the bad news of violence to female bodies by men, several of the girls said they had already heard of atrocities done to women. I realized that at least they didn't have to carry the burden of those thoughts all by themselves as I had to do as a child. Women who talked to me afterward considered the discussion a positive, clearing, cohesive experience for the children as well as for the adults. I learned something about the resiliency and strength of children.

My latest educational project, used as part of the sexism presentation at Califia, is a slide show about women's image in fashion, advertising, and pornography. I seek to expose the levels of misogyny in visual communications that we see and record in our minds daily.

I present information from a feminist photographer's point of view in talking about the meaning of up camera angles, down camera angles, the tensions produced by cropping at significant places on the body, truncation, symbolic visuals, and references to famous associations. I try to stimulate participation in the form of comments, expression of feelings, telling of stories, arguments, and sharing of information. The effect is one of increased power once the manipulation is exposed. Revealing technique immediately interrupts the stimulus/response effect.

Women have said to me, "I don't just see an ad anymore. I also see what the maker is doing in the ad." They can never look at images in quite the same innocent manner again.

Having seen the slide show, hopefully, feminist artists and photographers will do their own art work with more awareness and seek to prevent unconscious sexist and racist associations in their work. We can develop new, strong, healthy powers for the visual image of women.

At Califia, art is integrated into a political/social setting that encourages acquisition of knowledge, consciousness raising, and development of skills. The value system is feminist − that is to say, that which is good for the advancement of women. The requirement is to grow and take action accordingly. This unusual feminist environment produces some unusual and delightful results. And perhaps because of the all female presence, the events at Califia often have a cyclical nature: students learning from teachers and other students, on the way to becoming teachers who educate teachers and students, and learning from it all that it's wonderful to be a woman.

Women of Color Califia

by Carmen Silva

THE PURPOSE of this article is to shed some light on the herstorical Women of Color Califia Weekend of 1982. As light is shed on a precious jewel, the rays bend and twist and yet still manage to reflect some previously undetected surface. This jewel will be turned in the light of herstory and many of its facets will be seen. The reader will need to judge for herself which rays will touch her heart, move her to action, begin to unveil the power within. This account will not seek to convince you of any position. Many others will look at this camp, write about, rage or cry over it. For now, it is my turn.

I am a woman of color in a herstorically white collective. The definitions for woman of color in this article will be what we used for the camp. Asian, Black, Chicana, Latin, Native American or identifying with any nonwhite, non-European culture. The bicultural sisters came despite the arbitrary division. We acknowledge their courage and vision. At the time of our declaration (May of 1981), the women of color on the collective were: Chris Alvarez (Bicultural), Dawn Darington (Bicultural), Barbara Forrest (Bicultural), Carmen Silva (Chicana), and Anna Maria Soto (Chicana). When the vision was made real in May 1982, we had on our collective three more women of color: Ann Carino (Black), Marj Suarez (Chicana), and Lillian West (Black).

In the course of our work, the Califia collective was transformed from a group that was 36 percent women of color to its present 50 percent women of color. More significantly, the women of color on the collective have become bonded by a common experience of making a vision real. The full consequences of these events are still not known.

The issue of women of color gathering autonomously with allegiance to no one except to each other's well being is a radical issue. Such an issue pops up periodically in the white women's movement. This time something came of it. The camp is the result of women of color working in the Califia Community since the mid 1970s. It is the product of women of color who have sweated, risked, and angered their way through Califia camps in the past. We stand on their shoulders. Our work is made in the shadows of their struggle. I saw many of those women at the weekend. They seemed tired, and yet the gleam of a vision still escaped from their eyes. They worked hard and gave me strength. I love them, and it is to them that I dedicate my work.

When Anna Maria and I first went to Califia, it was on the advice of a white woman we know. This woman was a friend for many years, and we trusted her perspective in the matter. Both of us were ready to do some political work, yet we knew nothing about organizations or groups for women of color who happened to be radical.

Califia did indeed have an impact. However for us, as for many women of color before us, the impact was not as profound or transforming as the impact it had on white women. We went to all of the presentations, stayed up late, did all the readings and still did not get the point. White women were crying and arguing, and we were left with a sense of observing it all rather than experiencing it. We knew that *something* was happening and we knew that we had to have it. We had to have it for ourselves as well as for other women of color who would never touch the Califia experience.

The premise that Califia is based on is an educational one. The experience of Califia, beneath the theory and rhetoric, empowers the ability of women to realize certain personal and political planes of power. For women of color the premise is, of necessity, a transformational model. The circumstances in which we live (economic, cultural, institutionalized oppression) may not improve any time soon. And yet, within these circumstances, the strength must be ignited to continue on. Our experience together was one of bonding and nourishment. The lessons we learned have been many.

During our first year in the collective, we knew that we would be responsible for creating a program for women of color. It became our commitment to organize Support, Education and Action (SEA) groups, specifically for women of color, during all of the four camps that 1981 season, to determine what women of color wanted and needed in regard to programming.

The SEA groups were structured loosely. We began with our purpose for being there, talked to any feelings of alienation and/or isolation, and shared information about each other's lives. We met daily. What resulted was beyond our expectations. During the first such SEA group in Northern California, a vision was shared. Why doesn't Califia sponsor a Women of Color Camp? As collective members, we knew we now had a big enough project to create and nurture.

After our declaration at the Northern California camp, we were faced with our first organizational decision. How to organize a camp for women of color by a then predominantly white organization? An added dimension was that Califia itself, through actions of some white collective members, had been accused over the years of white, liberal, and overall ineffective attempts at dealing with racism both in the collective and at the camps. Whether these allegations were true or not is beside the point. That these conceptions and impressions were in the community is certainly true, and once we had begun to make public our dream, we were made aware of them rather quickly. It is this network of communication among women of color − this willingness to tell each other the truth of our experience, to take interpersonal risks because we have a higher purpose in mind − that is inspiring and quite effective in getting our projects done. The solution to this challenge was to have the camp organized by an independent, new, and multicultural network of women who shared our dream. We named ourselves the Women of Color Network.

Forming the Network allowed the second challenge to surface. What would be the nature of the relationship between the collective and the Network? There had been problems in the past with other projects that Califia had sponsored. If there was to be a "Califia Camp," then certain conditions needed to be present in the program as well as in the organizational work. Would the Network be an advisory committee? Could white collective members attend meetings? What about the money? These issues engendered many difficult discussions. At this point, any concerns white collective members would voice could have been labeled "obstructionist." Women of color on the collective were put in a very dangerous position within both groups since it was now our job to communicate to both groups what the other was thinking. If anything was left out in the planning, or if we were to make a logistical error, either group might have pulled out and the project would have died.

The solution to this challenge was based on communicating to each other our vision of the camp. The purpose of the camp was to share, discuss issues, empower, and contribute to each other in a meaningful way. We wanted this camp to make a difference. When we got stuck on a detail, such as on our policy about financial assistance (we were split along class lines), and when it seemed like this would be the argument that we would hate each other for, we would stop and take a look at our purpose – suddenly our positions would soften and we could reach consensus. Consensus came as a result of our love and respect for each other rather than our ability to bludgeon each other's opinions. From this cycle of solution to new problem to new solution, we came to discover three basic principles that contributed to our project's completion. We share these with our sisters as a model we can work from in our continued commitment to multicultural programs within an educational context.

To declare is to make real.

The Northern California SEA group declared it, and it was so. As women, the power of our words has long been kept from us. As feminists, we have begun to discover that what we say is powerful and it can cause change. As women of color, to give our word and to keep it is a crucial bond between us. Given the society we operate in, we can do nothing else except take great pride in our ability to do what we say. It takes courage to declare oneself. Our movement is courageous. When you declare yourself, the stage is set for the next principle.

To empower one another is critical to producing intended results.

We have long known that we cannot do it alone. The impact we wanted accomplished by the Women of Color Camp only came about by women who were clear about the purpose of the camp and were willing to hang together until the job got done. This takes communication, honesty, and a sense of trust. These conditions were created because we had a greater purpose in working together than merely personal satisfaction. We did not have to like each other or agree – but we did establish being-as-one with the purpose of the camp. This meant supporting each other whenever the load, tension, or anxiety was too much. It meant late night calls and a commitment to be there for your sisters no matter what.

To establish context is to make things happen.

There was only one thing greater than the purpose of the camp and that was the context that was created in our lives during our time together. The context was one of everyone's contribution being valued and supported. The camp grew and became more real during critical growth periods out of our discussions, fights, fears, and love.

Our way of viewing events that led up to the camp, as well as the groundwork laid for the next Women of Color Camp (May 1983), was based on the knowledge that everyone makes a difference, that every event is a contribution, and that everything will work out. Having such a context allowed us to handle any unexpected crisis with certainty and swiftness. It made us open to criticism and responsive to corrections.

With these three principles in mind, let us look at the realities of the camp. It was organized by a loose-knit coalition of groups and small clusters of individuals who would enter, give input, then leave. Such a coalition has its pitfalls and we discovered four critical ones for us.

Knowledge can oppress.

Just as a doctor can maintain certainty in his/her power and privilege over the patient by witholding certain options or pieces of information "for their own good," or a teacher may not give an entirely accurate picture of a child's progress because the parent "may not care anyway," so too can people who know how to do things fail to give out critical information on certain matters to people who don't know how to do those things. This "not knowing" can be and has been a barrier to women of color experiencing that certain projects are indeed within their realm of accomplishment. When information or techniques or background herstory is doled out piecemeal, or worse yet, simply forgotten, and when this information is critical to the success of a venture based on coalitions, there is a danger of miscommunication, misunderstandings, and misperceptions of motives as well as loyalties.

The challenge for all of us, as we engage more in coalitions that involve crosscultural connections, is to stay alert, to get to know how things are done, and to share that information with each other effectively.

There is power in confrontation — when context is established.

On the third morning of the camp, we were due to have a presentation on class issues as they relate to women of color. A small group of us had been meeting before camp to organize this presentation. When it came time to present it, only one of three women showed up to begin the talk. The presentation continued, although it was greatly modified. The community forgave us this organizational slip-up, although it was clear that the incident had greater significance than just the events themselves. We held a Network meeting later that day. Each day an open Network meeting was held in plain sight of the women so that we could monitor the tone of the camp as well as handle any situations that required immediate action.

The issue of the morning's presentation was brought up. The woman was angry and hurt that her two sisters did not show up and did not notify her. One sister did not realize she had to be present, and the other sister did not feel ready and slept-in. The meeting was tense and uncomfortable. What finally surfaced was the issue of responsibility. Who would be in charge? Who knows what's happening? Who are questions to be directed to? Past frustrations and disappointments were also shared. Some of it was hard to hear; yet it was heard. The experience of confrontation contributed to the group and allowed for suppressed anger to rise, be acknowledged, and be rechanneled to a better purpose.

Constructive criticism can recreate context.

At the end of every day, we would have a community meeting to make announcements and bring up issues relevant to the camp and the camp atmosphere. On the last night of the camp, the community wanted to do an oral evaluation. We had not planned this — our evaluations were on forms and we were ready to hand them out and collect them the next day. Many sisters needed to leave early so we modified our schedule. The criticism that followed was new to some of us. For every criticism, we had to hold back an answer, a reason, a fact that was left out. Had we not done that, it would have been a question and answer match rather than a community effort to analyze strengths and weaknesses of the gathering.

A Califia sister from San Francisco spoke about constructive criticism and suggested that we use it as a framework for our meeting. Immediately, the tone changed. The issues brought up by the community were now seen as challenges to be solved before next year's camp. The words themselves were the same yet it was not anger but love that was their context. This shift made our evaluations extremely valuable.

In conflict there is an opportunity to heal.

There were women at camp who had been to past Califias and who had vowed never to attend another. These women were very concerned and curious about the value of our camp. Was the Network a front? Were the collective members sellouts? There were deep wounds in the women's movement – wounds that had opened and not been allowed to heal. The courage to participate in an activity that may be emotionally risky is huge. Women took risks to attend – economical, political, and personal.

We took a stand on Califia and said that there *will* be a camp. However much time, however many women we would have to talk to, however many fundraisers – there would be a Women of Color Califia. This commitment allowed other women also to be strong. No matter that they vowed never to attend Califia, no matter how much money it would take, no matter if the car might not last the trip – women took a stand on themselves and attended.

Once this courage is recognized, once an organization taps into the respect and admiration it holds for *all* of its members, there is then an opportunity to create a profound impact on the quality of work that organization produces.

Wounds, anger, pain, loud words become a signal. When women share their grief and sorrow honestly and forthrightly, and those feelings are acknowledged, recognized, and respected, they become the basis from which we can continue our collective work over bridges rather than schisms.

From our experiences, we learned, too, about the theoretical underpinnings that we believe can serve as a model for working in multicultural radical feminist projects. There are four conditions that must be present for a project of this nature to be successfully planned, executed, and evaluated for future use.

There must be inspiration.

To inspire is to draw air into the lungs – to be inspiring is to breathe life into dreams and have them become real.

There must be role models.

There is a paradox in the nature of organizations. Although a project may be "new" or "unique," everything has been done before. We sought out women who could help us in formulating our ideas. We observed and reviewed other projects and networks to see how they functioned. These individuals and groups served as a springboard for our visions.

Every effort must be made for crosscultural representation.

Under no circumstances must the group be predominantly one culture. It will not work unless relationships have been established with women of various cultural backgrounds. Diversity must be built in from the very start. It is extremely difficult to build it in later when the context and tone have already been set around a single set of cultural values. Once a single culture predominates, it is impossible to distinguish the strands of thought that are culture-bound. The inability to make such distinctions plagues organizations constantly. It is worth the effort at the beginning to insure representation.

There must be evidence of the willingness to form coalitions.

Nothing of any impact will ever be done by one group. Working partnerships and short-term coalitions around key issues are necessary for our feminist future. It takes a flexibility and a clear sense of purpose to create solid coalitions that work. They don't need to last forever, but they do need to produce the intended result.

In closing, I would like to share with you my own visions for the future, which have been born out of my work with women throughout the country.

1. I want to devote my life to feminist principles and represent the power of these principles wherever I go.

2. I want to facilitate women talking, sharing, and experimenting with new forms of relating to each other without such strong attachments to patriarchal, heterosexual models.

3. Women of Color in this country are experiencing a breakthrough at the level of group interaction. We have bonds that will keep us safe (as they have in the past) and free (as they must in the future).

4. I declare that the Women of Color Network will represent what collective effort means. We will support one another and be there for each other.

5. I will, in my lifetime, become a part of a world-wide network of women whose purpose will be to empower other women to be all that they can be.

Now that I have declared myself, I invite you to do the same. We can do nothing less.

Feminist Education at the Feminist Studio Workshop*

by Ruth Iskin

BRIEF HISTORY

THE FEMINIST Studio Workshop (F.S.W.) was founded in Los Angeles in 1973 as an independent educational institution for women working in the arts and humanities.[1] Our goal was to create a learning environment for women that would be free of the constrictions of male-dominated institutions and that would nourish a feminist community in which women could generate feminist art – art that expresses women's experiences and perspectives. During the first three years, 105 full-time students from the U.S., Europe, and Canada participated in our one and two-year programs. Students could work on degrees through our affiliation with several nontraditional colleges – Goddard, Antioch, and International College. In addition, approximately fifteen hundred local women participated on a part-time basis in courses, workshops, and special programs.

The need to find a working space and a base for the Feminist Studio Workshop led to the concept of the Woman's Building – a center that would house various L.A. feminist groups, make a public statement about the strength and cohesiveness of the women's movement, provide a model for independent feminist institutions, and create a focal point for feminist activities in Los Angeles. The organizations which relocated at the Woman's Building were: Womanspace (the first independent gallery and

---

* Thanks to Kirsten Grimstad for help in editing this article.

performance space for women in the arts on the West Coast), Gallery 707 (a commercial gallery devoted to the exhibition of women's art), the L.A. Women's Switchboard (a telephone information service for feminist groups and services), a branch of Sisterhood Bookstore (a feminist bookstore), Grandview Gallery (a woman's cooperative gallery), and a feminist therapist who rented an office in the Building. Later on, new organizations joined: a chapter of N.O.W., a women's coffee shop, and Womantours (a woman's travel agency), while others left or closed down. The F.S.W. School, housed at the Woman's Building, included studios, a Woman's Graphic Center, and the Center for Feminist Art Historical Studies. The Woman's Building also provided for community gallery and performance spaces as well as the Extension Program.[2]

Our original plan for the organization of the Woman's Building was to create a Board of Lady Managers composed of representatives of the tenant organizations and community women.[3] We thought that the work of shaping and maintaining the Woman's Building would be the shared responsibility of individuals and their organizations. It became clear, however, that the tenant organizations preferred to defer leadership responsibility to the F.S.W. and to remain essentially in the role of renters. Thus, when we moved to a new location in the summer of 1975, the F.S.W. staff-collective formally assumed the responsibilities of directing and running the Woman's Building.

The move to a building in downtown Los Angeles in the center of several ethnic neighborhoods provided the opportunity for us to redefine our spaces and their purposes. Based on two years of experience, we were better able to shape the physical space to serve our needs, reflect our values, and implement the goals of the Building as an alternative feminist institution and as a public center for women's culture. The move also provided an impetus to search for additional feminist organizations to join the new Building, since by that time many of the organizations originally renting space had moved or disbanded. In the new building we were able to house four large community galleries, a spacious performance area with the capacity to hold four hundred people, the Woman's Cafe, the offices of two feminist therapists, a branch of Sisterhood Bookstore, Canis Gallery, Olivia Records storage space, a much expanded Extension Program, and the F.S.W. School. The School included a Graphics Center with printing and darkroom facilities, a Video Center, a tool room, and the Center for Feminist Art Historical Studies which provided access to women's art books and slide collections.

The Woman's Building and the F.S.W. have been funded primarily through tuition, membership fees, and admissions to events rather than through grants or outside fundraising. Those grants we have received have been earmarked for special projects rather than for regular day-to-day maintenance costs of the Building.[4] A major fundraiser, the "Building Women" concert financed the materials used for the renovation of the new building.[5] All the work – design of spaces, construction of walls, sanding of floors, scraping and painting – was done by volunteers from the F.S.W. and the larger L.A. women's community. Women learned construction skills and, in a concrete way, experienced one of the goals of the F.S.W. and the Woman's Building: creating a female community focused on work and shared values.

THE NEED FOR FEMINIST EDUCATION

All of us who teach at the F.S.W. were trained and have taught in traditional academic institutions, and it was because of our experiences as students that we created an alternative educational situation. We found that education has been hampered by the dominance of masculine values.

Women have not been educated to be the makers of culture and politics, but have instead been trained to better perform their roles as wives and mothers. In the field of art, women traditionally have been accepted as models, as inspirations, as subject matter, and as collectors – all functions which support male artists and their art. The assumption that female art students will not become artists themselves but rather end up marrying (an artist, perhaps) underlies the interaction of male art teachers with their female art students. Women have been discouraged from serious pursuit of a career and have been deprived of the kind of financial, emotional, and professional support that male students expect and receive.

Even if women are able to transcend the obstacles of male-dominated educational institutions and are able to use their skills in the world, they suffer from the constrictions of sexism in the kind of work they can create. Women's work is most likely to reflect the dominant values of culture or, at best, the struggles that women go through in their efforts to sustain a nuclear family and to gain recognition in a male system.

THE PURPOSE AND GOAL OF FEMINIST EDUCATION

The purpose of feminist education is to create and participate in cultural revolution. Towards that end, feminist creative activity takes place in the context of a community in which women can support one another, validate individual and common experience, create from that experience, and share their work with the public . . . . When women are primarily in a feminist support community, their work reflects female/female support and the different sense of identity which one has in that situation. This is a new and different kind of art, reflecting a new social structure – feminist community structure.[6]

At the F.S.W., feminist education is aimed primarily at the arts. We define the function of art as raising consciousness, inviting dialogue, and transforming culture. We believe that it is not possible to end women's oppression unless feminism reshapes culture, and that the creation of feminist art is essential to this process. Our goal for feminist education at the F.S.W. is to create a feminist learning structure/environment out of which women will emerge to participate in feminist leadership through their work. The focus of feminist education at the F.S.W. is to assist women in developing their strength, leadership, expertise, and creativity; to help them make a transition from victimized, powerless outsider to effective, powerful participator in reshaping the world according to feminist values.

THE F.S.W. STRUCTURE AND PROCESS

Women's conventional education and female role conditioning set up specific attitudes that have limited our aspirations and roles. Women have been brought up to expect that their lives will be shaped and that they will be taken care of by someone else, first by parents and then by husband. Women are taught to assume passive rather than independent roles in the world outside the home. Women are not expected to take risks or meet demands for achievement, success, competency. They are raised to be helping mates, to put their husbands' careers and their childrens' needs before their own.

Feminist education seeks to counteract and undo this kind of conditioning as a prerequisite for women attaining their full potential. The first-year program at the F.S.W. is designed to perform that function by giving support, demanding growth, work, and achievement, and encouraging a critical analysis of women's oppression. The F.S.W. is structured around the interactions of the whole group. Our work has encompassed such diverse fields as painting, drawing, sculpture, environmental work, performance, art history, photography, film, video, graphic design, printing, writing, dance, music, and organizing. The diversity of disciplines is determined by the interest and participation of students and not by the availability of a teacher in a certain field.[7]

The F.S.W. has four ongoing structures: the entire F.S.W. group (for all staff and students), community meetings and small consciousness-raising (CR) groups (both of which are conducted without staff participation), and staff meetings. Other forms such as the critique, the project-oriented group, skill classes, and a large-group project are generated at different times of the year or change format from term to term.

The school year is divided into three segments, each of which has its own emphasis. Initially, we focus on a large-scale group project which will culminate in a presentation to the public. In the second period, we concentrate on acquiring skills in small-group classes, followed by a month-long period of individual work during which students meet with staff members of their choice once a week. Finally, we emphasize bringing the work (both individual and collective) to completion and preparing for a group presentation to the public.

THE F.S.W. GROUP

Meeting regularly in the large group helps create a sense of group identity and community. Whenever possible we start and end the day with the entire group present. Much of the learning about leadership, organizing, identifying one's own feelings and power, and improving one's work, takes place in the group discussions of feelings, problems, and ideas. These discussions challenge the assumption that women should not assert themselves and provide a space for women to overcome their fears of speaking in a large group. At times we use CR (even in meetings of fifty people) to provide a safe, supportive, nonjudgmental atmosphere in which women can articulate their thoughts and feelings.

The focus of the large group varies during the year. Sometimes there are joint presentations by staff members about women's culture; at other times there are brainstorming sessions about the group project. Different periods are used for sharing work and receiving feedback. Each year, the first day of the F.S.W. is devoted to a marathon in which each woman introduces herself to the group by showing her work. Later, after a period of independent study, the women bring in new work to share their development and achievements. The group as a whole tries to move forward and grow in much the same way that individuals move forward in struggles with their own work.

THE COMMUNITY MEETINGS

In the community meetings, the students use the time as they see fit. Students have chosen to explore different modes of intragroup communication and organization or to discuss their relationship to the Woman's Building. The meetings play an important role in forming a sense of camaraderie and self-sufficiency, a feeling of caring, power, and responsibility. The fact that the staff is not present may enable students to express uncomfortable feelings about the F.S.W. and its staff before the women are ready to share these feelings in the presence of the staff.

CONSCIOUSNESS RAISING

During their first days in the F.S.W., women are divided into small CR groups which meet once a week throughout the year. The CR group in the F.S.W. functions as it does elsewhere – as a safe and appropriate setting for the expression of feelings and as a politicizing experience through which women identify with each other. But as one part of the larger educational structure of the F.S.W., CR takes on an additional role in the process of feminist education. Through CR women connect with their personal experiences and realize the commonality of those experiences. This both frees the women to do work and provides material from which work is made. Thus CR is used as a technique in the process of making feminist art. Because CR is a leaderless structure, each woman can give and receive support. At the same time, CR exists here within an overall structure of feminist education which is not leaderless. The leaders (the staff) combine giving support with making demands. The combination of the two is what accelerates progress.

Four CR topics – money, work, sexuality, and authority – appear to be the basic and most charged issues that come up in the process of feminist education. We deal with these topics at the beginning of the program in a marathon CR day in which the staff also participates. In a feminist structure outside the patriarchal commercial system, the issue of money is a subject for careful analysis and a source of strong feelings. Since women have been prevented from fully participating in society in terms of *both* making money and making decisions about spending it, they face material and emotional difficulties around this subject. Important questions get raised: Should we charge money? How do we charge without excluding some women? Is it all right to value feminist services in monetary terms? What about the need to recycle money inside the feminist community? Our purpose is to deal with the issue of feminism and money responsibly and at the same time make it possible for women to survive in the present monetary structure. We face the fact that a fixed tuition fee is required to participate in the F.S.W. program. Ideally each woman should be able to pay according to her means, but it simply would not be possible to operate the school or the Woman's Building without minimum funds for expenses and salaries. We ask women concerned with this issue to join us in the work of obtaining funds rather than remaining immobilized and angry about it. (Recently we were awarded a grant from the National Endowment for the Arts for scholarship funds.)

The topic of work is related to money. We need to work in order to survive. But other issues related to work are also raised: How can we do our own work? How is our work linked with our professional identity? How do we receive criticism and recognition for our work? How do we respect and value that work?

Sexuality, another subject for CR discussions, is dealt with as it is related to work: How is sexuality seen as a theme in women's work? How has it been used to divert women's attention from work and achievement? (For example, women often seek power through sexual affiliations rather than through their own accomplishments.)

The discussion of authority centers on the difficulty women have in asserting their own authority and in accepting authority exercised by other women. We make a distinction between having authority in a certain area (e.g. education, art, writing) and being authoritarian or dictatorial. Since women are not raised to command authority but rather to support and be subject to the authority of others, this issue lies at the heart of every feminist's struggle. For women, the taboo against having authority is so strong that they feel threatened and fearful when they see another woman who represents authority. They identify with her, and the initial reaction is to rebel against and to stop the female authority. Through the process of feminist education, this response can turn into an understanding that we can each have authority. Our purpose is to get a woman to the point where she can be her own authority and also support other women's growth.

THE CRITIQUE

It is primarily through the critique that women learn to improve their work. We have experimented with both large and small groups and have found that the small, ongoing critique class, in which each member agrees to bring work to every session and give as well as receive criticism, works best. Regular and punctual attendance is required in order for the critique to work. The sole function of criticism in the F.S.W. is to assist the student in developing her work. Effective criticism takes place when we face directly and are able to eliminate dynamics that usually go unacknowledged in critiques: unarticulated positions, biases, and feelings from which the person giving criticism speaks, power plays, and a sense of competition between students as well as between teacher and student.

The student whose work is up for criticism usually experiences fear connected to her work: fear of being inadequate and inarticulate, fear that the work is unclear or inferior because it does not speak for itself, fear that the work is trivial, unprofessional, or not feminist. In a traditional critique situation these feelings are left unspoken; each participant acts upon them, while not fully recognizing them, and assumes that the experience is unique to her. The first step toward clearing the way for helpful criticism is to prompt the sharing of these feelings at the beginning. For example, the first session in which we ask women to show their work is preceded by a session in which the women express their best and worst fantasies about showing their work to the group. When everyone realizes the commonality of their apprehensions and hopes, the shared experience creates a comfortable feeling – and even comic relief. This frees the women to actually look at the work, hear the criticism, and participate in giving feedback.

Because hearing responses to one's own work is such a charged experience and therefore selective, some women tape record the feedback and listen to it again later on.

At the beginning of the critique, the artist is asked to present her work and to explain her intentions and process, the content and the formal means she chose. After her presentation the group gives feedback. In order for the artist to be able to listen to criticism, it is important to start out by acknowledging what is there in the work before talking about what is not there. Then suggestions can be given about ways to improve the work and additional directions it could take. These might include other awarenesses that could be brought to the work in terms of content, examining whether the media is used in a way that is appropriate to the work, asking whether and how the work communicates what the artist intended, and discussing if she is satisfied with what the work expresses.

Sharing information on how a similar topic has been treated by other artists, both male and female, helps clarify the consciousness that is brought into the work and the tradition through which the work will be apprehended. For example, one of the participants shared a series of four photographs showing herself and her children viewed through the bars of a child's playpen, as if both mother and children were prisoners inside the playpen.[8] The artist was dealing with the topic of motherhood and expressing her identification with her children with whom she felt equally confined. We began by articulating this feeling and then analyzed the similarities and differences between the way this artist dealt with the subject and the way it has been dealt with in feminist literature and in visual art. [Treatment of the theme of mother and child in Western art includes religious glorification and expression of pain in the subject of Mary with the infant Christ; the child and mother as objects glorifying the head of the household —the father — even in his absence from the painting (Renoir); the child and mother as victims of sickness, poverty, general social injustice, and human misery (Käthe Kollwitz); the mother and child as a complete world to themselves, with a heightened element of consciousness in their interactions, (Mary Cassatt); and finally, the shattering of the idyllic mystique of mother and children in the family context (Marisol and Dorothea Tanning).] The artist who brought her photographs to the critique was acknowledged for her own point of view, and her work was also set in a historical perspective through comparison with other treatments of the theme. Then we discussed aspects which were not fully present in the work and which could broaden its content such as: How is the mother not only similar to the children in feeling restricted but also different in her role of responsibility and power? What is the relationship of the sense of confinement of mother and children to the social structure in which this is experienced? And how can that context be integrally expressed?

This example demonstrates how we facilitate the creation of feminist art. Each artist is encouraged to develop her work by expressing her personal experience with a consciousness of the social context in which it occurs. We do not prescribe or favor the expression of one experience over another, nor of certain media to express the experience. Rather, we see our role as assisting the exploration and expression of women's experience and points of view through art.

THE GROUP PROJECT AND THE NATURE
OF COLLABORATION

Group projects have always played an important role in feminist education. In 1971, women in the feminist program at California Institute of the Arts, their teachers Miriam Schapiro and Judy Chicago, and several invited artists from L.A. transformed an old condemned house into "Womanhouse."[9] Womanhouse was an environmental art work that reflected women's feelings, sense of oppression, fantasies, and dreams associated with "the home." At the F.S.W. we build upon this heritage.

During the first and third year of the F.S.W. program, the group project was the renovation of the building in which our program was housed — the transformation of the space into which we had moved into a "building of our own." Planning the spaces to serve our needs and making a public statement about our identity and values, as well as doing the physical renovation, were integral aspects of the group project. The women in the program participated in all stages of the work. They learned how to build walls by constructing frames and attaching sheet rock; they learned how to tape, plaster, scrape, and paint walls, sand and varnish floors; they learned how to use power tools, paint signs, and organize for the opening to the public. The women who worked on the project began to overcome the sense of alienation that most women have about using the strength of their bodies and learning the simple skills needed to use power tools. The group renovation project also provided an opportunity for the women to confront their fears, frustrations, and discouragement about being able to complete a large-scale project. This experience was a valuable prelude to the struggle that they would undergo in the remaining part of the year in doing their art work.

The most important aspect of the experience of the group project is the transformation of the physical activity of the project into a sense of building a community: the feeling of pride in collaboration, the sense of pushing beyond one's limits, the experience of the power of the group as a whole, the kind of sisterhood that develops among women covered with dust, scraping the same ceiling while sitting on the same scaffolding. This sharing of responsibility and effort among women, of exhilaration mixed with exhaustion, cannot be adequately described in words.

In addition to working on the building, the F.S.W. women were doing CR, making their art, and receiving critiques on their work. By the time the building was opened to the public, they had completed work for an exhibition, installed it in the gallery, and presented performances and readings of their own writings.

The experience of the group project transformed the forty-five women, who two and one-half months earlier had come from different parts of the country, into a community. It became a community in which women cared for one another and supported one another on a project that reflected their common goals and values, overcoming difficulties and sharing successes.

Each group project is timed so that we begin and end the year with an experience of collaboration. At the beginning of the year, the function of the project is to encourage large-scale endeavors on the part of individuals and the group. Toward the end of the year, (after a period of learning skills and doing one's individual work), the group effort demonstrates the students' accomplishments. Once again, this work is shared with the public. The group project reunites the group while at the same time providing space for each individual's work. It shifts the emphasis from each student's wish to please the teacher to each woman's responsibility to herself and to the group. The competition among students − encouraged in traditional education by the measuring of individual achievement only, through exams and grades − is eliminated by placing a high value on cooperation and the success of the group effort, while at the same time allowing for individual achievement.

The group project provides a format in which women can confront not only the problems that arise in working collaboratively but also those connected with their independent work. The two issues which surface specifically around collaboration are women's fears of losing their identity to someone else or to the group and of taking over and imposing their ideas on others or on the group. Most women experience both fears at various stages of the project. The group project allows the women to work collaboratively, individually, and in a combination of the two.

Various forms and modes of collaboration have been explored by women at the F.S.W. In one collaborative effort, women wove their individual writings, which had been reworked numerous times with the group's input, into one coherent reading presentation. They had previously presented a public reading that was the result of even more direct collaboration. Each woman wrote on the same theme, the experience of losing her virginity. Then they passed their work on to another woman whose task it was to discover what the essence of that experience was for *her* and to alter only those parts that could not possibly have applied to her. Then the papers went through the process once more. What remained was a distillation of the experience. Women saw their similarities and differences, and what they finally expressed was a fusion of their experiences.[10]

Another collaborative effort was created for the opening exhibition of the new building. Five artists (Ann Isolde, Cynthia Ann, Meridee Mandio, Anne Gaulden, and Emily Chaison) created about twenty-five small images of women corresponding to some of those invoked in Anne Waldman's poem "Fast Speaking Woman." Initially, they planned to weave the images together in a quiltlike manner. But as the number of images grew, and each woman's style and focus became evident, they decided to preserve their individual identities by assembling each artist's images on a separate panel and hanging the five panels (identical in size and format) next to each other. They included small square mirrors (the same size as each image) interspersed among their images on each panel in order to extend the creation of images to the spectator, allowing the viewer to literally view her or himself among those images. The result was a collective work which also exhibited each artist's work independently.

Ann Isolde, one of the five women who originated the piece, recounted the experience:

We were trying to work collaboratively and stay independent at the same time. There were enough images for a large number of people to work on, and we decided to collaborate because it would have taken one person too long to do it alone. We were able to work in our own private space and then get together for meetings where we made various group decisions, like what the format would be, how many images each person would do, what the theme was, what materials we would use. After that we selected our images from the poem, democratically, by going around the room, each woman choosing an image when her turn came.

When we brought the images to the F.S.W., the collaboration went beyond our group, as we got critiques from others. This gave my imagery and work a whole new direction. When there are a lot of ideas, and various people are involved, the project is enriched. All along we were communicating on the phone about how we felt and what images we were making. This kept us going, and we inspired each other. Finally we got together to decide how to put all the images together. At first we were going to do it like a quilt, with each person giving her images to someone else; then we decided to keep each person's work together in order to keep individual styles apparent.

There were difficulties in that collaboration takes a lot of time; you have to find out what everyone feels and thinks, which is hard under deadline pressure. We had problems around money, buying materials and making sure that we kept track so that each person got paid back what we owed her, etc. We got along pretty well; people helped each other. We were not just making our own piece. The collaboration was a teaching/learning situation.

SKILL PROJECT-ORIENTED AND THEORY CLASSES

In the skill and project-oriented classes, the traditional classroom dichotomy between student and teacher is transformed. Designer Sheila de Bretteville described this in a graphics workshop on typography:

I asked the women to bring a statement from their journals, which they would then set in type. The task was to deal with how you make the private public through graphics; what is the effect — tone and form — when you make your work available to a broad audience, rather than to yourself. They transformed their statements into a poster, a billboard, or a multiple-printed piece. The class became a community with the class time and place giving the structure, rather than a teacher giving information. Each week they were the audience for each others' work and gave each other responses as to whether the message could evoke a response from a broad audience.

Since one of the goals was to enter into a dialogue with the audience, they did not want to yell the idea so loudly that there would be no place for the response of the viewer. We dealt with the importance of the conversational tone, and the interactional mode in graphics. Each student found her own solution, did her own piece, and what was shared was time and space. Interaction between all members of the class provided the form.

Learning from others in the group, including the authority figure, decentralizes authority and knowledge. In an all-female group the project-oriented class resulted in much more exuberant participation than in the male/female group at Cal Arts. There we tended to find more defined jobs for everyone, whereas in the all-female context we worked more closely together, and women often changed jobs.

Education in feminist theory took place in the Issues class, which was also a training ground for leadership. Women learned to overcome obstructive group dynamics and purely personal investments. They also learned to listen to, and to forcefully articulate, points of view. Arlene Raven, who led the class, described its purpose and process:

> The purpose of the Issues class was to allow us to deal with important topics in the women's movement, the peace movement, the humanistic movement, and in art, in a way that would place us in a specific relationship to those issues. Instead of simply articulating our positions, presenting the issue, and relating the bibliography (the academic approach), we assumed ourselves to be people who are particularly concerned with *acting* on those issues in terms of how we lead our lives, do our work. First, we separated our own psychology from the discussion of the issues. One of the things we did was to find out what our attachment to the whole area of debate was. We sought to make sure that we were, in fact, talking about the issue at hand rather than giving other messages, such as: "I want attention," or "I am smart," or "I feel stupid." We discussed the interaction among ourselves and cleared that away through exercises such as pretending that we had points of view that we didn't really have, and arguing from those. Then we looked at people debating in the class and analyzed the interaction . . . . The issues that we discussed had to do with political life, with the women's movement, and art. Some of the issues were trashing, lesbianism, the power of art, and the difference between politics and culture, which is an ongoing debate in the F.S.W. We never reached any particular conclusions because that was not what the class was about. The class was meant to encourage acceptance of different points of view and an ability to articulate them in such a way that we could really see what those

points of view were. Each woman arrived at a conclusion when it was appropriate for her. We opened up the field for discussion . . . . Women were listening to each other, and this respect for one another created flexibility. The need to have one narrow point of view subsided when women did not have to fight for that respect any more. Then we were able to really understand some issues.

THE PROCESS OF FEMINIST EDUCATION

Each year at the F.S.W. women go through what we have named "the process of feminist education." Briefly described, it is the fear, anger, anxiety, and pain women experience when they first face their own feelings of being oppressed, powerless, and immobilized. These feelings are stimulated when a woman sees herself in relation to other women who are leaders – women who appear to be strong, powerful, capable, and self-confident. Anger is usually directed at the woman who represents the realization of a taboo: a *woman* who is in charge of her own power which is manifested in leadership. These women are seen as symbols of the power figures of the family and of society and are therefore mistaken as oppressors by women who have not yet freed themselves to use their own power and leadership abilities. This process, which we have recognized in our experience of feminist education at the F.S.W., is a crucial one for each woman to work through. Within the women's movement, it has often brought out feelings of disillusionment and deep pain, and it has been responded to by what is called "trashing" and pinpointed as a partial result of "the tyranny of structurelessness."[11]

This problem is the experience that any oppressed person has when first coming into consciousness about being oppressed, and it is behavior that can be the first step toward liberation. Because we see this process as an inherent and necessary part of feminist education at this point in history (however tired we are from playing a part in it over and over again), we have developed ways in which we feel it can be dealt with actively, rather than simply *reacted* to. The method we use is twofold (and works well in the context of an educational environment with recognized leaders): we give permission for the feelings to arise and encourage the expression of pain and anger. At the same time, we analyze the source of those feelings in the oppression of women in society.

The second part of this process is to assist each woman in moving from a position of feeling oppressed, which is at the source of her anger and pain, to transforming her sense of oppression into an ability to take leadership and power and to act on those abilities rather than on her feelings of victimization. After listening supportively to the expression of the feelings that come up, and after introducing an awareness of women's oppression, we make demands on her to grow and change. We demand that each woman take full responsibility for her feelings of immobilization and powerlessness, granting the recognition of oppression. We demand that each woman move from a position of blaming another (society, parent, teacher/leader, stronger peer, etc.) to a recognition that only she herself can ultimately make things different for herself. We are there to support growth and change, as well as to demand the transition from "mutual oppression to mutual support."[12]

During this process, blame tends to be directed at the authority figure in the situation. Most women tend to get stuck, even if temporarily, in the anger stage, out of fear of moving forward in a direction utterly contradictory to everything that women have been educated to be. While it is important to recognize the role that male-dominated sexist society plays in women's oppression, it is counterproductive for women to continually indulge in the role of the victim. This simply perpetuates victimization and oppression. Support for women developing their potential, their work, their leadership abilities, and their capacity to exercise those in the world are at the heart of feminist education.

By the end of the first year at the F.S.W., the students are stronger and know from their own experience what the process of feminist education is. The women who return for their second year are most likely to complete the process successfully. During the second year they are able to devote most of their energy to the development of their work, as well as being able to play an important role in helping the first-year students through this painful process. It is easier for the women who are in their first year at the F.S.W. to listen to women who have moved through the process recently than it is to hear it when voiced by the figure who symbolizes authority – the teacher. It is useful also for the second year women to have a chance to experience themselves in comparison to women who are in the initial stages. The counteracting of female role conditioning and the constructive development of work and leadership are simultaneous parts of feminist education.

Artist Bia Lowe describes her experience of this success at the F.S.W.:

When I came to the F.S.W., I felt like I was exposed physically. I felt a constant sensation of weakness and vulnerability which was overwhelming. It frightened me, but mostly it generated feelings of anger; and maybe it was just that for the first time there was permission to be angry. Being allowed to express myself stimulated a lot of old pain about my oppression. After a while, I dealt consciously with a lot of stuff about authority; before, I had reacted to authority by acting out, and sometimes by being rebellious.

My experience in the second year had a lot to do with seeing other women from the first year at a different stage. A lot of them were not in touch with their oppression, and/or their sexual identification as women, which made me feel less helpless, and also a little bored. It was a process that I recognized, one that I didn't necessarily want to reenact. I felt like I had more opportunity to make choices – whether or not I wanted to continue to feel helpless and other-identified. I wanted to take on responsibility for the Building – the Building being a metaphor for *my* development – and I realized nobody else was going to take care of me unless I was willing to. I was angry at the Building when I first came because it wasn't taking care of me, or itself in some ways. And then, later on, I wanted to take responsibility and felt crazed because I was so worried that *it* (i.e., *me*) wasn't going to succeed. When I took more active responsibility for certain aspects of the Woman's Building, I experienced other women's anger at the Building and at me. I realized that the success of the Building was only as good as the ability of the women participating to move out of the space of our own frustration. Finally, the issue of anger and helplessness gave way to just getting the job done. At that point I became involved in seeing what value my efforts really have.

NOTES

1. The methods and ideas discussed in this article are based on my experience as a member of the staff collective of the F.S.W. and were developed with my colleagues. The F.S.W. was founded by designer Sheila de Bretteville, art historian Arlene Raven, and artist Judy Chicago. Chicago left at the end of the first year, and at that point artist Suzanne Lacy, printer and graphic artist Helen Roth, writer Deena Metzger, and I joined the staff.

2. This is a description of the Women's Building during its first two years of existence.

3. Modeled after the Board of Lady Managers which initiated the Woman's Building in Chicago in 1893 (part of the World Columbian Exposition). The name Woman's Building was also chosen as a tribute to the 1893 building – a feminist,

woman-governed building dedicated to women's history, culture, work, and achievement. The 1893 Woman's Building was a temporary structure on the World's Fair grounds. It housed exhibitions, statistical data, women's writings, and patents of the work of women in over forty countries. Arlene Raven and I created a documentary exhibition of the 1893 Chicago Building.

4. We brought in and spent about $134,000 during the year 1975-76. This was a significant growth compared to the $47,000 of the previous year. Only 15 percent of the 1975-76 budget came from grants. We were astonished at the size of these figures since the Woman's Building is always running on minimal survival funds and much of the work is either volunteered or severely underpaid. We realize that we must build a solid financial base since the kind of energy and work needed to sustain an institution like the F.S.W. does not make it possible to hold an additional job.

5. The "Building Women" concert was organized by women from the L.A. community and the Woman's Building: Olivia Records, Bobbie Birleffi, Kate McDonough, and Cheryl Swannack. The performers, like the organizers, donated their work. They were Holly Near, Lily Tomlin, Meg Christian, Margie Adam, and Miss Alice Stone's Ladies Society Orchestra.

6. Arlene Raven, member of the F.S.W. staff collective, "Notes on Feminist Education," unpublished.

7. Through the Extension Program we offer a wide range of courses and workshops taught by experts in their fields. One of the purposes of the Extension Program is to augment and complete the course offerings for the women in the F.S.W. For example, when two dancers came to participate in the F.S.W. last year and we did not have a dancer on the staff, we scheduled additional dance classes in the Extension Program.

8. The photographs were made by Terri Hawthorne, one of the participants in a special ten-day intensive workshop, "Feminist Education: Methods and Techniques," held in June 1976.

9. See Judy Chicago's description of the process of Womanhouse in *Through the Flower, My Struggle as a Woman Artist* (Doubleday, New York, 1975). The California Institute of the Arts, Valencia, California, has published a catalogue and a slide package, and Johanna Demetrakas has made a film about Womanhouse.

10. This description comes from Deena Metzger who guided the process in the Journal Workshop.

11. See articles by Joreen (Jo Freeman), "Tyranny of Structurelessness," *Second Wave*, vol. II, no. 1 (1972) and "When Sisters Turn on Each Other," *Ms. Magazine,* April 1976 and readers' responses to her article in *Ms. Magazine,* September 1976. See also, "What Future for Leadership?" *Quest: A Feminist Quarterly,* vol. II, no. 4 (1976), interview with Charlotte Bunch and Beverly Fisher. The problem in the women's movement is magnified because women are so prone to see themselves as the cause of the problem and by extension see the women's movement as the cause. We need to understand that the problem stems from women's oppression and the struggle to solve it is necessary to the process of making possible work relationships among feminists.

12. Term coined by Arlene Raven to describe this process.

Unlearning Complicity, Remembering Resistance: White Women's Anti-Racism Education*

by Terry Wolverton

A working definition of white racism: racism is a lie. The lie asserts that white people (people of European ancestry) are innately superior morally, intellectually, and culturally to other racial/cultural groups.

Everyone born into a racist society learns this misinformation. We do not ask to learn it; we often resist learning it. Once we learn this lie, we perpetuate it through creating or participating in institutions which legislate privilege to white people. These institutions bestow economic, legal, political, educational, and social power to white people, while robbing people of color of their labor, natural resources, cultures, and right to self-determination.

Eliminating racism involves exposing and unlearning the lie, and dismantling the institutions which keep the lie intact.

---

* I want to acknowledge and thank the following women who, by their words and/or by their presence, have influenced me in the development of my anti-racist consciousness: Elly Bulkin, Doris Davenport, Maria Díaz, Kris Holm, Yvonne King, Robin Podolsky, Yolanda Retter, Aleida Rodríguez, Suzanne Shelton, Ricky Sherover-Marcuse, Nancy Taylor, the women of White Women Against Racism, and all the women who've been part of my group: Pat Carey, Cindy Cleary, Jacqueline DeAngelis, Mary-Linn Hughes, Cyndi Kahn, Ginny Kish, Judith Lausten, Bia Lowe, Barbara Margolies, Tracy Moore, Patt Riese, Louise Sherley, and Jane Thurmond. This listing in no way makes them responsible for the content of what is expressed here, nor does it presume that these women are in complete agreement with the ideas I've articulated or with one another.

I especially want to thank Bia Lowe, Mary-Linn Hughes, and Jane Thurmond for their support and feedback on this article.

I am a white woman working to unlearn racism.

In order to do this, I must first be willing to acknowledge the racism that I have learned and the impact such learning has on my life, shaping my identity, relationships, world view, visions.

I must love and value myself enough to believe that I can change, to know that I am not intrinsically stupid or cruel for being white. For a white woman who has internalized oppression and self-hatred through sexism (female role conditioning), this lack of belief in my own worth must be overcome before I can effectively fight racism.

I must also overcome my silence. White women are taught not to talk about racism, especially not to acknowledge or protest its occurrence. We learn instead to deny it ("I'm not racist"); hide it ("I don't want anyone to *know* I'm racist"); or resort to guilt and helplessness ("I'm so bad for being white, I can't do anything.") I have seen these same behaviors – self-hatred, denial, guilt, helplessness, silence – keep me tied to my oppression as a woman, and I now see them keep me obedient to racism.

Since October 1980, I have been working with other white women in an anti-racism consciousness-raising group.* We came together out of a desire to examine and rid ourselves of the racist misinformation we have been taught, and to learn how better to work against racism in the women's community and in the world. We also wanted to create new bonding among white women on the basis of anti-racism, rather than continuing to bond around tacit complicity with racism.

We have been consciously developing an educational process which can be used by other white women. Our process has been inspired by the models of self-education and community education which many of us have experienced at the Woman's Building in Los Angeles. Over the two years we've been meeting, we have expanded our activities and deepened our self-examination. As our insights have grown, so have our strategies for change.

I became aware of my need for this group after spending a year working on a national lesbian project, the Great American Les-

---

* Consciousness raising, or CR, is one of the most widely-used communication and learning processes in the feminist movement. Using this structure, each woman gets an equal amount of uninterrupted time to speak about her own experience. Women then discuss and analyze both the commonalities and differences expressed. It is a process rooted in the belief that the theory we develop must come from our real, lived experience.

bian Art Show (GALAS). I was part of a collective of six white lesbians in Los Angeles who organized the project with the goals of increasing the visibility of lesbian art and artists, and inspiring more lesbians to make and exhibit artwork. To achieve this, we publicized an open invitation to lesbians across the United States to join a national network of lesbian artists exhibiting their work all over the country in the spring of 1980.

Our group saw no particular significance in the fact that we were all white. If we thought about it at all, we had convenient excuses: the project required tremendous amounts of volunteer labor, and women of color can't afford to donate that; or women of color don't have the time and money to make art a priority in their lives; or lesbians of color can't risk being out as lesbians in a public exhibition. Although these statements might be true for some women, our thinking was stereotypical, reducing individuality and erasing all the women of color who *do* volunteer, who *are* artists, who *are* out as lesbians.

We had made token efforts to do "outreach"* to lesbians of color, but most of us did not know many, or any, women of color personally well enough to ask them to work with us. Instead we sent out press releases to names on a list. Still we did not see how our whiteness had anything to do with the way the project was structured or with our lack of success in involving large numbers of lesbians of color. We told each other we had done our best.

When one of us received an angry phone call from a woman of color who asserted that we and the project were racist in our lack of inclusion of women of color, we got very upset. We felt attacked, unappreciated, misunderstood, defensive. And unprepared. We hadn't *meant* to be racist: therefore, we felt unjustly accused. It was not our fault, we reasoned, that lesbians of color had not responded to our outreach. Because we had been observing the typical pattern among white women to *not* talk about racism, we were unconscious of the racism that was occurring.

A few days later, we received a call from a white woman who was a member of a group of white women working against racism. She denounced our project and our ignorance and angrily accused us of being racist. During this conversation the woman gave no sign that she felt any identification with us as white

---

* It has been pointed out by women of color that the concept of outreach assumes that one is at the center of something, and that those outside the center should gravitate toward it.

women. We felt she was trying to "politically-correct" us. She lacked information about the project, including the fact that there *were* lesbians of color participating in the exhibitions. She showed no support for the intention of the project and suggested that art was only relevant to middle-class elitists. It was very difficult to accept the criticism when we could see no investment in the aims of the project from her.

Some members of the GALAS collective were beginning to understand the truth in the criticisms we were receiving. Other members wanted to deny the racism, defend our good intentions, or discredit the women who had delivered the criticism. The disunity we experienced was painful and confusing to all of us and revealed that we had no basis to trust one another on this issue.

We did set up a meeting with the white woman who had called us and two other members of her group. We spoke about our desire to understand and implement the comments we'd received. We also stated our need to know that their criticism came from a desire to support and improve our work, not to destroy it. This meeting produced a significant exchange among us. We were able to acknowledge both the positive efforts and the mistakes we had made. They responded with validation and support as well as suggestions of other possibilities for action. In experiencing a sense of unity as white women, we could work on our racism as a shared problem, rather than scapegoating one another.

Throughout the completion of the project, I was moved by the generosity of a number of women of color who did participate in GALAS by showing their artwork, curating a show, promoting the project, attending fundraisers, and spending time talking to members of the collective about their perspectives on racism. This challenged my previous assumption that "women of color don't want anything to do with us anyway." One of the strongest realizations I had was about the way in which my separation from women of color was reinforcing and perpetuating my racism.

I learned other lessons as well:

- that I could be, and often was, racist without meaning to be;

- that unconscious racism undermined the work I was doing for social change;

- that I had denied my racism to the extent that I was surprised when criticized for it and was unprepared to respond to being criticized;

• that this denial has been ingrained in white women and the white women's movement, and that it keeps us racist;

• that white women need to identify with and support one another to move out of silence and denial, instead of disassociating from one another out of shared but unspoken guilt, or the desire to see ourselves as "the exceptional white woman";

• that I needed to actively start educating myself about my own racism and work to unlearn it.

Not long after GALAS was completed, I had a classic women's movement experience: reading just the right articulation of theory at just the time I needed it to move to a new level of consciousness and action. I came across Elly Bulkin's article "On Racism and Writing: Some Implications for White Lesbian Critics" in *Sinister Wisdom no. 13* (1980). I read:

> . . . I assume that I/we do not have to be *non-racist* in order to be *anti-racist* (italics mine). For me, this has been a crucial realization. As a vocal critic of heterosexism I have been able to raise my own voice confident in the knowledge that my own actions, my own words do not reflect that very bias. In taking an anti-racist position, I can make no such claim. Yet I can hardly wait to take these positions until the day when I will be free of all I have been taught about race and when I will no longer reap the benefits of having white skin in this particular society. Increasingly, I am aware that such deferring of anti-racist actions effectively silences me.
>
> I think it is essential that as white women, as white lesbians, we break out of that silence, that inaction, that wait for the never-never day when we will be blameless enough to speak.

Bulkin's distinction between *non-racism* and *anti-racism* helped me to see an obstacle in my own approach to racism: I had confused the act of trying to *appear* not to be racist with actively working to eliminate racism. Trying to appear not racist had made me deny my racism, and therefore exclude the possibility of change. The alternative was to work to unlearn the racist misinformation I had been taught and to replace it with true information about people of color and myself.

Bulkin says in this article that her understanding of racism has developed through participating in anti-racism workshops and in a consciousness-raising group for white women.

At that point, I determined to start an anti-racism CR group for white women and approached the Woman's Building Educational

Programs about sponsoring it. I felt strongly that I wanted to place this work in the context of feminist education, to assert the relationship between anti-racism and women's liberation.

I put notices in the local women's press advertising a group that would meet at the Woman's Building once a week for eight weeks. I felt nervous taking this action: in doing something about racism I risked exposing my own racism. I feared that advertising a group specifically for white women would be misinterpreted as exclusionary and therefore racist. One white woman told me I was "playing it safe" by being in an all-white group, avoiding having to deal with women of color about racism. I saw the formation of the group as an opportunity to "do my homework," as white women have been exhorted to do by women of color who are sick and tired of trying to jolt or cajole us into consciousness. In seeing racism as a white problem, I wanted white women to begin to take responsibility for advancing solutions. I saw, and still see, the group as part of a process of whites working effectively with people of color.

Seven women came together in October 1980 to be part of this group. After eight weeks, we evaluated our progress and made a new commitment for another period of time. Because confronting racism is such an overwhelming (and seemingly endless) task, we have found it more manageable to commit ourselves to the group for specific amounts of time. At the end of each time period, we assess our activities, analyses, process, and progress, and restate the needs we have for being in the group. We also set new goals or recommit to on-going goals we've established and decide on new topics for the group to explore.

At the first meeting, I indicated that although I had initiated the group, I did not intend to be its leader or its teacher. My desire to be there sprang from my own need to learn and to change and to do that with other white women. Mutual responsibility has been shared in the group since its beginning.

Much of our first few sessions were spent establishing a sense of trust and safety in this group. We have been careful to distinguish *safety* from *comfort* (we do not expect to be totally comfortable talking about racism). We needed a basis for understanding what had motivated each of us to undertake this work and what each woman believed she had to gain from examining her racism. We needed to know that we would value and validate one another as sincere in our desire to learn. We wanted to trust that none of us would be condemned as intractable, hopeless, or innately bad for revealing her racism. We wanted to know that criticism would be delivered in a spirit of identification and with the honest intention to help each other better understand racism and act with integrity.

When we first met, we discussed the different emotions we experienced when talking or thinking about racism. These feelings ranged from sadness to embarrassment, confusion to guilt, helplessness to rage. Each woman talked about the effect of these emotions: whether they served to motivate us or keep us passive.

We used CR to discuss our early experiences of racism, and how we learned racism as children. Although our backgrounds differed — from working to upper class, from Baptist to Jewish to atheist, from urban to rural environments, loving or abusive families — none of us escaped learning racism. Many of us had never told these stories to anyone before or had never reflected on their meanings.

We also used written materials to provide information that was missing from our own education or experience. Most white people are taught only European history, geography, and culture. After reading an article on "Racism in the English Language,"[1] we talked about how racist misinformation infiltrates our speech and therefore our thoughts. We lack even an adequate language with which to talk about people of other cultures. We stumbled around with our search for appropriate words: third world (doesn't this enforce the dominance of the "first" and "second" worlds?); people of color (does it sound too much like "colored people"?); nonwhite (assumes whiteness as the norm); minorities (a misnomer in terms of statistical reality — white people are a minority of the world's population — and a diminutive, as in *major* and *minor*).* Our silence multiplies due to a lack of language. In looking at what resulted from this dearth of vocabulary, we could see that we had often identified people of color with racism (i.e. associated people of color with the racism *we feel* around them). We had no other information, no other definitions; our racism was all we knew about people of color.

We have spent many sessions exploring our relationships with people of color. The first time we discussed this, we gave ourselves the assignment of making personal lists of all the people of

---

* I've chosen to use the term "people of color" because it is in the vernacular of my women's community (Los Angeles).

color we had ever known, then used CR to talk about the things we had learned from making the list. We were reminded of the many connections we have had and do have with people of color, and we were made aware of the separation and loss we feel as well. We remembered significant relationships we had forgotten, usually because we had received no positive acknowledgment, and sometimes outright punishment, for having those attachments.

We have all made it a goal to expand our relationships with people of color — in our work and social lives, in our personal spheres, and in our community. We share a desire to be allies in the fight against racism, and we know that this begins with making personal connection.

Over the two years we have developed other processes, including more focus on dealing with current situations. We begin our meetings with a ritual of "checking in" by talking about something we have read in the newspaper or heard on a news broadcast, a situation we've witnessed, an interaction in which we took part, or an event we have attended. We may express our feelings about the occurrence or discuss the dynamics of racism at work in the situation. This process also helps us keep both the issue of racism and our goal of connecting with people of color uppermost in our minds, and gives us concrete material to work with.

We also function as a problem-solving group when one of us is confronted with a situation in which she does not know how to act. The group makes suggestions, helps clarify the ways racism may be operating, and offers support for the woman to act in a positive and anti-racist way.

We sometimes engage in roleplaying, literally rehearsing interactions with others about racism. In practicing our strategies for interrupting racism, we can test out different approaches and responses. When we first started to do this, the rest of us would often be tongue-tied when one of us portrayed the person making racist statements — we felt embarrassed, fearful, guilty. We saw how our silence gives added power to the expression of racism.

We also found that an accusatory or argumentative response is not very effective. Both parties end up more firmly polarized and entrenched in their points of view. In roleplaying we can experiment with other ways of responding, being both honest and compassionate, using our own experiences (mistakes and successes) to dispel the other's misinformation.

Over the two years we have been meeting, we have spent many sessions discussing the relationship of feminism and racism. We started out reading Lorraine Bethel's poem "What Chou Mean *We*, White Girl?" which appears in *Conditions Five*. The poem is an arrow-sharp and humorous critique of the white women's movement from the point of view of a black lesbian feminist who is fed up. It is guaranteed to bring any white woman's guilt reflexes right out into the open. We talked about what in the poem was on target, what hurt us, and about racist errors we had made in our work in the women's movement. We also talked about the futility of guilt, how guilt is the opposite of responsibility since guilt immobilizes us. Additionally, we gave ourselves the opportunity to acknowledge the actions we take that are anti-racist and congratulated one another for them.

After reading two articles − Angela Davis' "Rape, Racism and the Capitalist Setting" (*The Black Scholar,* April 1978) and Deb Friedman's "Rape, Racism and Reality" (*Quest,* Summer 1979) − we talked about our sexual fear of men of color. Many of us felt that this is an area where we most strongly experience racist feelings. There are women in the group who have been sexually assaulted by men of color and who felt a conflict between their desire to defend themselves and their wish not to appear racist. Others said they are more afraid of the sexism of men of color than of white men. In sharing our histories, particularly our adolescent experiences, we realized the ways our fears have been cultivated in the messages we received about men of color from our parents and from society. We were promised punishment if we related to men of color, or warned that we would be violated if we became too friendly with them.

Davis and Friedman illustrate in their writings how white men have manipulated these fears to their advantage: to inflame other whites into supporting racism; to terrorize white women into accepting the "protection" of white men; and to reverse and disguise the acts of sexual violence by white men against women of color (and white women). This information should encourage white women to reassess how we can conduct our fight against violence against women without falling into complicity with racism. While we must resist any man's assault on any woman, we must also resist the scapegoating of men of color by white men.

There are some issues we have returned to over and over again, and one of them is white identity. This has consistently been one of the most difficult topics we've addressed. When asked to talk about our white culture, many of us could only speak derisively of ourselves as the products of hot dogs, pop tarts, dippity-do, uptightness, racism. We felt shame about being white, or vagueness about whether we had any culture at all. We had judgments about other white people and did not want to be identified with them. One of us finally suggested that we make a rule that we could only speak positively about our cultures. This dumbfounded us; we believed we had nothing to say.

Two women in the group devised an exercise which asked us to look at our backgrounds by answering several questions. These included: What is the geography of the place where you grew up? What kinds of food do you associate with your family? Describe a particular family ritual in which you enjoyed taking part, and tell about a family member you feel proud of. This exercise reminded us that our cultures are made up of very personal, complex, and diverse elements. Although there has been pressure to assimilate, we are not the products of some monolithic White assembly line. We also realize that we have lost aspects of our cultures; many of us know little of our ancestors, the language or customs they practiced, the rituals of their daily lives, or their own resistance to oppression.

We see that the cultural void in which we find ourselves is one result of racism. We have been taught to base our self-perceptions and world view on a lie — racism — which prevents us from knowing ourselves and from knowing others.

One manifestation of this loss of our cultural centers is cultural imperialism:* the assumption of access to, understanding of, or familiarity with another culture in order to absorb it. If we feel bereft of our own culture, we will try to fill the void with something. In a consumer society, we're taught to buy things to fill the void. Especially if we feel critical of white culture, we may try to disassociate from it and become, in the words of Lorraine

---

* Much of the analysis we've developed about this issue comes from the research and thinking of group member Bia Lowe.

Bethel, "racial transvestites." We act as if talking Black English, listening to soul music, wearing (or making) "Indian" jewelry, or wearing "Mexican peasant" clothing could transform us into more colorful versions of ourselves.

I'm not suggesting that it's bad to learn about or participate with other cultures. I think that is essential. What debilitates us is forgetting who we are, believing that we can absorb the spirit of a culture through material consumption of it. What results is a perpetuation of inauthenticity on our parts and a reduction of peoples to artifacts. It causes us to romanticize/objectify those peoples and supports their economic exploitation.

The difficulty we have in identifying as white or feeling positively about our culture acts as a barrier to identifying and empathizing with other whites, even those with whom we may feel closely identified in other ways. I have been to feminist gatherings where, in the middle of a discussion, a white woman says something racist. Often the comment comes from misinformation, not malice or the intention to be racist. There is generally a collective shudder of embarrassment from the other white women gathered who feel they *know better,* and a perceptible moving away from the speaker. We are afraid she is going to make us look bad (expose our racism), especially if there are women of color around. Occasionally someone will speak up and denounce the woman for being racist, ending any dialogue before it begins. Most often, though, there will be an awkward silence and a change of subject. The former approach is accusatory and is likely to provoke mistrust and defensiveness. The latter approach takes no responsibility at all: we do not claim the speaker as one of our own. We do not express what we really think and provide an opportunity for education. We do not clarify for the speaker that racism is perpetuated whether one means to or not. We confuse *appearance* with *being*; we are disturbed that racism has been revealed, but take no action to dispel the misinformation. Neither response to the situation moves white women any further in anti-racist practice.

The insights of Ricky Sherover-Marcuse, a white anti-racism theorist and educator, have helped us to understand better our behavior as white people regarding racism.[2] Sherover-Marcuse bases her beliefs in the practices of Re-evaluation Counseling, also called Co-counseling, one of the few psychological movements to include a progressive political analysis.

She states that everyone is taught racism at a young age, against our wills. Because we know, in the wisdom of children, that racism is wrong, we resist it. However, our resistance is squelched by adult authority. We feel pain and rage and powerlessness. Add to this the taboo on talking about racism, and what we have is people in pain who feel helpless and cannot acknowledge what they know.

Sherover-Marcuse insists that white people must remember that we did not start out racist, we did not want to learn racism, and that we did resist it. She believes that white people will be motivated to work against racism once we can "reclaim our innocence" and acknowledge how we too have been hurt by racism. She is careful to distinguish that this hurt is neither qualitatively nor quantitatively the same as the oppression experienced by people of color. She sees it as essential for us to be compassionate with ourselves and with one another.

After taking a workshop with Ricky Sherover-Marcuse (in which we joined forces with another local group, White Women Against Racism), our group began to work with some of her ideas. Especially rewarding have been the sessions we've spent on remembering our resistance to racism as children: the six-year-old girl in Texas who had to be bodily restrained from drinking at the "colored" water fountain; the eleven-year-old who was banished from the dinner table by her father when she refused to stop arguing with an adult male guest who was making racist remarks; the fourteen-year-old girl in an all-white suburb who registered for a Negro History class in summer school when all her friends were taking Pre-Algebra; the fifteen-year-old who attended the funeral of her high school friend − a young Black man − even though her father threatened her with death if she did so.

Reclaiming our resistance helps to challenge our notions of our "helplessness" as white women. At the same time, remembering the punishment we received for our resistance helps us know how and why we came to comply with oppression. This work has also given rise to deeper emotional expression, and we are risking more with one another. We have begun using other communication techniques after some women began to feel limited by the CR process. They felt the time agreements and tight structure sometimes kept the discussions too intellectual and inhibited the depth of our exploration. Our structure is now more relaxed, and we feel more comfortable spending longer amounts of time on one individual. We're also more forthright about giving input to each woman's story, asking her to role play parts of it or describe her feelings about the situation.

The setting of personal and social goals has been an important activity of the group since our beginning. In the last year, we created an action component to the group. While we still feel the need for education, we also feel an urgency to manifest what we have learned. Each of us defines the actions we want to undertake, sometimes out of wanting to address a particular situation or need, sometimes out of wanting to practice a particular insight or analysis.

We work individually, or in units of two, three, or four (as of this writing, we've not done anything together as an entire group). These actions have included writing letters to protest racist advertising, writing articles about racism and anti-racism, conducting workshops for other women, making anti-racist artwork, criticizing racism in the work or behavior of other whites (and attempting to be compassionate and maintain a feeling of identification). We're working to support some projects that women of color are doing, networking with other white women anti-racists, and building an affirmative action program at the Woman's Building. One member has begun a Jewish women's CR group, inspired by the working model of our group. Several of us marched in this year's Christopher Street West Parade (gay pride) with women of color under a banner proclaiming "Third World and white lesbians united against racism."

As a group, we help one another refine and develop our actions, evaluate their effectiveness in terms of our overall goals, problem solve about troublesome areas, set time lines, and work on each other's projects in primary or supportive ways. We also cheer each other on, giving recognition and validation to all the small steps and big leaps we are taking.

NOTES

1. "Racism in the English Language," available from Racism/Sexism Resource Center for Educators, 1841 Broadway, New York, New York 10023.

2. "Thinking About Racism: Twelve Working Assumptions," available from Unlearning Racism Workshops, Ricky Sherover-Marcuse, 6538 Dana Street, Oakland, California 94609.

The Women's Writer's Center: An Interview with the Directors*

by Sue Dove Gambill
with Rachel DeVries and Rita Speicher

Dove: Would you begin by telling us the focus of the work you are doing at the Women's Writer's Center?

Rita: We have created a feminist environment for educating women who want to be writers. One primary concern is to see ourselves in an historical context; another is to prepare women in a realistic way to deal with the struggles of being a writer; and third, to have women recognize that we exist within a community. We don't see artists as passive, isolated individuals within society, which is so often the tradition, for example, of the male writer. As feminist writers we have an active and reciprocal relationship with the entire feminist community.

We do writing alone, but once that work is completed our responsibility is to contribute it to the wider community through

---

* This interview was conducted in May 1981. I wanted to look at how an independent feminist institute and the women within it are being affected by the climate and changes in the United States in the 80s. I was particularly interested in looking at women in art and education. The Women's Writer's Center in Cazenovia, New York, where I had been studying for one year, gave me a view of both.

The Women's Writer's Center (1975-1982) offered a nine-month program of concentrated study in writing, women's literature, feminist aesthetics, and criticism. Women came from all parts of the country bringing with them a diversity of age, educational and writing experience, race, ethnicity, culture, work, sexual preference, and lifestyle. While in Cazenovia they met in classes with residential faculty and several times throughout the year studied in week-long sessions with well known feminist writers such as Olga Broumas, Rita Mae Brown, Michelle Cliff, Judy Grahn, Audre Lorde, and Adrienne Rich. Students were also given the opportunity to read their own work in public and to learn the business side of a writer's life.

Though the Center has since dissolved as a corporation, it has served as the seed for a new program, which is referred to in closing.

publishing and readings, connecting with the community, and getting a response. We do not see art as an elite function. It is a potent political act. Whether the actual content addresses what might be seemingly political topics or not, what women have to say is political.

Dove: You were saying that art is not a passive and isolated experience, but do you see in working with women, when they first come in, that passivity or lack of confidence in their own work is a problem?

Rachel: There is a wide range of women who come, with different kinds of backgrounds. There are still women who come who are operating primarily out of passivity, and that is something which needs to be acknowledged before it can be changed.

Rita: All of us have been subject to the prevalent patriarchal attitudes and institutions in society. That's the reason we began the Center. We were writers who were existing within patriarchal institutions, and the primary impulse came out of our own needs and what has been talked about for so many years in the women's movement: the validity of women's voices and women's experiences within literature, and the forms that develop out of that. Ten years ago there was no place for us, but then women began to come together in small groups and writing workshops, many of which still exist throughout the country. In order to break that passivity, which is a learned response to the conditions in which we are educated, we have to create our own institutions and our own environments that begin with the assumptions that what women have to say is valid, important, and absolutely necessary for our lives. Very often before the establishment of so many women's writing workshops, we existed in isolated places within the patriarchal community and our content was often considered "unimportant and irrational."

Dove: Is that why you decided to remain as an independent institute rather than be connected to a university?

Rachel: One reason is that we can make our own rules. There doesn't need to be a fixed and prescribed way of running the institute nor does there have to be absolute and fixed criteria for the kinds of people we decide to accept in the program. We can make those decisions based on what our needs are. I think there is always an attraction to a major university for obvious economic reasons. But the realities that this would involve diminish the attractiveness because we would not be able to continue to run the program the way we think is best for women. We'd immediately fall under that hierarchy which insists, by its very nature, that what we have to say is not really important.

Dove: Some of the students who come to the program do get credits through their home-base universities. Do you find that sets limits on your program?

Rachel: I don't think it sets any limits on our program but sometimes it sets limits on the students' ability to experience the program in a natural way. In coming from within the context of a more traditional university, sometimes they come imbued with notions about credit being the norm, and they have to work it through. We operate on a double-edged sword with students — they seek the feminist environment at the same time they distrust it. In making the decision to come to a feminist institute, the impulse is absolutely correct, but that doesn't mean that any given woman has overcome her training in terms of passivity, or the effects of living in an environment which validates everything that is patriarchal and invalidates everything that is feminist.

The fact that we do not confer degrees or certification is absolutely essential to the program. Writing is not something you can learn in nine months and go out and be a finished, proficient, and professional writer, whatever that means. It's a lifetime, ongoing process.

Rita: We are not diminishing the importance of women's programs within traditional universities. It's necessary to reach women wherever they are. The existence of women's studies programs, in jeopardy now as always, is important to us. We recognize that we choose to be agents of change in a different form. We prefer to take on the difficulties of being independent for the rewards we see in terms of the structure which we have created. Aspects of our program can change very quickly, based on our experience and what we perceive to be the needs of our students. We are accountable to the wider community rather than to a bureaucracy. While we are held back by the financial difficulties of being independent, we are propelled forward by our sense that we control everything that has to be done. We don't have to appeal to deans to change something. Change is built into our structure.

Dove: What is the connection between women's studies programs and the Women's Writer's Center? How do you see that there can be support and challenge between these programs?

Rita: We connect by exchanging students, philosophies and ideas, resources, support communities, and by supporting the newspapers, magazines, and feminist presses which are absolutely essential. Ideally, we should be challenging ourselves back and forth. "Is it better to work within the system or outside?" is a reactionary and wasteful kind of question. The questions should be: "What are we working for?" "How are we working?" "How well are we achieving our goals?" "How can we help each other?"

There are women who may never make it to an academic environment. We need institutions that will recognize and serve these women. There are women who've never had the opportunity to go to college. Yet they come here and can write with brilliance and vision. We've had women who've dropped out of college and others who've gone through and have law degrees.

Dove: With the economic situation worsening in this country, do you see a change in the students who are coming to the program?

Rachel: I remember a specific phone call from a student before she came who wanted to know what she was going to do when she left the Center. What I did was throw the question back at her. What do you think you're going to do? She wanted to know how she was going to earn a living. I don't think we pretend to offer something like job training in the traditional sense of the word. When you get done with the Center, you're not necessarily going to be hired as an advertising copywriter or be writing a weekly column for some magazine and raking in the money. Women who come here have got to begin to see themselves as emerging writers. We all have had to work at other jobs to make a living and that's part of what happens in this society where writers are not valued as workers. Before deciding to be a writer, it is necessary to think about the realities of the world in which you live.

Rita: This is not a receptive or safe world for an artist. This is not a society that values its artists. To be a woman writing with a feminist consciousness is to recognize the tremendous risks that one must take. It is necessary to respond to that risk with courage, to connect to the community for support, to be willing to give up illusions that often exist about being a writer, and to accept the hard, arduous work and the years of apprenticeship that are necessary. There are few feminist presses, and there are few feminists who have ever been published by major publishing houses.

Dove: So the question isn't just how to be a writer and make a living, but how to be a feminist writer?

Rita: Exactly. What are our resources? We don't have fifteen presses to send to. Not only are we learning to develop our creative skills and our ability to express ourselves, but also we are deciding what we do with it afterwards. That's what I mean by the responsibility we take on by seeing ourselves as members of a community. We have to create the presses and support them. We tell our students, "You had best spend your money, as little as it might be, buying the books put out by feminist presses." We have to accept the fact that we have to write, produce, distribute, sell, and review our own work, and that is quite a task. It can be very frustrating because you want to be able to write your novel and then let it go. However, every step along the way has to be done by us and that is a tremendous challenge and frustration. But the rewards are also valuable.

Rachel: I think it's important to talk about passivity and action. I often see women making a move and then from that one move deciding they've crossed the barrier of passivity and are now in the realm of action. I think, particularly now as things are working against us politically, that this will be magnified — taking any action at all is going to feel like moving from passivity to action. This feeling needs to be explored very carefully. To take a single move, whether it's to come to the Center, or to decide to come to consciousness, or to decide to spend your energies working with women is only *just* a first step. Every step of the way is going to be just as difficult. I think it is becoming more obvious in women's groups across the country that some women will turn against the very women who are trying to move us forward. That to me is a distortion of action rather than taking one's life seriously.

Dove: I think what you're saying relates to the historical moment. I'm meeting a lot of women who have come to political consciousness just in the past year or so, and a lot of them take so much for granted. They can't see what you're saying because they think we have always been at this same place.

Rachel: True. At the Rita Mae Brown reading there were women in the audience who didn't realize that Rita Mae was one of the founders of this most recent women's movement. They had no sense of our own history, no sense of who that woman was who was reading to them.

Dove: Another important point that I saw in that situation was that there was no understanding or acknowledgment that being a writer is a political action.

Rita: There is a divisiveness that we are experiencing within this movement. Our initial impulse of coming together (during the past fifteen years) encompassed a wide range of political ideologies and personal behaviors. Although there were always problems and disagreements, still there was the sense of making a movement, evolving, and developing. And now there's much more negative criticism. I don't stand against criticism. I don't think a movement can sustain itself without positive and constructive criticism. But there is this one upsmanship – and I choose that word very carefully – of who is more "politically correct." And I think part of that is an impulse to stop history.

Rachel: I think there is a lot of talk right now about being open, and the willingness to take risks, and a lot of talk about acceptance of differences, but what I often see happening is exactly the opposite. Differences, I think, are interpreted for the most part as argument, and not workable.

Dove: How do you see the Women's Writer's Center and women's studies programs responding to this situation?

Rita: First we need to analyze why there's factionalism now, and we have to see it in the context of the conditions of the world in which we live. This has not happened randomly. If we look at the world, we see that it is becoming more reactionary and dangerous. It makes sense that people are scared and want a place of safety.

Rachel: For example, when we look at the current emphasis on fat liberation and the movement of the physically challenged, I think it's very significant that these two movements are springing up at a time when the mobility of all women is being encroached upon and endangered every minute. This is not an ahistorical happening. However, I don't think that as a movement we're looking at it that way. In saying this, I am not speaking against these groups because they're definitely relevant and valid. But I think, as women, we become more immobilized every single day, and we need to look historically at why these movements are gaining significance right now. In some ways the narrower questions allow us a way to not deal with our own immobility but to focus on those people who are actually rendered immobile by society at large. However, such discussion would be seen as a shift in focus from the physically challenged to the able bodied and would be seen as selfish. But I think that is a crucial error. We need to look at those movements as ways of looking at all of our immobilities and in-capacities. I don't have a sense that this is what is going on. I think that any discussion of that would render you "politically incorrect" and therefore would stop movement. There's an awful lot happening right now that stops movement and stops logical thought.

Rita: Something which has happened historically in any political movement is the co-optation of language. As writers we become acutely aware of that. There's a language that developed with the women's movement. It was and is a functional language; it's a language designed to describe, in realistic terms, our own ex-periences. For example, behind the word *support* is a recognition of the necessity for women to hold ourselves up by sharing our strength. Support becomes a way of challenging and helping us move forward, not simply holding hands so that we can remain at rest and feel comfortable in that. And yet that word can so easily be turned against somebody. For example, if I say, "I demand more of you and that's the best way I can support you," and you turn to me and say, "That's not supportive at all. I want you to ac-cept my most meager and humble expression. I don't want you to challenge me." As many have pointed out, when they used the word revolutionary to sell pantyhose, we knew we were in trouble. Co-optation of language is a very astute political manuever which can immobilize a movement quickly.

Dove: As writers, and as a writer's institute, where do you go from here?

Rachel: Even though language is being taken away, we need to con-tinue redefining it. For example, we need to define the meaning of support. If we keep asking where's our safety, where's our support, then we're still looking for a cushion, and it just doesn't exist. Women need to see that the notion of support is not a nice little soft place but that which is going to keep on pushing us to do our very best. The woman who challenges what you've written is really doing you a favor; she is helping you shape your craft so that you do not stop at the first draft.

As writers we can't fail. I say that because that's what I feel in my own life. It doesn't mean I'm going to get money or that I'm going to get any accolades or good reviews any place in the traditional press or even in the feminist press. But I take what I do very seriously and with the sense of risk implicit — that there is no place of safety guaranteed me. I still continue with my own writing, and that is the position I think all of us have to get to as women. We exist in a world that will not support us in a way we would like to think of getting support.

Rita: We have to be aware of what happens in a society that controls women's voices and how women have always fought against that, have always used the overt and covert methods to speak the truth of our lives. I don't see how any woman could survive as a writer without first knowing her history within this tradition.

The second thing is to analyze our circumstances. What have they been and what are they now? We must analyze them differently from the way the patriarchal newspapers, or even the politically left journals do.

Then we must determine what skills we need and develop those skills. We've developed a form called consciousness raising that led to radical changes in individuals' lives and helped in the creation of a whole political movement. Now we need to develop new skills. They may come from past experiences, but they have to be skills that are going to continue to move us forward. There has to be a recognition of what kind of community it is that we are trying to create, what are the problems, and how do we address and solve those problems. What is our vision for the future? We need to recognize the individual voice that contributes to all of that. We're not interested in creating an institution that's going to turn out clones of any political ideology. I think our best moments have come when we read the work of women and we talk to women about the truths of their own lives — and we talk about what has prevented us from speaking, who has erased our experiences, the kinds of amnesia that exist. We have to move through all of these to a place of action. The history, the analysis, the development of the tools ultimately lead us to ask: who is going to work actively now?

Dove: So you are saying that it's not just one action; it's continual, the rest of our lives.

Rita: Yes. Behind all of this we come to a serious recognition of what we call women's power. It can be a frightening thing when a woman first conceives of herself as a woman who has power that comes from her ability to speak and act. I'm amazed sometimes when I'm in the classroom after the students have given their first public reading and I am looking at a room filled with changed women. They have taken some truth from themselves, have drawn from the experiences of their lives in a very hard and difficult way, and have then chosen to speak to a group of women. We are all strengthened by that; we're ready for the next step, and that can be frightening as well as marvelous and inspiriting. We need to recognize that we do have power and we need not be fearful of each other's power. There's good reason to be suspicious because power has been used against us, but it's nothing to exorcise from the movement. It's the very basis of what we're choosing to do in this world, wield our own power to change the world.

I've heard women say that feminism is limiting. We've had the original humanism, the new humanism, and now the neo-new humanism. You will be criticized in this society if you call yourself a feminist. If you are a humanist you can always go back to a place of safety. Once you call yourself a feminist you have that brand − the scarlet F. Feminism, though, is not a limiting vision of the world. We need to recognize women as feminists who work in different facets of society and who experience different kinds of oppression.

Dove: I think some women are saying they don't want to be called feminists anymore because they are terrified by the conflicts that we are going through. They don't know how to handle it and they run.

Rachel: And that's exactly what the patriarchy wants to have happen.

Rita: It's like white women saying, I don't want to write about racism because it's not part of my experience. How can you live in a society that is racist and not say racism is a part of your experience? The foremost thing is that I don't think anyone can be a warrior in this conflict unless they can accept who they are. We are each born into a particular class, race, sex. We do not have to be guilty about that. I have to, however, be willing to tell the truth of that experience.

Dove: Not only being true to it, but also being responsible within it.

Rachel: And we must question the assumptions that we're imbued with, question them and challenge them and work on changing that which feels wrong.

Dove: I find there is a real push right now to be unified, trying to be a "melting pot," without going through the struggle of our differences.

Rita: It's important to recognize that there are going to be hard times ahead of us and we need to be aware of the effects of the outside world and to be conscious of how and where we want our movement to continue. What is the next stage? We've gone through a number of stages in an extremely short period of time, and I think sometimes there is a certain frantic scrambling to know with certainty what the next step is. By the nature of making revolution, we don't always know what that will be.*

---

* The Women's Writer's Center has gone through many changes during the past year. Those involved in the Center decided to dissolve the corporation out of the recognition that its structure, having served the needs of its students, faculty, and community for seven years, has fulfilled a cycle and must be transformed to reflect what has been learned and perfected over those years. FREEHAND: An Independent Learning Community of Women Writers and Photographers is a new program, started by a group of artists. It began its first year in October 1982. For further information write: FREEHAND, Provincetown, Massachusetts 02657.

A Feminist Chautauqua
for a Rural State

by Diane Sands, Judy Smith,
and Jennifer Thompson

DURING THE SUMMER of 1977, we took women's studies on the road. Previously we had been teaching an introductory course in women's studies at the University of Montana in Missoula, where we had struggled for a number of years with the administration over establishing an on-going program. Our model was quite different from standard academic approaches, and we had no success in getting funding even though most of our students were enthusiastic about the course and had taken questions and issues raised there into other classes. They appreciated the discussion of the personal implications of what they were studying, and several of them convinced us that we should try to make women's studies available to many kinds of women in Montana.

Montana is a rural state, and many women live in very isolated communities where exposure to new controversial ideas and opportunities for postsecondary education are limited. The great distances across the state and seasonal bad weather inhibit travel, and many Montanans feel removed from the activities and political issues of the rest of the country. We thought it especially challenging, therefore, to make the material we covered in women's studies available to community women of different ages and educational backgrounds.

We chose to do this with a two-week traveling course called, "Woman: New Definitions, New Directions." Our brochure described the course as a two-week intensive, interdisciplinary experience. "The first week will focus on 'Woman Changing Herself,' the second week on 'Woman Changing Her World.' Lectures, panels, discussions, workshops, and films will present new information about the role and status of women, promote an exchange of ideas about causes and consequences of traditional and contemporary women's roles, and examine the growing movement for change in traditional sex roles." We advertised the course for four locations: Missoula and Great Falls, which are urban centers in Montana (populations 60,000-80,000); and Kalispell and Glendive, two rural communities (populations under 25,000).

The course could be taken for the full two weeks or on a daily drop-in basis. Cost was $10 per day or $100 for two weeks. We also made it possible for women to barter rather than pay cash. Undergraduate and graduate credit was available from the University of Montana extension program.

Our schedule was designed to:

1. Provide exposure to new ideas and research and different approaches to old ideas. We would try to raise basic questions of feminism and demonstrate in nonacademic language how an interdisciplinary approach can be useful for understanding sexual inequality.

2. Initiate a discussion of how to apply women's studies to participants' personal experiences and provide space for personal reflection.

3. Describe to women in Montana communities the nationwide women's movement and its effects in order to break down their isolation. We wanted to expose participants to new books, films, and other resources, and to discuss various groups around the country. We also focused on activities at the local and state level and included community women as resource people.

4. Create a classroom situation in which barriers are broken down between "experts" and "learners." While instructors have valuable information, class participants also have opinions and experiences. We wanted to avoid "talking down," yet felt that it was up to us to make material available and understandable.

5. Provide direct experience with issues. Local women would help with publicity and act as resources for the course. We discussed such issues as how to organize a women's center, how to get materials on rape and abortion into local

libraries, how to talk to friends and family about feminist issues.

We felt that the traditional classroom situation did not provide the most impetus for learning or involve all the participants, so we planned a daily mixture of formats: lectures, groups, films, personal exercises, and readings. We divided each day into smaller units and made sure that no lecture or presentation of material lasted more than two hours. We included at least one personal discussion or exercise each day (these included exercises in assertiveness training, values clarification, fantasies, discussions of family, sexuality, and career expectations). We also invited in a variety of speakers. Each day handouts were distributed to read at home, and occasionally there was homework.

In the end, the course was offered only twice, in Missoula and Kalispell. We canceled the Great Falls session before we realized that there were enough registrants to have gone ahead. Though we made efforts not to conflict with harvest, we were not surprised when the Glendive course did not happen because there was only a small population of a couple of thousand people within a few hundred miles to draw upon.

Women with diverse backgrounds, ages, jobs, educational experience, and exposure to feminism enrolled in the two courses. They included a seventy-seven-year-old suffrage activist with fifty years of clippings about women; a perfectly coiffured owner of a dress shop; a thirty-year-old unemployed teacher; an anthropology professor; a Bureau of Reclamation supply clerk on her annual two-week vacation; a thirty-eight-year-old mother of three who was finishing a social work degree, and a feminist art student. This diversity was important to the course, where we sought to create a setting in which respect and a sense of continuity between generations could develop. Participants reported that the older women provided role models of "feeling good about growing older," being "active and changing," and showed a "challenging way to live after retirement." The older women expressed how supportive the class was for them. As the early suffrage supporter commented, "I've tried to keep up but it's been lonely. Finding out what's going on is very gratifying. The younger set is carrying the banner on."

EVALUATION OF STRUCTURE

For those few women who wanted credit for the course, we designed two brief take-home essay exams, mostly covering material in *Women: A Feminist Perspective* edited by Jo Freeman.* For graduate credit, we required a research project as well. As there were only limited research and library facilities, we encouraged projects focusing on elements of women's lives in their own community, such as public schools, women offenders, or violence against women. Everyone who attended the class was asked to fill out an evaluation form, and student evaluations, for the most part, dealt with personal benefits of the course: "For the first time I felt the positiveness of being female"; "It has made my life more interesting and hopeful"; and "It was the best class I've ever taken. It changed my life." In addition to personal growth, the comments also reflected an increased commitment to becoming active. Women expressed a determination to "write and have my say for our kind," "to speak out," and "to stay on top of what is happening in the school because I know I can make change." Our favorite comment was the classic: "Before the course, I couldn't believe there would be two weeks of stuff to know about women." (The woman who said this enrolled in a women's history Ph.D. program a month later.)

As active feminists, we are concerned that feminist education be more than entertaining and more than a catalyst for personal change. As feminist educators, we see women's studies providing new information and analysis of traditional ideas; developing a feminist methodology for analyzing our experiences; breaking down power relationships between "experts" and "learners," thereby equipping women to transform society. Women's studies has at its core the intention to restructure society. Feminist education should produce an activist commitment.

Our biggest problems were time and money. "Women: New Definitions, New Directions" was termed "self-supporting" by the University of Montana — women who wanted it had to pay. Money is always a problem for women, especially for the community women we were trying to reach. Since we valued our time and neither of us had a regular source of income, we could not do this course for free. We felt that $100 per person for the course was not exorbitant, and we attempted to arrange time payment

---

* Mayfield Publishing Co., Palo Alto, California, 1975.

plans and barter systems. We got good barter, including huckleberry jam and fresh eggs. However, in the end, the cash was still a problem for women. We each received $137 after expenses for one month of instruction plus months of preparation.

A bigger problem than money for some women was the time involved. Many women, especially women working outside the home, had difficulty arranging more than a day or two free. (One woman had her government employer give her the time and money to attend as part of its affirmative action commitment. Others used their vacation time.) For the future, we have discussed traveling models made up of weekend workshops or evening courses. However, a weekend doesn't allow for covering materials very deeply or developing ties within the community, and evening courses mean immense amounts of travel for limited contact hours. A one-week version of the "feminist chautauqua"[1] is our preferred alternative. This would demand less financial and time commitment from participants, yet still allow for intensive contact.

The course functioned well on the drop-in basis we had set up. Two-thirds of our students dropped in for one day to one week, and the other third completed the full two weeks. Since each day's topic was self-contained, continuity was not a problem. Few women wanted credit for the course, and it was clear that they took it for their own stimulation.

In the spring of 1978 the course was offered again, this time with half of the participants coming from the Missoula community and half from the University of Montana. We met once a week for three hours a day and covered a compacted version of the summer course. Several of the students have since made women a primary interest in their other courses, often insisting that faculty make women's perspectives visible. The community women, especially those involved in feminist projects, claimed that the course gave them a broader feminist context in which to understand their work. Plans were made to teach the course in the spring of 1979 in Helena, 150 miles away from Missoula.

CONTENT EVALUATION

While we went deeply into a few subjects and made an overview of others, our goal was to present an introductory, interdisciplinary course. Questions, not answers, were emphasized. We sought to develop an inquiring feminist perspective in our students. We did this through activities such as a presentation on Montana women's history. This combined material from archival research and oral history accounts with panels on ethnic groups and personal discussions of family histories by students. We also had discussions of women and the health care system which integrated both material on historical conceptions of the biological nature of women and an analysis of the medical model of health care with an activist component stressing the contemporary women's health movement and what women are doing to make change on local and national levels. By the end of two weeks, students commented with amazement at the regularity with which the same questions arose in different subject areas: perspectives on violence, defining and redefining power, economics, and reproductive control.

Each day we included material which informed students of national women's projects committed to changing the role of women. In discussing these projects and their political perspectives, we emphasized the diversity of approaches as a strength of the women's movement rather than as movement factionalism. This approach conveyed respect for the ability of students to understand diversity and to arrive at their own perspectives.

We also planned evening sessions of films, poetry, music, and other activities in Missoula, but the turnout was small. After the first week, we made room for all these activities during the day. Films, for example, which were an important part of the course and originally scheduled as evening events, were rescheduled to make sure that everyone saw them.

We made an effort to encourage physical activity as an integrated part of the course by scheduling a participatory feminist theatre and a body movement workshop. Although attendance was low (they were held in the evening), enthusiasm was high, and in the future we plan to include noontime volleyball, a self-defense workshop, and daily fifteen-thirty minute bodywork breaks of yoga, relaxation, and drama exercises. These activities provide a forum for discussing what the channeling of women out of physical activities and sports has meant, including exclusion from strenuous jobs, the myth of feminine physical weakness, and the role of women as victims of violence.

An introductory, interdisciplinary course such as this is best taught by a women's studies generalist – someone with experience in both teaching and activism. If such a person has kept up on women's studies in many fields, she has less need for extensive preparation, can discuss a variety of topics, and can fill in when, for example, the speaker on legal rights is called into court at the last minute. A feminist generalist also has the kind of overview of women's studies and experience in women's projects which allows her to integrate the academic and the practical and keep the theoretical questions of feminist education before the participants.

The only minority of significant size in Montana is Native Americans. There are several reasons why this group didn't participate in the course. First, neither session was situated on any of Montana's seven reservations. Missoula and Kalispell have small Native American populations and we did not direct special advertising toward this population. In addition, Native American women's double oppression of sex and race results in little free time or money for courses or workshops. Native American women with resources for educational activities often have Native American studies as a more immediate priority. We hope to find ways to involve them more in future courses.

IMPLICATIONS OF THIS MODEL

In analyzing the course, we realize that the central concept in our feminist educational model is "capacity building."[2] We see in our isolated area a lack of basic feminist education, both as a way into the women's movement and as a way of growing once in the movement. Montana women lack a knowledge of their history, an overview of women's issues, and a sense of feminist principles on which to act in a disciplined way. The course attempted to deal with these problems by "capacity building" for Montana women and the women's movement at several levels.

The course was most successful in building the capacity of individual women by broadening each woman's consciousness of the choices open to her in lifestyle, etc. This was done by seeking to improve a woman's self-concept through increased knowledge of the proud heritage of women and positive identification with women's culture. We validated each woman's personal experiences as much as possible in the many discussions. We also increased the individual's ability to deal with choices by teaching some assertiveness skills and by increasing knowledge of available resources.

The capacity building aspect of the course increased the base for women's studies and the women's movement in the local community. This was especially true in Kalispell where women from the class continued to meet and where course participants helped start a women's center, became the community speakers on the ERA, and organized to monitor sexism in the school. One of the older student's comments reflected this growing awareness of a local base for action: "I go to Missoula to the University to find an intellectual community. I have felt so isolated here. Then I take this course and say, wow, these people live here. This is happening in Kalispell, not just at the University!"

Community resource women are important for our program, and their involvement increases the number of women with experience in feminist education techniques who will identify with feminist issues. In addition, resource women, often not identified primarily as feminists, were exposed to feminist ideas by being involved in the course. In the future these women can be called on for more active involvement or support. Resource women worked especially well on the "changing lifestyles" panel and as speakers on growing-up-ethnic-in-Montana. Particularly moving was a presentation by a sixty-year-old organizer of a maid's strike who spoke of the realities of traditional women's service jobs. Presentations on the law, feminist therapy, child development, and art were also made by women whose primary commitments are in those areas.

Feminist education is one way to build the strength of the women's movement in our state. For women with minimal exposure to the movement, an introductory women's studies course provides a nonthreatening structured environment in which to explore feminism. It encourages women to become active in areas central to their own lives, as demonstrated by the growth of activism among the Kalispell women.

The course also served to build the capacity of women already involved in some aspect of the women's movement. Feminists working in one area — such as health, education, violence — often lack information about other issues and can benefit from an overview of what is happening in other parts of the women's movement. Gaining this perspective strengthens the women's movement by increasing the bonds between feminist projects. The course can also increase feminists' awareness of other projects which work on issues that effect women — Native American, low income, and environmental issues in Montana. In addition, for women already involved in a feminist project, the course increased their capacity to explore issues by exposing them to printed resources and by identifying community women who could be resources for them. Information on feminism nationally, or even regionally, is especially important to feminists in a rural state. Because our course was a feminist project, we stressed the importance of feminist principles and processes by demonstration and by discussion. In all of these ways, "Woman: New Definitions, New Directions" strengthened the women's movement in Montana.

NOTES

1. Chautauqua: the term originated as an annual summer educational program for adults in rural New York State in the late nineteenth century.

2. Capacity Building: as used in grant proposals, to increase the ability of a group/population to meet its objectives by increasing the skills/numbers of people involved.

Creative Teaching Spaces: Home Movies

by Barbara Hammer

I was struggling to be hired as a teacher. I pleaded with the authority, the chairman of the film department, to tell me why I wasn't hired. He didn't say a thing about my being a lesbian but I was sure that was the reason.

I dressed up in my straightest two-piece jacket and skirt, nylons, and high heels to attend the teachers' meeting. I wobbled in the heels as I hadn't worn them for years and was out of practice.

The chair of the department confesses to me that he feels guilty teaching the five hour a week class on film as art because he is not an artist. My heart surges with imagination and expectation. I'm hungry for just such a teaching position. But he hires a man for the job.

I HAD THIS DREAM on the morning I set aside to begin writing this essay on teaching outside the patriarchal institutions of learning, on teaching at home.

I am a radical lesbian-feminist and my films reflect my politics. When I apply for a teaching position at a university, although I have the educational and teaching credentials required, I am inevitably turned down with a form letter noting the number of applicants, the difficulty of decision making, the hopes that I will find rewarding and gainful employment elsewhere. Nowhere does the letter say I am too radical, feminist, or lesbian.

It is important to examine feminist education outside of a traditional institution as many of us find ourselves too radical for the existing mode of pedagogy. I decided to open my live-in studio to women who want to learn the skills of filmmaking.

To connect with students, I generally post flyers around town, advertise in the local women's newspaper, and rely on word-of-mouth advertising by former students. The class meets for three-hour sessions once a week in the evenings as many women are employed during the daytime hours. The financial costs for the student depend on how many are taking the class, but I try to figure on earning between $20 and $30 an hour. The students pay for their film and related materials, and I provide my personal equipment for their use.

I find that the women who choose to study outside an institution are empowering themselves through their choice of private lessons in a subject area usually discouraged for women. I am interested in their personal struggles, ambitions, and decision making. The intimate setting of my studio, with thrift shop rug, comfortable furniture, and used projector and editing tools helps relax their inhibitions around filmmaking as prestigious, expensive, and impossible. I am able to teach methods for inexpensive filmmaking, and I can cover a particular technique until each class member understands. Usually no one is left behind in such an intimate grouping. Finally, I am rewarded by self-activating students who advertise, arrange, and show their films in a public setting.

I hear a knock at the door. The six women who have decided to study Feminist Filmmaking arrive. Their faces are open and excited, filled with expectation and hope. Surely in this private class in a home/studio environment they won't be disappointed. I tell them they can make any film they wish and that their fantasies may become their realities. They needn't worry about the equipment and skill building for I will be beside them in a one-to-one teaching situation as the class progresses. Now it is time to find out why they have come to make cinema.

Some come to class with a conscious intention to tell us their stories, dreams, and descriptions of visual pictures. Others want to be filmmakers but are not sure what form or content they want their film to take. One of the important beginning lessons for me as teacher is conveying that film is simply narrow strips of celluloid with gelatin layers holding disparate pieces of silver grains or color sensitive dyes. It is necessary to see film beyond the "Hollywood presence" and recognize that film is not a story, a document, or a poem. It can be any of these but it can be something else, too. It is a plastic and transparent medium that, when developed, is capable of accepting an image or nonimage. When used with apparatus, electricity, and a projection system of transport motor, lens, and light, it is capable of displaying a magnification at a distance from its plastic self. That approach allows the student to see film for what it is and then recognize that what she wants to do with it is her projection on the medium. This overall realistic view provides opportunity and consciousness, two determinants for effective choice

The students have introduced themselves and I have introduced "film." We sit in a circle on the floor. The informality, as well as the round form, encourage a sense of comfort and "at homeness" and help set an attitude of equal consideration for all. We will work as a group, I explain, and each woman will contribute a part to the content of the film as well as to the physical making of the film. I will facilitate the processing of the class and act as resource person and equipment/technique teacher, but the form and content of the film will be up to them.

Believing that images are at our disposal within ourselves and only need to be retrieved and brought to consciousness, I begin a guided meditation to facilitate this process: first a relaxation exercise so that each woman feels herself relaxed and lying on the floor without tensions; then a "dropping into" herself deeply through a countback or a leaf-falling image until there is a deep inner resting place for each woman. I ask her to allow an image to come to mind on a blank screen of her mind. I ask her to note it, to notice how she sees, from what angle she is seeing, what the colors and smells are. This is an awareness exercise in noticing and remembering. Can she imagine then another image following the first, I ask, leaving silences for her to see and note. I remind her that this is a place available to her whenever she wishes to return to it, and then I ask her to come back to an awareness of her body and surroundings and her breathing. With the lights now on, she sits up and takes as much time as she needs to write down the images she has seen. The images become her personal script.

While they are scripting, I prepare tea for the group. Then each woman shares her script with the others. They arrive at a common theme, selecting from their individual scripts an image or sequence that will fit the theme. With relief and pleasure they laugh at completing an emotionally demanding task of personal image finding and group decision making.

That describes a typical first session in the home/studio classes I have been teaching for the past three years in North Oakland, California. The individual attention, the teacher's "seeing" of each woman, the small class size, the informality, the chance to explore, experiment, and take risks with provocative teaching methods, the personal availability of teacher to student as well as group process would be difficult to achieve in the traditional instructional setting.

Teaching filmmaking or artmaking in a nontraditional setting reduces anxiety. As women, we have been led to believe that we do not have an aptitude for mechanical skills. Many women approach cameras, tape recorders, and editing equipment with trepidation and sometimes even with terror. Students have told me that they have dreams of accidents leading to equipment destruction while they are learning filmmaking. Introduction to personal cameras in a home setting is less threatening. The student has the opportunity to express fears, take her time, and handle equipment in a relaxed atmosphere.

"Educational anxiety" may take the form of floating fear provoked by memories of competition, judgment, and potential failure. Many of us have been victims of a quantitative system that pushes students through as fast as possible, proclaiming itself to be providing equal opportunity but providing rushed incompetency instead. We were not allowed the opportunities to test ourselves with our own projects. We were tested with information or skill building that others, usually men, thought important. This does not imply that the feminist educator accepts the work of her students without critical thinking or evaluation. Many times I am tempted, in a world that so little acknowledges the efforts of women, to nod my head and appreciate the smallest effort. This is unfair. As a feminist educator, I must see the potential in my student for her greater work, stronger achievement, and continuing effort by envisioning a grander scope of her possibilities. I cannot take the easy way out with bland acceptance of the mediocre but must expect from her work that has the potential to be revolutionary.

This quality of "being seen," this taking in, this sense of recognition of student by teacher and vice versa is the prime modality of effective feminist teaching. This is teaching according to the needs and capacities of the student. One teaching mode will not do for all. Individual recognition was imperative to me in my own education. Two "Master Teachers" with whom I have studied taught outside of a traditional institution. I studied with Terry Sendgraff who developed the movement form "Motivity" based on body movement in accordance with the forces of gravity, often using trapezes and other suspended apparatus to emphasize the natural principles of motion. With gentle guidance in an informal structure, I was able to create, improvise, and invent while "being seen." In addition, I was privileged to study poetry with Deena Metzger, known for her evocative symbolic imagery, who pointed out pathways to an inner journey. She was an audience to our own work and led many of us to see that we could identify ourselves as poets were we to accept the work and discipline demanded for that designation. For each of us, whether studying movement, poetry, or film, the task of individual work begins when the class ends.

Feminist education must stimulate the inner guide and voice, the self-recognition of the need for expression, the commitment to demand of ourselves long and arduous hours of concentration, and the courage and practice of sharing completed work. That is a tall order for a short class. The teacher will be participating in the reciprocal process of feminist education by demystifying equipment, reducing anxiety around movement/words, and demonstrating through her practice a commitment to work as a belief in self-expression, while simultaneously recognizing the same potential and practice in her students.

If Feminist Art is included in national and international women's studies curricula, the scope and the vision of education can be expanded for the entire community of scholars, artists, and activists. As a feminist teacher, I am responsible not only to my continuing choices as an image-maker but to the enhancement of possibilities for other women to make those choices and to become part of a community of self-responsive and responsible cultural workers. In unofficial, self-created classes we, as feminist educators, reach for new ways to combine reason, intellect, emotion, and intuition for a clearer direction and comprehension of our lives.

The Women's School of Planning and Architecture

by Leslie Kanes Weisman
and Noel Phyllis Birkby

The Women's School of Planning and Architecture (WSPA) is an alternative learning experience for women in all environmental design fields – architecture, planning, landscape architecture, urban design, environmental psychology, etc.

Our intent is to create a personally supportive and stimulating exchange of ideas. We believe both personal and professional growth can be fostered through a fuller integration of our values and identities as women with our values and identities as designers. Our aim is the creation and expansion of a forum within which we may discover and define the particular qualities, concerns and abilities that we, as women, bring to the environmental design professions.

WSPA is a *school* in the sense that it is a place to learn – but not a school in the traditional sense. The learning experience we offer is not available in conventional professional schools where learning is often considered a one-way transfer of information and skills, from teacher to student, and where the educational system is often considered a training ground for the hierarchical framework that rules most of our working lives. At WSPA, we opt for more cooperative, fulfilling, and productive forms of education and practice. Each WSPA participant is encouraged to share her knowledge, skills, ideas and questions.

WSPA is a twenty-four hour school. We believe that learning goes on at all hours, and in lots of ways, so we have chosen to hold two-week residential sessions in order to facilitate a variety of learning experiences, and to create a sense of community.

From 1979 Brochure

224

WSPA GREW FROM the experience and convictions of seven women – architects and planners, teachers and practitioners – who met through their participation in women's professional organizations and conferences from 1972-1974. Plans for the school developed out of our discovery that we shared common goals and interests not being met within the existing professional contexts, where women are in the minority. We wanted to extend the exciting and supportive experiences of these conferences to a longer period of time. We wanted to finish unfinished conversations and to explore the ways in which our concerns overlapped and reinforced each other. WSPA was organized to create a forum within which the participants could explore the particular concerns which they, as women, brought to the environmental design professions. The Women's School of Planning and Architecture was the first such school in America to be completely founded, funded, and run by women.

We worked on plans for the first session from March 1974 through July 1975. The original planners were Katrin Adam, Ellen Perry Berkeley, Noel Phyllis Birkby, Bobbie Sue Hood, Marie Kennedy, Joan Forrester Sprague, and Leslie Kanes Weisman, based in the Boston, New York, Detroit, and San Francisco areas.

Communication was made through telephone calls, letters, and a few meetings which, with the exception of our last one, were held on the way to or during various "professional" conferences in Los Angeles, St. Louis, Eugene (Oregon), and Lincoln (Nebraska). Some of us paid our own way (and were not reimbursed by WSPA), while others came as "delegates" (members of the press, representatives of academic institutions, and/or speakers) whose expenses were paid. No more than four of us ever met at any of these conferences. At our final planning session in early July 1975, the six coordinators from the East met at a coordinator's home in Vermont. We were unable to afford the transportation costs for our seventh member from California to attend. It was not until the day before the participants arrived at the school in August that all seven of us met together.

IN PROCESS

March 1974 "Let's have a school."

June 2, 1974 "The idea of our own school seems more real and necessary."

June 29, 1974 "We are planning a school for next summer to take place somewhere in the Northeast (preferably near the beach)."

September 1, 1974 "A school for women, by women . . . a different locale each year where women congregate to teach in teams and/or individually for varying lengths of time . . . an entirely different kind of class scheduling than the traditional ones . . . . If we can sustain a budget without seeking other types of funding (grants, gifts, etc.), it allows us very critical independent action."

September 22, 1974 "There is very clearly a need for women in the design fields to have a forum where they can exchange knowledge and questions as fully accepted human beings. No such place currently exists nor are any of the existing institutions likely to become such places during this century . . . . We should not distinguish between faculty and students. All good teachers remain good students and vice versa."

October 23, 1974 "A lot will take place in the interstices around and between any formally scheduled program. I am, therefore, less concerned about where it takes place and what the specific offerings are than that it *does* take place."

November 1974 "It looks like it may be Mt. Holyoke, not exactly Spain, but it's supposed to be very pretty."

December 1974 "We are concerned with the self-actualization and growth of all participants . . . we are nonhierarchical in concept . . . we do not try to duplicate existing programs in conventional schools."

December 27, 1974 "Name of school should be plain and simple . . . School of Design for Women/Design School for Women/Women's Design School . . . maybe more specific − The Women's School of Planning and Architecture."

January 14, 1975 "Regarding the rental of your campus, what is required to reserve space? What is the latest date to do this? 'Ninety days before the beginning of your program.' "

January 1975 "Tentatively scheduled for two weeks in August. Hopefully we may attract women who are practicing and want to take a vacation, as well as students who have summer jobs."

February 2, 1975 "Childcare facilities . . . as a school for women, we must address ourselves to this issue."

February 20, 1975 "We should not set academic standards but we should consider some process of selection to provide a mix of abilities, ages, lifestyles, geography, and special professional interests. . . . I am really impressed with the way a resolution of the complicated issues seems to be creeping across all the dangling questions."

March 4, 1975 "News releases will go out tomorrow."

March 15, 1975 "Walked through main building at Biddeford, which seems to house almost all classes and seminar rooms, laboratories, video lab, projection rooms, office and cafeteria . . . Ooh, a pool table! . . . and the tennis courts are right on the water . . . Can I be the recreation director? . . . What about the school sweatshirts? . . . It's like going to camp, all the good parts . . . ."

WSPA 75: BIDDEFORD, MAINE

Our first session was held for two weeks in August of 1975 in Biddeford, Maine. More than fifty women participated, ranging in age from eighteen to forty-eight. They came from twenty-one states and Canada, and represented varied ethnic and economic backgrounds, as well as diverse lifestyles. They brought with them a rich blend of ideas, skills, and energy. The enthusiasm generated by this first session prompted a desire for another.

INTENTIONS AND GOALS

- To provide an opportunity to more fully integrate our values and identities as women with our values and identities as designers;

- To discover and define the particular qualities, concerns, and abilities that we, as women, bring to our work;

- To create our own national support network of women within and interested in the environmental design fields, and thus end our isolation from each other;

- To achieve a collective visibility and power base within which to effect a change in priorities and practices within environmental design;

- To offer to women a separatist experience that is supportive and analytical of our unique experiences, perceptions, and common concerns as women within male-dominated fields;

- To provide a forum within which to examine and redefine the nature of professionalism and professional practice;

- To reevaluate the processes, priorities, and content of traditional education, and to develop alternatives to them;

- To eliminate some of the effects of our competitive, male-defined and male-identified educations and to rediscover, validate, and affirm our own processes as women;

- To become a mobile community. Each WSPA is to be held in a different geographic location in order to maintain flexibility, avoid localization, reach more women, prevent the institutionalization of either people or environment, and provide a unique experience each time;

- To establish a mode of organization within which the participants at the WSPA session can influence and participate in the evolution and direction of the school;

- To develop an organization that is not based upon volunteerism.

ON WOMEN, FEMINISM, AND WORK IDENTITIES

"We need to find ways of sharing skills, exercising judgment, and influencing the shape of the environments in which we live and work within the political consciousness and framework of the women's movement. We need to explore the possibilities for designing and building new environments for an evolving women's culture – spaces for self-help health clinics, resource centers, women's workspaces, lesbian centers, alternative living environments, and social spaces . . . . Separatism is not an escape from or avoidance of reality. Rather it offers a critical distance from which to gain a clearer vision, and a greater chance for a careful analysis through contrast." *Leslie*

"Environmental design professions are perfect for exploring lifestyles because we deal with lifestyles." *Susan*

"It has been a private and long-time fantasy of mine to see a women's school run by women and evolved by women that was different from traditional women's colleges, which were and still are usually run by men. This is the first time I think we have anything close to that fantasy coming true . . . . If women are really going to change anything, they need the space and time to think it through and experiment without the constraints of the establishment breathing down our backs." *Phyllis*

"In the same way that I felt hesitant about starting an office of my own, I felt hesitant about teaching. I think it was the thought of the supportive environment of women that gave me the confidence to take a chance. So for the first time in fifteen years, I will be able to share my knowledge of tools and cabinetmaking – something that I have never been able to share with anybody before." *Katrin*

"I have been so afraid of being an architect – that's why I've pursued other branches like education. Finally examining the technical and practical, using tools, has given me a different perspective. Now I'm ready to deal with this – I do want to be an architect." *Wendy*

"Can architects be radicals, given the prerequisite of clients who pay? How can we support ourselves while organizing? Where can we work? Can/must our livelihood be separate from our politics? How do you live as a woman in a society and in a profession and not get into competitiveness and individualism?" *Jill and Marie*

THE COORDINATORS

WSPA is, to a great extent, a design problem. The planning process, the school session, and our continuing evolution are experiments in new ways of creating and organizing. The school session was both a by-product of our problem solving and an aggregate of our attitudes, priorities, and actions during the planning process. Our tacit agreement to avoid preconceptions and reliance upon existing male-defined structures and methods made us more flexible and responsive to things as we experienced them. On the other hand, careful analysis and consensus were required in almost every situation, and the consequent demands of time, emotional energy, and long-distance communication created a high level of anxiety for most of us at one time or another. We were always working under the pressure of deadlines and communication problems stemming from our geographic distribution.

Collectively, we constituted a peer group. Despite our diverse politics, lifestyles, ages, geographical backgrounds, educations, and work experiences, we accepted each other as equally responsible and equally capable of making a contribution toward creating and running the school. In fact, we perceived our diversity as an exciting advantage, since each of us was concerned with innovation in one way or another. Seeing ourselves as a peer group minimized feelings of superiority or inferiority, defensiveness or ego tripping. It's much easier to work cooperatively and to accept group identity when the individualistic, competitive mode is diminished.

All of us were involved in every level of WSPA, in decision making, conceptualizing, administrating, and in teaching. There was no hierarchical separation between decisions, responsibility, and implementation, or between risk and reward. Decisions were made by consensus, and we tried to balance the amount of work among ourselves. The work load was distributed through self-selection. As a task arose or was anticipated, one or two of us would volunteer to assume the major responsibility for it, with the idea that the group would be consulted on important or difficult decisions, and that the responsible person would use her own judgment on less complicated issues. The factors upon which self-selection depended were available time, interest in the task, and/or previous knowledge or personal aptitude in a given area.

WSPA was always envisioned as a group effort. We made every attempt to create a cooperative rather than an individualistic public image. Many of our decisions clearly reflect the importance we placed on the avoidance of a star headset, either among ourselves or in the way we were perceived by others.

We chose to list our credentials jointly under categories in our brochure (e.g., "Our formal educations include . . . . We have taught or are teaching at . . . . Our designs and articles have been published in . . . ."), and listed our names alphabetically. The impact of our cumulative achievements was much greater than the effect of our separate resumes anyway. In our course descriptions, we did not list the names of the people conducting the courses. We wanted participants to select courses according to their interest in the subject rather than focusing on any of us as personalities.

Our policy regarding publicity also reflected our desire to avoid the divisiveness that is inevitably created by competitive star tripping. No reporters were permitted at the school during the session because of our concern about potential disruption of the relationships within the entire WSPA community. (Two local reporters did do stories on us, but only as a result of our having invited them to visit as a part of one of our courses. We interviewed *them* first.) During interviews, two or more of us were present if possible, and we always requested that reporters phone all the coordinators about any article that they wanted to write about WSPA. After the session we also suggested contacting participants and gave reporters a complete list of their names, addresses, and phone numbers. We always requested women reporters.

It is important to add that we saw ourselves as having a collective identity in the sense that we were a collection of strong and very different individuals who supported and complemented each other. We did not subsume or fuse our separate identities.

LEGAL AND FINANCIAL STRUCTURES

We formed a legal partnership for several reasons. It was a means of formalizing our agreement to assume equal personal liability and share equally in the assets. It was a legal conduit through which to funnel all monies, establish our books, open our checking account, and purchase insurance. And, of critical importance, it expressed the partners' strong personal commitment to WSPA and to each other. The fact that we all signed a legal document (even though it was very simple and brief) helped establish a trust in each other's commitment to seeing that WSPA really would happen. Because the organizers were concerned so specifically with the goal of getting WSPA going, and because of the problems inherent in long-distance communication, we were rarely able to deal effectively with the personal pressures and concerns each of us felt at one time or another while we were organizing. It may well be that the formal, legal expression of the mutuality of our financial, personal, and professional investment greatly increased our individual tolerance and anxiety thresholds during the planning and running of the school.

We also publicly claimed responsibility for WSPA by listing our names on the announcement poster and press releases. WSPA was unknown, unproven, and unprecedented. By personalizing the school, it became more real to us and to the public.

Coordinators put up seed money (mostly for postage and printing costs) in accordance with our various incomes and resources. We each kept a record of our reimbursable expenses, such as phone calls, xeroxing, and transportation. All income was generated through participant tuition. The cost to the participants for the first two-week session was $380. Approximately half of that amount was for room and board and went directly to the college from whom we rented all our facilities. The remaining half represented tuition, from which all out-of-pocket expenses and seed money was reimbursed and a stipend of $250 per coordinator was paid. The stipend and the amount and kind of expenses which would be considered reimbursable were determined by group consensus at the end of the session. We decided to leave $500 in our account toward the operation of the second session.

The idea of giving work/study grants developed when we found that we did not have enough full-paying participants enrolled to create the community of fifty or so women which we had decided was our optimum size (although we had enough participant tuition to break even and pay ourselves a modest salary because we had kept our overhead low). Work/study was a way of bringing in women who had indicated on their application that they could not afford the whole fee but with some financial assistance would be able to attend. Participants receiving these grants paid their own room and board and WSPA waived payment of their tuition. Women with these grants did some sort of work during the school session that we would either have had to do for ourselves or pay someone else to do. Work/study tasks included documenting activities with video, still photography, or film, helping with childcare, keeping a record of each course (being the course scribe), and organizing a library of reading materials which we had brought with us.

The work/study grants proved to be important tools for implementing the principles of the WSPA. They provided at least a partial solution to our concern with elitism because they allowed us to subsidize about one-third of the participants without sacrificing our autonomy through obligations to other institutions or funding sources. They were helpful in diminishing the differences in roles and responsibilities between coordinators and participants, and they helped eliminate volunteerism. If we as coordinators did less work, then we could afford to pay ourselves less, and participants who did work for WSPA were in effect being paid the amount of their tuition.

There were, however, certain problems with the notion of work/study. The work load and time demands for different jobs were not equal. Childcare was very demanding while other tasks were not. Since the ultimate responsibility and liability did rest with the coordinators, we frequently became involved in most of the work/study tasks anyway. Still, with better organization and the benefit of our experience, it is a feasible concept.

CHILDCARE

Participants paid for room and board for each of their children. WSPA absorbed the cost of daycare through having some of the participants who had received work/study grants do daycare work. We tried to be sensitive in selecting these women. While we were not overly concerned with someone ruining a roll of film, children are something else. There were lots of inquiries and discussions. We were fortunate in that the women who finally did do daycare work were especially sympathetic to children. Still, there were problems that arose among the children that none of us knew how to cope with. We decided that a combination of one or two full-time trained professionals with some work/study assistants is a better solution.

ON REDEFINING EDUCATION AND PROFESSIONALISM

"We used to talk about how it was an asset that women had not been socialized completely into what male professionals have always been. Now, in fact, I think it is our responsibility to change the profession." *Joan*

"It was easy to find the women, private citizens mostly, unpaid members of town boards and local associations. Several weeks before WSPA, I contacted each one asking her if she'd be a resource person, sit with us, and answer our questions about how things worked. Most of them immediately apologized for not being professionals. I explained that this was precisely what made them interesting to us." *Ellen*

August 14, 1975 "Met with Lily and Paulette in York at the country-clubish Stage Neck Inn. Talked about saving wilderness as we wasted our waistlines. Very sophisticated political group to battle the planned development. Amazing what women (non-professional, nonpaid) can and will do!"

August 21, 1975 "Met with the group over breakfast to discuss questions for Virginia M.'s interview and general info about interviewing and note taking . . . . She's a 'professional' volunteer – chair*man* of the planning board. Says 'it's a title, not anything to do with sex.' Sharp lady, though. After thirty years of volunteering, she's piqued at having to train a $10,000-a-year CETA assistant." *Charlotte*

"Architecture, architectural education, and many of the related professions traditionally have been elitist male clubs, embracing sexism, racism, and classism. Not only are women few in number, but our conditioning has typically been overwhelmingly male-identified." *Leslie*

"Traditional schools of architecture don't discriminate. Most tend to graduate white, middle-class male designers regardless of whether you were Third World and/or a woman when you entered!" *Phyllis*

"One of the things I was interested in exploring personally in WSPA was how architectural education could be different (having had some unhappy experiences in teaching). I felt I wanted to explore how you could teach in a less hierarchical manner, how you could work with students as a group. I wanted to try a more intuitive approach to learning." *Marie*

METHODS

Participants selected one course as their core course, representing their primary focus of study. This provided the opportunity for sustained and focused study in small groups.

Cooperative teaching was encouraged. Two of the five core courses were jointly coordinated and team taught. The lecture mode was eliminated. Emphasis was on the active participation of all members of the group, minimizing the role of coordinators as experts or authorities, and maximizing our roles as information sources and organizers. Purely theoretical discussions within the group were discouraged, and theorizing generally was placed in the context of real experience. We maintained about a 6:1 participant to coordinator ratio to ensure optimum personal interaction among everyone in the courses. Each person's presence and contribution in a group that size is noticed and necessary.

SCHEDULING

Throughout the two weeks, the eight three-hour sessions for each of the core courses were scheduled erratically (not in a repetitious pattern such as Monday, Wednesday, Thursday, Friday, 9:00 A.M.-12:00 P.M.). Once each week all core courses were scheduled at the same time so that only those "enrolled" in a core course would be attending those sessions. This kept at least two of the eight sessions very small and intimate. Four sessions per course were scheduled opposite one of each of the other courses. This did two things. First, it allowed members of each course to meet with members of each of the other courses at least once for a joint session. Second, it meant that if you were not enrolled or teaching in either of the two scheduled courses for any given time slot, you could participate in either of the courses, play tennis, study, take a side trip, or do whatever else you wanted to do. The remaining two sessions per course were scheduled alone, when no other courses were in session, and were called "all school" sessions. The idea was to make it possible for everyone to interact with one another several times during the two weeks and for each of us to feel related in some way to all of the courses. Participation was never mandatory, and the extent and nature of the group's participation in the sessions varied from course to course.

Many coordinators, where subject matter allowed, organized the eight sessions of their core course topically, so that participants could easily drop in or out and still remain involved rather than merely observe. This also helped maintain the relationship of each individual to the entire WSPA community and discouraged the development of small cliques of women within separate courses.

By providing a flexible system for scheduling, we encouraged everyone to contribute. The calendar for our two-week schedule was about seven-feet tall and twenty-feet long and divided into a large grid of squares with the days listed on the horizontal axis and the time slots on the vertical axis. Each day had three time slots: morning, afternoon, and evening. All meal times were fixed and recorded on the calendar between the time slots. Other information, such as the hours of core course sessions, open time, presentation time, and the schedules for meetings, was written on pieces of paper and taped into the appropriate day and time slot in the grid. Anything could then be moved easily, and anyone who wished to fill in an open time slot with a workshop, or schedule an event, or sign up for a presentation could do so on their own without consulting the coordinators. Everyone checked the calendar each day to determine her own schedule for that day.

While we were brainstorming together on these scheduling concepts, we used the analogies of musical composition, orchestration, and choreography. We were trying to achieve a loose, nonlinear rhythm and sequence within a very discernible structure. The basic elements were relationships among curricular content, group size, and personal options. We considered the latter element a critical one. The flexibility of our scheduling allowed people to be self-directing with regard to their own interests, the amount of information they wished to be exposed to, the pace at which they could absorb information, and their need for relaxation and privacy.

CURRICULUM

Course offerings evolved from the specific interests, experiences, and knowledge of each of the coordinators. The diversity of the curriculum was a reflection of the diversity of the coordinators and not the result of theoretical discussions about an "ideal curriculum." We agreed generally not to offer anything which duplicated something that was available in the same way within traditional academic and/or work settings. Because we were working outside of the system, we were able to experiment with both content and methods, to test ideas, to get critical feedback, and to investigate things that we could not explore for one reason or another within the establishment. Many of us have found that as a result of the supportive, brief teaching/learning experience at WSPA, our self-confidence and our willingness to experiment and take risks have been enhanced. Many ideas first explored at WSPA have been filtered back into our work and our lives.

The curriculum consisted of the following five core courses:

The Community Context of Town Development (Ellen Perry Berkeley)

Demystification of Tools in Relation to Design (Katrin Adam)

Professionalism Redefined (Marie Kennedy and Joan Forrester Sprague, with Jill Hamburg)

Urban Design: The Outside of Inside (Bobbie Sue Hood)

Women and the Built Environment: Personal, Social, and Professional Perceptions (Noel Phyllis Birkby and Leslie Kanes Weisman)

ON TEACHING METHODS

"The beginning was rough for me. I was used to paying my money, then sitting back and watching other people perform, but I just couldn't be passive in this process. Too much of me had to loosen up." *Margo*

"WSPA meant a lot to me, influenced me, educated me. I felt not at all comfortable most of the time. Even though I felt a little odd, I learned a great deal about taking responsibility for myself . . . . So much that I do is on a schedule because of the demands of my family. I've accepted the responsibility, making life fairly easy if I choose to go along with it and a mess when I choose not to. In Maine, whatever I did affected only myself, which turned out to be a heavy learning experience – and scary." *Nan Ellen*

"Participants in the class reacted in different ways to the unstructured format. I'm still thinking about individual variations in being able to work in a more or less structured way. I think you have to include a more structured option." *Mari*

"We always think of either/or, structured or nonstructured, and it's so hard to say, Why can't we do both? Why can't we be really pluralistic about our approaches? Not have one exist at the expense of the other – which is what usually happens . . . . Part of what I understood from the experience was that although you can begin to explore theories of organization in a short period of time, it's a very small beginning of an ongoing process, and in a way it's frustrating not to be able to keep in touch with that group of people and have that process continue. You can't have instant group!" *Joan*

"I saw new starts and approaches to problem solving here – creative blockbusting, organizational development – maybe not new words but a new context." *Heidi*

"In the first session of Women and the Built Environment, when we talked about our memories of the neighborhoods and homes that we grew up in as children, we learned a lot about each other, and maybe something about where our environmental perceptions and values come from too." *Phyllis*

"Learning by analyzing your own experiences is the greatest motivator I know of . . . . Another thing that I learned from our course at WSPA was that it is possible to have fun and learn at the same time. Too much of learning is humorless and heavy. I remember the all-school session we set up as 'an experimental design problem using unusual materials' – all those groups of women with all those cakes and gumdrops and marshmallows and vats of icing, making three-dimensional 'architectural' models of their concepts for the future of WSPA as a 'living/learning environment'!" *Leslie*

"In Urban Design, the ten women met and discussed what we wanted from the course. At the onset, we were project-oriented and wanted to combine talents and experiences into a simulated work situation. Bobbie Sue proposed an interview technique – we each wrote a resume and submitted it to the group as prospective members of a design team . . . . We had a beach expedition where we built scale (or near-scale) models of areas of the campus in the sand, using pebbles and roseships. We moved and replaced and tried different solutions to the three problems we'd identified until we formalized our ideas in time to escape incoming tides and rush back to record our solutions on paper." *Scribe's notes on Urban Design*

"I wanted the women to know that there should be no mystique about tools – there is a lot of information available in books and from people, but the best and nicest way to learn is to pick up a tool and use it yourself." *Katrin*

"The really important thing for me is the kind of thinking that's gone on since WSPA – the ways in which some of the things that happened there have turned into usable information for me now." *Marie*

CREATING THE WSPA LIVING/LEARNING ENVIRONMENT

Participants were self-selected according to their mutual interest in the environment as a bonding mechanism to create a community. Their diverse ages, experiences, and backgrounds were crucial learning resources. The only admission requirement was that participants be working in, studying, or genuinely interested in some environmental design field. Other reasons for participating were an interest in an all women's community, interest in feminism, interest in exploring and experiencing alternatives to traditional learning environments.

The serenity of a vacation-like setting counterbalanced the intensity of the group experience. Relaxation, playing, and socializing are components in learning and also help create a feeling of community. We used the natural environment as a classroom within which to study and as subject matter for study. This strong natural environment was balanced by a "built" environment. Living in ordinary, plain buildings that are not architecturally, historically, or symbolically strong in character allowed us more easily to infuse our own identity into our surroundings. Calendars, schedules, personal messages, graffiti, tools, books, cartoons, banners, etc., all transformed our immediate environment into one that we had created as a community.

The facilities we rented were relatively isolated geographically yet within close reach of many attractions. The group itself had closed boundaries; there were no guests, no part-time participants, no publicity. We wanted to minimize distractions in order to focus on developing relationships with each other. All participants, coordinators, and children lived in the same building, shared rooms, and ate meals together.

We developed and used rituals for personal introductions and celebrations. When they arrived at WSPA, all participants (including coordinators), filled out a form in which they very loosely described both their personal and work backgrounds and their interests. These forms were posted alphabetically in our main meeting/lounge room for everyone to browse through at their convenience and to refer back to as we got to know each other better.

The Prix de Biddeford was our spoof on competition and awards — the world's first nonhierarchical award, where everyone won. Presented by the coordinators as a surprise at our celebration dinner the last evening of the school session, it consisted of two brightly painted wooden toy towers which came apart like jigsaw puzzles into exactly the same number of pieces as there were participants in the WSPA. Each of us went away with her random piece and WSPA was left with the job of storing the empty spindles and base (for "class reunions"?). Special pieces were made by one of the coordinators for each of the children at the school. One of the participants typed in the award on her curriculum vitae recently when applying for a job! Various window frames, chimneys, and tower clocks are now being worn as "WSPA chic" necklaces around the country.

ON THE ENVIRONMENT

"Because it took such a great effort to get here, it was as though we had preselected ourselves as people who would have a lot to give to each other when we got together." *Bobbie Sue*

"My journey into self-discovery was catalyzed by WSPA – a woman-identified, woman-oriented environment, without the hierarchical, male trappings of a conference. Unique because there was no competition and no need to be competitive; no leaders, all teachers, all students, open, supportive – and daycare!" *Margo*

"A bed in the library – of course! Doesn't everybody love reading in bed?" *Charlotte*

"The information sheets helped to break down the differences due to age with the emphasis on ideas and thoughts as opposed to the accomplishments one has racked up . . . . I feel here an atmosphere of acceptance for you as a person, as a woman. In a man's world you are constantly having to prove yourself, to justify your very existence. Most of the time you are judged on the position you hold, your age, your appearance. While I have found I can deal with that world, what a pleasure it is to be away from it!" *Gina*

"One thing we learned very quickly is that we all had very different lifestyles, incredibly different needs, and here we all were, a group of women professionals at this school in Maine and you'd think if anybody in the world would be similar, we would be . . . ." *Joan*

"For years in the women's movement I had been talking about and learning about the meaning of sisterhood. But it was only in being with other women who share my work interests and experiences that I've been able to know the meaning of personhood. For the first time, I've been able to integrate the fragmented pieces of myself, to fuse my work identity with my feminist consciousness, to feel like a whole person." *Leslie*

"I feel more comfortable now. I felt like sort of an oddball at first in that I'm not working. I'm not professional. I mean I am working (I have three children and a husband who's an architect), I just don't get paid for it. And so that's a little different than almost everybody else here, and yet I don't have any problem relating to anybody. This is just what I needed. I used to think that no one around understood the things that I do and feel." *Nan Ellen*

"Dammit! I'm not the only one. It's not me that's weird. I am not alone. There are others too who think that there's more to life than dedicating it to just one thing – one career. There are fuller, more balanced, more humane ways to approach living and working – and this attitude does not mean one is less dedicated, efficient, and productive, not to mention imaginative and creative, with a more varied background and a greater range of choice as to when to work, where, or if to work at all at times." *Gina*

"This school as an alternative can substantiate your life as an alternative." *Marrian*

WSPA 76: SANTA CRUZ, CALIFORNIA

Our evolution continues to reflect our original intentions and has been challenging and difficult. During the planning for our second session, we integrated ten participants from the first session into our coordinating group (two of them offered core courses at the second session). Three of our cofounders rotated out for a year and we added three new teaching coordinators. This organizational change from a peer group whose members shared equal responsibility, work, risk, and commitment, to a coordinating group whose members differed in the degree and kind of involvement in WSPA, presented us with many new questions about decision making, payment, and communication between the two groups which emerged (one on the East Coast and one on the West Coast). The old partnership agreement was dissolved, and WSPA is now a tax-exempt, nonprofit corporation.

We offered seven new or revised core courses at the second session:

Architectural Design (Cathy Simon)

Basic Woodworking Techniques (Charlotte Hitchcock)

Design and Construction of Architectural Tapestry (Patti Glazer)

Energy Conscious Design (Polly Cooper)

The Politics and Ideology of the Planning Process (Harriet Cohen)

Women and the Built Environment (Noel Phyllis Birkby and Leslie Kanes Weisman)

The Writing Process: A Designer's Approach? (Ellen Perry Berkeley)

The scheduling made it possible for each participant to be fully involved in at least two courses and for teaching coordinators to take each other's courses, a goal we were unable to fully achieve the first year. In lieu of the 1975 Prix de Biddeford spoof on competition and awards, in 1976 we granted all participants the S.O.E. (Sister of the Environment) degree, our sardonic comment on academic credentials.

WSPA continued to successfully create a setting in which women of different social and political orientations could communicate. Our lifestyles ranged from the nuclear family to the radical lesbian. Our involvement in design and the environment and our need for mutual support in our work in male-dominated fields enabled us to meet on common ground and move toward an acceptance of our differences.

In 1977, we undertook a reassessment of previous sessions to determine the best direction for the future of WSPA. Several women on the East Coast designed a questionnaire which was distributed to everyone who had inquired about WSPA, our past participants, and to those on our mailing lists of women in the environmental design and related fields, schools of architecture and planning, and women's organizations. We surveyed opinions in the areas of content, preferences in length and time of year, geographic locations, money, and childcare needs. Response to the questionnaire indicated that the majority preferred to attend a summer session in the Northeast. A great many women were interested in a weekend program, although many others opted for a longer program, similar to our previous sessions. The major interests of those who responded were in energy-conscious design, the feminist analysis of the built environment, the politics of architecture and planning, as well as issues, programs, and techniques for rehabilitation of housing and work environments. The format and program offered in the next session were in direct response to those interests.

WSPA 78: BRISTOL, RHODE ISLAND

In order to be more accessible to working women, WSPA 78 in Bristol, Rhode Island, was designed to permit participation in a special weekend session between the first and second weeks as an alternative to the full two-week program. This third WSPA session – "Work Places and Dwellings: Implications for Women" – was well attended and had a very high energy level, but the full-session participants felt that the weekend portion was disruptive. We decided that the following year we would keep the weekend concept but place it at the beginning. This proved to work much better in terms of overall energy and group identity, important WSPA factors.

It was at this third session that WSPA began to deal with the realities of Washington bureaucracy by inviting women from the HUD Women's Program and Policy Division to come and explain how the system works (or doesn't, as the case may be).

WSPA 79: DENVER, COLORADO

This session — "Designing the Future as if Women Mattered" — was the first time we had a "barrier-free" environment and built ramps for a participant who was wheelchair bound. The choice of this year's theme was based on the expectation that the next few decades will witness a critical juncture in history — the transition from a rapidly growing and resource-consumptive industrial society to a postindustrial society. There are many possible political, social, and psychological responses to the changes ahead. Our intent was to investigate the many ways that we, as women and architects, planners, and designers, can facilitate the transition toward a new social, physical, and spiritual order. This was done by identifying key trends, exploring alternative visions of the future, and developing strategies for change.

Though there was some conflict over the use of speakers and the possibility of a star system developing, this session as a whole offered a nice balance between theory and practice with ongoing classes in recycling buildings, building solar hot water systems, changing environmental needs of women, designing for diversity, building redesign, and a feminist analysis of housing.

The Denver session left WSPA $1,000 in the acount as planning money for the next session. This was cause for celebration as we had never been able to accumulate that much before in planning funds. The sad tale, however, was that the next session slated for Frederick, Maryland, in 1980 was cancelled for fear of under-registration. Two factors seem to have played a part in having to make this decision:

1. Publicity was inordinately late and many former participants never got a notice or knew a session was planned. Unfortunately, not enough former coordinators or participants with WSPA planning experience from other sessions were involved

in planning for the 1980 session. From this experience, however, we developed a set of guidelines explaining procedures and pitfalls for future coordinators.

2. The other possible factor was that there was, lurking in the background, a possible grant of some decent size from HUD in Washington. Some members of the planning group felt that they would have a better chance for the grant if the session was postponed in order to give them time to pursue these funds.

The original intention in seeking outside funding (something we were adamantly opposed to originally) was to enable us to offer travel money and tuition at the next WSPA session to women who could otherwise never afford to attend. We realized we professional and academic women had to collaborate with community based grassroots women if we were to really effectuate meaningful change. We felt we were ready to move from consciousness raising, skill building, and theory, to political activism; and we decided to let the government pay for it! However, the price WSPA paid for the cancelled Maryland session was fatigue and alienation among many of its most valuable coordinators. The next session was left in the hands of a few less experienced women without the usual guidance and review.

WSPA 81: WASHINGTON, D.C.

WSPA's fifth session – "A National Symposium: Community Based Alternatives and Women in the Eighties" – was conceived as a three-day weekend session funded by a HUD grant for $10,000. Many WSPA people thought of this as something other than a WSPA session. Most of our sensitive concerns with how a session should operate based on feminist principles were violated. The conference was quite conventional in format. The $1000 from the Denver session was absorbed and never recouped. However, the content was significant, and an outstanding network of diverse women and groups was brought together. Among them were: The American Indian National Bank, The Coalition of 100 Black Women of D.C., Center for Community Change, Clearinghouse for Community Based Free Standing Educational Institutions, National Association of Community Cooperatives, National Congress of Neighborhood Women, National Council of Negro Women, National Hispanic Housing Coalition, Rural American Women, and Southeast Women's Employment Coalition. This network, and its ongoing work and collaboration, is our biggest hope for real environmental change for women.

THE FUTURE

After the 1981 weekend session, WSPA formed a policy group to reassess our purpose and goals. Letters of inquiry continue to come in all the time: offers of places to hold sessions have been received, but lack of money and interest among those most capable of organizing a session are causing our current inactivity. There is much interest in WSPA in Europe, and proposals for an international session have been written. Though we are inactive now, the machinery is there waiting to be utilized, the network is a good one, and the connections can be picked up rapidly to organize a session or event in the future. WSPA remains an experiment and an ongoing learning process. We have not become static or repetitious. Our "solutions" have often led us to more experiments. We have thrown out, let go, taken risks, used intuition, made mistakes; we have had to cope with our own conditioning, insecurity, and paranoia.

In retrospect, one of the things that WSPA affirms and clarifies most strongly is that a feminist education must consist of two equally important factors. One is the analysis and evolution of information, theory, and ideology. The other is the development of an actual context which reflects those values. A feminist analysis, and even the generation of new ideas, can take place in many environments, including establishment academic institutions. A feminist education cannot. It must synthesize the two factors of analysis and context: the intellectual with the experiential, the facts with the behavior, the ideology with the structure. The evolution of a feminist ideology is critical. But the impact of feminist values is significant only when they are reflected through changes in behavior and action. Learning in this sense is holistic, and it cannot be achieved under a traditional, hierarchical system whose organization and methods deny the fundamental tenets of feminism — no matter how radical the concepts, rhetoric, and visions are, or who expresses them.

PART III

Approaches to Feminist Education

Not By Degrees: Feminist Theory and Education

By Charlotte Bunch

THE DEVELOPMENT of feminist theory and a rigorous analysis of society are more important for us today than ever before. Feminists need to understand the forces working against us, as well as to analyze our experiences as a movement, if we are to survive the anti-woman backlash and keep our visions alive. When feminists despair, burn out, or give up, it is often because the forces against us are strong and because our theoretical framework does not give us a sense of how individual activities contribute to significant victories in the future. A solid feminist theory would help us understand present events in a way that would enable us to develop the visions and plans for change that sustain people engaged in day-to-day political activity.

When I left the university to do full-time work in "the movement" in the 1960s, it didn't occur to me that I would return one day to teach or write feminist theory. Like many others who chose to become movement activists then, I felt that I was leaving behind not only the academic world, but also what I saw as irrelevant theorizing. However, as I experienced the problems of movement organizing when an overall analysis was lacking, felt the frustration of conflicts where issues were not clear, and observed people dropping out of political activity, I became aware of the critical role of theory in the movement. I began to see feminist theory not as academic, but as a process based on understanding and advancing the activist movement.

---

*This essay first appeared in *Quest: A Feminist Quarterly,* vol. 5 no. 1 (Summer 1979).

While my growing sense of the importance of theory applied to all my feminist work, the urgency that I felt about it became clearest during my involvement with lesbian-feminism. When the lesbian issue became a major controversy in the women's movement in the early 1970s, I realized that in order for lesbians to function openly, we would have to understand *why* there was so much resistance to this issue. It was not enough to document discrimination against homosexuals or to appeal to fairness. We had to figure out why lesbianism was taboo, why it was a threat to feminists, and then devise strategies accordingly. I saw that my life as a lesbian in the movement depended on, among other things, the development of a theory that would explain our immediate conflicts in the context of a long-term view of feminism. This theoretical perspective developed along with our activism, but it required us to consciously ask certain questions, to look at our experiences in and out of the movement, and to consider existing feminist theory in new ways. Through this process, new interpretations of the relationship between lesbianism and feminism, and new strategies for ending lesbian oppression emerged.

For example, as we examined feminists' fear of being called lesbians, we were able to confront directly the role that such name calling played in the oppression of all women. Having a theory about lesbian oppression did not tell us what to do tactically, but it did provide a framework for understanding situations, for placing them in a broader context, and for evaluating possible courses of action. This experience showed me that theory was not simply intellectually interesting, but was crucial to the survival of feminism.

THE FUNCTIONS OF FEMINIST THEORY

Theory enables us to see immediate needs in terms of long-range goals and an overall perspective on the world.[1] It thus gives us a framework for evaluating various strategies in both the long and the short run, and for seeing the types of changes that they are likely to produce. Theory is not just a body of facts or a set of personal opinions. It involves explanations and hypotheses that are based on available knowledge and experience. It is also dependent on conjecture and insight about how to interpret those facts and experiences and their significance.

No theory is totally "objective," since it reflects the interests, values, and assumptions of those who created it. Feminist theory relies on the underlying assumption that it will aid the liberation of women. Feminist theory, therefore, is not an unengaged study of women. It is an effort to bring insights from the movement and from various female experiences together with research and data gathering to produce new approaches to understanding and ending female oppression.

While feminist theory begins with the immediate need to end women's oppression, it is also a way of viewing the world. Feminism is an entire world view or *gestalt,* not just a laundry list of "women's issues." Feminist theory provides a basis for understanding every area of our lives, and a feminist perspective can affect the world politically, culturally, economically, and spiritually. The initial tenets of feminism have already been established – the idea that power is based on gender differences and that men's illegitimate power over women taints all aspects of society, for instance. But now we face the arduous task of systematically working through these ideas, fleshing them out and discovering new ones.

When the development of feminist theory seems too slow for the changes that we seek, feminists are tempted to submerge our insights into one of the century's two dominant progressive theories of reality and change: democratic liberalism or Marxist socialism.[2] However, the limitations of both of these systems are increasingly obvious. While feminism can learn from both of them, it must not be tied to either because its greatest strength lies in providing an alternative view of the world.

The full implications of feminism will evolve over time, as we organize, experiment, think, analyze, and revise our ideas and strategies in light of our experiences. No theory emerges in full detail overnight; the dominant theories of our day have expanded and changed over many decades. That it will take time should not discourage us. That we might fail to pursue our ideas – given the enormous need for them in society today – is unconscionable.

Because feminist theory is still emerging and does not have agreed upon answers (or even approaches to many questions), it is difficult to work out strategies based on that theory. This difficulty can lead feminists to rely on the other theories of change or to fall into the "any action/no action" bind. When caught in this bind, one may go ahead with action – any action – for its own sake, or be paralyzed, taking no action for lack of a sense of what is "right." To escape this bind, we must remember that we do not need, and indeed never will have, all the answers before we act, and that it is often only through taking action that we can discover some of them. The purpose of theory, then, is not to provide a pat set of answers about what to do, but to guide us in sorting out options, and to keep us out of the "any action/no action" bind. Theory also keeps us aware of the questions that need to be asked, so that what we learn in each activity will lead to more effective strategies in the future. Theory thus both grows out of and guides activism in a continuous, spiraling process.

In pursing feminist theory as an activist, I have become increasingly aware of the need to demystify it. Theory is not something set apart from our lives. Our assumptions about reality and change influence our actions constantly. The question is not whether we have a theory, but how aware we are of the assumptions behind our actions, and how conscious we are of the choices we make – daily – among different theories. For example, when we decide whether to put our energies into a rape crisis center or into efforts to change rape laws, we are acting according to certain theories about how service projects and legislation affect change. These theories may be implicit or explicit, but they are always there.

A MODEL FOR THEORY

Theory doesn't necessarily progress in a linear fashion, but examining its components is useful in understanding existing political theory as well as in developing new insights. In the model I have developed, I divide theory into four interrelated parts: description, analysis, vision, and strategy.

1. Description: *Describing what exists* may sound simple, but the choices that we make about interpreting and naming reality provide the basis for the rest of our theory. Changing people's perceptions of the world through new descriptions of reality is usually a prerequisite for altering that reality. For example, fifteen years ago, few people would say that women in the U.S. were oppressed. Today, the oppression of women is acknowledged by a large number of people, primarily because of feminist work which described that oppression in a number of ways. This work has involved consciousness raising, as well as gathering and interpreting facts about women in order to substantiate our assertions. Description is necessary for all theory; unfortunately for feminism, much of our work has not yet gone beyond this point.

2. Analysis: *Analyzing why that reality exists* involves determining its origins and the reasons for its perpetuation. This is perhaps

the most complex task of theory and is often seen as its entire function. In seeking to understand the sources of women's oppression and why it is perpetuated, we have to examine biology, economics, psychology, sexuality, and so on. We must also look at what groups and institutions benefit from oppression, and why they will, therefore, strive to maintain it. Analyzing why women are oppressed involves such things as sorting out how the forms of oppression change over time while the basic fact of oppression remains, or probing how the forms of oppression vary in different cultures while there are cross-cultural similarities.

Analysis of why something happens sometimes gets short-circuited by the temptation to ascribe everything to one single factor, such as capitalism or motherhood. In developing an analysis, I find that it is useful to focus initially on a phenomenon in a limited context and consider a wide range of factors that may affect it. Then, as that context is understood, the analysis can be expanded. Above all, we need not feel that we must answer the "why" of everything all at once with a single explanation.

3. Vision: *Determining what should exist* requires establishing principles (or values) and setting goals. In taking action to bring about change, we operate consciously or unconsciously out of certain assumptions about what is right or what we value (principles), and out of our sense of what society ought to be (goals). This aspect of theory involves making a conscious choice about those principles in order to make our visions and goals concrete. We must look at our basic assumptions about such things as "human nature" and how it can be changed, about the relationships of individuals to groups, about whether men and women are essentially different, for example. We may choose not to address some of these issues yet, but since every action carries implicit assumptions, we must be conscious of them so that we do not operate out of old theoretical frameworks by default. The clearer we are about our principles – for example, whether we think that women should gain as much power as possible in every area, or believe, instead, that power itself should be eliminated – the more easily we can set our long-term goals. Immediate goals can then be based on an assessment of what can be accomplished that may be short of our long-term vision, but moves toward, not away, from it. Visions, principles, and goals will change with experience, but the more explicit we make them, the more our actions can be directed toward creating the society we want, as well as reacting to what we don't like.

4. Strategy: *Hypothesizing how to change what is to what should be* moves directly into questions of changing reality. Some people see strategy not as part of theory, but rather as a planning process based on theory. But I include strategy here in its broadest sense – the overall approach one takes to how to accomplish one's goals. The descriptive and analytic process of theory help develop a more systematic understanding of the way things work, but they usually do not make obvious what one should do. Developing a strategy requires that we draw out the consequences of our theory and suggest general directions for change.

Like the other aspects of theory, this involves a combination of information gathering and creative speculation. It entails making judgments about what will lead to change – judgments that are based both on description and analysis of reality, and on visions, principles, and goals. Developing a strategy also involves examining various tools for change – legislative, military, spiritual – and determining which are most effective in what situations. There are many questions to consider, such as what sectors of society can best be mobilized to carry out which types of action. And in working out which strategies will be most effective, the interaction between developing theory and actively experimenting with it becomes most clear. For in all aspects of theory development, theory and activism continually inform and alter each other.

USING THE MODEL

This four-part model for theory can be used in many ways. In my feminist theory classes, we have tried to understand different theories by outlining how various authors address each of its developmental parts. For example, we take Shulamith Firestone's *Dialectic of Sex* and discuss her approach to description, analysis, vision, and strategy. Then we compare her ideas in each area with those of other radical feminists, in an effort to see the common tenets of radical feminism, the important areas of disagreement, and the strategy implications of those differences. We then take the same approach to socialist-feminist authors, compare them to each other and to radical feminist works, etc.

Another way to use this approach to theory is to examine possible ways of addressing a specific issue in terms of these processes. For example, on the issue of reproductive freedom, we can use theoretical work to understand the implications behind various strategies. Considerable work has been done detailing the variety of ways in which women lack control over reproduction, from forced sterilization to negligence in the development of contraceptives. Several analyses of why women do not have control over our bodies have been suggested. These range from the idea that men fear women's powers to create life and therefore compensate by controlling reproduction, to the proposition that capitalism is the primary cause because it must control the number of workers produced, to the view that the Catholic Church is the dominant perpetuator of this situation because its control over reproduction and matters of family life is central to its power. Most analyses also look at which institutions are most influential and which are most vulnerable to change, and the relations between them – e.g., how the Catholic Church affects hospital and government policies.

There are considerable differences of opinion about how reproduction should be treated. Some feminists argue that women should have absolute control over our bodies and reproduction at all times and in all circumstances. Others contend that there can be some legitimate limits on an individual woman's control; in the case of abortion, for example, limiting a woman's right to abortion on demand to the first trimester. Some argue that the state should prescribe standards of control that "protect" women such as the requirement of a thirty-day waiting period of any sterilization; and still others hold that a woman's control must be subordinate to the obligation of government to supervise overall population growth.

The practical consequences of these differences in theory become clear when strategies for gaining women's reproductive rights are discussed. Even among those who agree that women's lack of control over reproduction is central to our oppression, there are differences in strategy based on differences in analysis and vision. Those who think that the Catholic Church is the primary enemy of women's reproductive rights may focus on efforts to remove Church influence on the state, the fight against religious tax exemptions, and so on, while those who see multinational corporations as the primary controller of population issues would focus on them. The controversy among feminists over whether having the government require a thirty-day waiting period for all sterilizations would protect women or further abridge our rights to control our bodies illustrates how disagreement over vision and goals leads to different strategies and often to conflict over what we will demand.

This example, though simplified here, illustrates how the four-part model in particular, and theory in general, can be used to clarify practical political problems. When we understand the basis of our disagreements and the nature of the forces against us, we are better equipped to come to some agreement or to realize when compromise may not be possible. Theory helps clarify how things work and what our choices are, and thus aids in determining where to put our energies and how to challenge the sources of our oppression most effectively.

Theory is also a tool for passing on the knowledge we have gained from our life experiences and movement projects. Feminists need to analyze personal experiences as well as political developments – to sort out our initial assumptions about goals and analysis, to look at the strategies we used and why, and to evaluate the results in terms of what could be learned for the future. Making such feminist analysis accessible to others usually involves writing it down, which brings us to feminist education.

TEACHING FEMINIST THEORY

My approach to teaching feminist theory assumes that it is part of an educational process that is connected to the feminist political struggle. As such, feminist theory underlies all feminist education: a course on women artists, when taught from a feminist perspective, for example, should not only include the work of particular artists but also a political analysis of why women's art has not received proper attention. Feminist theory should be present in this way throughout a feminist curriculum, but it also needs to be taught as a separate subject where political theories can be explored in depth.

A feminist theory course begins with teaching the basic skills of how to read, analyze, and think about ideas. The course must also give information about existing feminist theory, about how that theory affects our lives, and about where to go to learn more theory. To get students personally involved, a teacher must challenge them to develop their own ideas and to analyze the assumptions behind their actions.

These are the central tasks of teaching feminist theory as I see them, after doing it in a variety of settings since 1970. I have taught women in universities and women's centers and summer institutes, in public and private institutions, as undergraduates, graduates in women's studies, seminarians, and feminist activists, and I have worked on transmitting theory through feminist publications. What I have found in all these cases is that women's problems with theory most often grow out of their trouble with thinking about ideas, and their view that their own thoughts and experiences are not important enough to be the basis of theory. Or, to put it in a slightly different way, many women have difficulty both in systematically pursuing thoughts and in believing that what they think makes any difference. These problems with thinking and with believing in the importance of one's thoughts and experience are related.

When teaching feminist theory, one must counter such attitudes and find ways to encourage women to think systematically about the world. Our society trains only a few people to think in this manner, mostly those from the classes it expects to control the social order. Certainly most women are not expected to take control and, in consequence, are not encouraged to think analytically. In fact, critical thinking is the antithesis of women's traditional role. Women are supposed to worry about mundane survival problems, to brood about fate, and to fantasize in a personal manner. We are not meant to think analytically about society, to question the way things are, or to consider how things could be different. Such thinking involves an active, not a passive, relationship to the world. It requires confidence that your thoughts are worth pursuing and that you can make a difference. And it demands looking beyond how to make do and into how to make "making do" different – how to change the structures that control our lives. My goal in teaching feminist theory is to provoke women to think about their lives and society in this way.

To counter women's negativity toward and fear of theory, it has to be presented as something with practical consequences for one's life and as something that can be made accessible to anyone. One of the ways women misunderstand, and thereby avoid, theory is manifested in the "too hard/too easy" paradox. Many women assume that theory is esoteric and concerns matters that are removed from daily life. As a consequence, they regard something as properly theoretical only if it is very abstract and they don't understand it very well – implying that it can't be real theory unless it is "too hard" for them to grasp. The flip side of this attitude is wanting all theory to be "easy" – implying that if it requires reading slowly, or returning to it later, or looking up words in the dictionary, then it is of no use. Both attitudes prevent a realistic approach to theory. Reading and writing theory is not easy, but it can be done, and it can be made comprehensible.

Underlying some women's difficulties with theory are problems of literacy – of reading, writing, and thinking. Without the basic skills of reading and writing, women face limits on how actively they can engage in theory. In my experience, people who do not see reading and writing as basic are usually those who can take them for granted.[3] Revolutionary movements have almost always seen developing a general literacy as one of their most important tasks. Yet in this country, where we assume that most of us can read and write, it is often overlooked. In fact, not only are many people illiterate, but we are also rapidly moving into a generally postliterate era.

Reading and writing are valuable in and of themselves, and women should have access to their pleasures. Beyond that, they are vital to change for several reasons. First, they provide a means of conveying ideas and information that may not be readily available in the popular media. For example, the ideas of women's liberation first spread through mimeographed articles that were passed around long before it was possible to get the attention of the mass media – and with more clarity than that with which the mass media later portrayed feminism. Second, reading and writing help develop an individual's imagination and ability to think, whereas much of mass culture, especially television, pacifies and encourages conformity rather than creativity. (Studies of the effects TV has on children, such as the way it emphasizes the immediate dramatic moment at the expense of reflective thought, have demonstrated these consequences.) Third, an individual's access through reading to a variety of interpretations of reality increases that person's capacity to think for herself, to go against the norms of the culture, and to conceive of alternatives for society – all of which are fundamental to acting politically. Fourth, reading and writing aid each woman's individual survival and success in the world, by increasing her ability to function in her chosen endeavors. And finally, the written word is still the cheapest and most accessible form of mass communication. This makes it useful to those who have limited resources. Feminists should, of course, use other mediums as well, but I emphasize the political importance of literacy because it is often overlooked. When we recall why literacy is important to movements, it becomes clear that we should neither assume that women are already literate, nor ignore the value of teaching women to read, write, and think as part of feminist education.

TEACHING TECHNIQUES

In most of my courses, I have not had to teach the basic skills of reading and writing so much as the skills of reading and writing *critically* as part of learning to think in new ways. There is no one method for thinking and there is no one way to teach it. I have used several techniques to encourage thinking and to provide women with tools for analyzing the world.[4]

I begin by introducing the four-part model of theory, and then encourage students to use the model in looking at everything around them, as well as in reading "theory." For example, in one classroom exercise I pass out a variety of feminist and nonfeminist women's magazines. Each student examines one during class and uses the four-part model to tell the rest of us what theoretical assumptions are embodied in that magazine: what is its view of reality for women? What does it imply about how, why or whether that reality needs to change? What are its approaches to those changes? What values does it espouse? The exercise can be adapted to popular movies or TV series, to comic books – anything. The point is to demystify theory by showing that theory underlies everything and does not exist only in books. At a simple level, the exercise also makes a student aware of how she thinks and analyzes for herself.

There are many situational assignments which enable students to explore the link between theory and action or which require them to think through the strategic implications of a theoretical position. For instance, one can set up a specific situation and assign people theoretical positions within it. The situation might be a women's center board of directors meeting where it has to be decided how to use a $20,000 gift it has just received. This situation can be designed leaving the students to devise their own options, or it can be narrowly defined so that students must choose between a given set of options. At a Washington, D.C. Feminist Alliance workshop on theory, for example, the group had to choose between using the money for a lesbian mother's defense fund, dividing it equally among groups affiliated with the organization, or using it for office space and staff for the organization.

Once a situation is defined, each student is assigned a theoretical position to represent in the discussion: she must be an anarchist-feminist, a liberal-feminist, or a particular person whose theories have been studied, such as Elizabeth Cady Stanton or Juliet Mitchell. After the exercise, we discuss why each thought that a particular theory would lead to a certain position on the issues and what questions it raised for her.

Another variation on the situational approach is to break into small groups, assign each a particular identity, and ask each to take positions on certain issues: e.g., you are a socialist-feminist women's union and you must decide whether to join with other groups to demand wages for housework. After we study various feminist theories, I have turned the situation approach around by giving students a particular issue to resolve in which they represent their own opinions, asking, for example, "do you favor a wages-for-housework demand?" Afterwards, we discuss what assumptions and theories they found themselves using to arrive at a decision.

The situations can be varied any number of ways and carried out in a few minutes or over several weeks. I have often found that what may have seemed abstract when first discussed in class comes alive during these exercises. The exercises also train students to think systematically and help them to gain confidence in applying theory to real life situations.

To get students to think creatively, a teacher must convince them that they should not try to figure out the "right" thing to say. Those most oriented toward politics seek the "correct line," while those oriented to the academy seek the "correct answer." The effect is usually the same. Concentrating on what is "right" or expected stymies creative thought. I often create situational assignments and give examples in my lectures where there is clearly no right answer, but rather a number of options that depend on deciding between different approaches and values instead of finding the so-called truth. Getting away from the right answer or correct line mentality is particularly important in a theory course because comprehending theory and its role depends so much on understanding the importance of interpretation and speculation. Since theory is primarily about interpreting reality, it depends on leaps of perception, speculation, and imagination — most of which get stifled by trying to be "correct."

I want to see women creating more theory, and to do this I have used techniques in the classroom that come out of my experiences in seeking women to write theoretical articles for *Quest: A*

Feminist Quarterly. To assist someone in her efforts to put her analysis on paper, we have found it useful to ask for responses to other articles or to provide concrete questions to address. In my classes, I initially asked for term papers in which students were to analyze a particular topic, but this generally meant that they pulled together some facts with others' opinions and did not make their own efforts at analysis. Now I require a journal in which students outline the basic ideas of all the readings assigned to the class and give their responses to those ideas. This approach has yielded both more originality and more systematic work on classroom readings. I now provide specific questions for papers to address and/or position papers to respond to, rather than free-form topics. These approaches help students work out what they think, just as they enable activists who seldom write to record insights and analysis which would otherwise be lost. Giving someone something to start with besides a blank page helps her to write.

The crux of teaching feminist theory is getting women to analyze and think about others' ideas as well as to develop their own. I also want to teach specific feminist theories, and most of the classroom time is used in lectures and discussions of such theories. But I have found that giving information is the easiest part of teaching. The real challenge is to teach skills and inspire an interest that enables students to understand that content more fully during the course, and to take that understanding with them into the rest of their lives.

NOTES

1. There are many approaches to theory, and those interested in exploring more about how theory is constructed should look at the literature of political philosophy. A model for feminist theory similar to the one that I discuss in this paper was developed by Judy Smith of the Women's Resource Center, in Missoula, Montana.

2. For more discussion of this problem and of nonaligned feminism as a response to it, see Charlotte Bunch, "Beyond Either/Or: Feminist Options," *Quest: A Feminist Quarterly,* vol. 3, no. 1 (Summer 1976), pp. 2-17.

3. Discussing the relationship of literacy to politics is not unique to feminism. The topic has been widely debated in political circles, and for recent opinions, I recommend "The Politics of Literacy," in a special issue of *The Radical Teacher,* no. 8 (May 1978).

4. There are volumes of literature on teaching the basis of how to read and write. The most useful exploration of teaching reading and writing along with political and analytic skills is Paulo Freire's *Pedagogy of the Oppressed* (Seabury Press, New York, 1970). Freire describes an educational process that is similar to consciousness raising.

Feminist Values: Guidelines for Teaching Methodology in Women's Studies*

by Nancy Schniedewind

THERE IS SUBSTANTIAL creative discussion on academic content in women's studies, but much less attention is given to *how* we teach. Florence Howe notes in her "Seven Years Later: Women's Studies Programs in 1976" that she observed surprisingly few innovative teaching methods in her visits to women's studies programs.[1] Students, I believe, learn as much from the process of a course — its hidden curriculum — as from the explicit content. The more classroom interaction reflects feminist principles and the greater the congruence between process and content, the *more* consistent and powerful students' learning can be.

At least some agreement exists as to appropriate content. Women's studies courses analyze (1) scholarship by and about women both in the traditional disciplines and in the interdisciplinary forms, (2) the structure and conditions of the oppression of women and contrasting models of, and processes for, self-determination, and (3) the relationship between the personal subordination of women and broader political, economic, and social structures, including examples and visions of egalitarian alternatives. Additionally, we hope students will gain the knowledge and skills to better control their lives. Finally, we encourage women to push themselves toward academic and personal excellence.

---

*An earlier version of this article appeared in *The Radical Teacher, #18* (Box 102, Kendall Square, Post Office, Cambridge, Massachusetts 02142).

261

In this paper, I examine those educational *processes* which reflect certain feminist principles, as I see them. I define five process goals that have implications for teaching methodology and give examples of how I use such methods in my women's studies classes at the State University of New York, at New Paltz. Many academics mistrust anything that is not lecture-discussion. I once did. Yet feminism necessitates not only the development of new knowledge, but also new forms of relationships between people. The classroom offers one arena to experience those relationships.

The emphasis on democratic classroom processes implicit in feminist pedagogy is similar to other egalitarian forms of education that have been proposed historically by theorists and practitioners. However, progressive educational methods have been, and can be, used to teach content that is antidemocratic and patriarchal. Jonathan Kozol's *Free Schools* articulated such a critique of the subject matter and values of the mainstream free school movement of the late 1960s and early 1970s.[2] Feminist pedagogy demands the integration of egalitarian content and process.

DEVELOPMENT OF AN ATMOSPHERE OF MUTUAL RESPECT, TRUST, AND COMMUNITY IN THE CLASSROOM

When women have opportunities to come to know each other as people, speak honestly, take risks, and support each other in the classroom, feminist values of community, communication, equality, and mutual nurturance are reinforced. While the subject matter in women's studies itself is often conducive to such community building, particular teaching methodologies expedite the process.

At the beginning of a course, I use interpersonal activities so students become acquainted quickly. I ask students to pair up with a person they don't know and talk to her about a woman who has been a role model for them. Discuss the qualities you respect about this woman. What attributes of hers do you see in yourself? Which would you like to develop? Through this process, students not only share perceptions of women role models, but gain personal insights about themselves and their partners.

To encourage honesty, I teach a simple interpersonal communication skill that is a vehicle for feedback throughout the course: *I-messages* offer women a means for giving positive or constructively critical feedback to each other in a supportive way.[3] The format for an I-message is: "When you _____ (behavior), I feel _____ (feeling) because _____ (consequence)." For example, "Sue, when you dominate the class discussion, I feel annoyed because I'm interested in hearing the thoughts of everyone here." This enables a person to tell another how a particular behavior makes her feel without generalizing about her. It doesn't demand, but gives the receiver the choice to change her behavior. I-messages are easy to learn, can be shared among peers and between students and instructor, and are very effective in producing an honest classroom atmosphere.

Democratic processes among students are important for community and mutual respect. (I will discuss democracy between students and teachers in the next section.) The more aware each woman is of her use or abuse of time, attention, and power within the class, the more potentially democratic the group process. A useful way to make students conscious of one aspect of group dynamics is to brainstorm a list of function-roles people play in groups − organizer, devil's advocate, includer, clarifier, withdrawer − and ask them to decide which they typically play. Explain that a group is most effective when its members take on the function-role that is needed at the time, and that people become leaders by taking on these roles. Give students a task to try such shared leadership. Since leadership can rotate among all group members, this theory of group democratizes typically hierarchical views of leadership. It also gives women an opportunity to try unfamiliar roles in a supportive setting. Student alertness to the group dynamics during the course stimulates democratic participation.

During some semsters, I taught process skills at the beginning of the course but failed to continually help students focus on them as we moved along. I have since learned that the little time it takes to raise and have students respond to questions like "To what extent did leadership rotate today?" or, "Does anyone want to give an I-message before we leave?" is well worth it in furthering feminist process.

Finally, festive procedures are community-builders. Refreshments during breaks, a potluck dinner, and the integration of poetry and songs into the course, all catalyze energy and build commmunity.

SHARED LEADERSHIP

Feminist values support the replacing of hierarchical forms of authority with participatory decision making. This does not imply structurelessness, but structure that is democratic. In the classroom it is possible for a teacher to share leadership with both students and other instructors.

Initially, I take primary responsibility for structuring my courses. Once they are underway, I involve students in two ways. At the outset, students divide into small groups and list on one-half of a sheet of newsprint what they want from the course and on the other half, what they don't want. I do this as well. We post the lists around the room and read and discuss them as a group. I often list expectations that are both academic and personal: I want everyone to come to class having done all the reading; I want us all to take responsibility for both our learning and that of others; I don't want to start or end late; I don't want gossip (people talking about each other behind their backs rather than to their faces). Students' expectations often include those that are content-oriented, as well as general ones: I want to learn how housework became women's work; I want to learn ways of dealing with racism and sexism in the classroom; I don't want assignments that are busy-work; I want what I learn to have meaning for me in my life.

When any expectation is unacceptable to me, I suggest that the student insisting on it withdraw from the course. Examples of expectations that I have found unacceptable have been: (1) not wanting to participate in small groups, (2) wanting to do an independent paper instead of attending class, (3) not writing any papers. I may modify some of my own expectations to meet student needs. For example, I've included a journal in some course expectations and students convinced me that they have had an overdose of journals in women's studies. I understood that and deleted the expectation. We discuss with gusto the ingredients of a challenging class. In the process, we set some clear, mutually agreed upon expectations.

During the semester, I periodically ask students for feedback about the course. While this can be done orally, I prefer students to write anonymously. Typical questions I ask include (1) What is helping your learning in this course. What is hindering it? (2) To improve this course, I should _____; the instructor should _____. Representative responses might be: What is helping my learning is the variety of activities, the energetic pace of the course, and the stimulating subject matter. What is hindering my learning is too much reading, or domination of the discussion by the same people. To improve the course, I should spend more time on the reading, or be more assertive in class. The instructor should allow more time for small group work, or invite other guest speakers. Then I ask a few questions about specific problem areas I've noted. For example: One thing the group/I could do to encourage participation in discussion from everyone is _____. Examples might be to talk less, ask other people for their opinion, speak out more, or tell Joan how her critical manner inhibits me from speaking.

I read, tally, and make notes of these responses and report them back to the class the next session. In discussing them, we try to work through problem areas and make needed changes. The written feedback takes only ten minutes and the subsequent discussion somewhat longer. I have found this time to be well spent in my effort to share decision making.

While I share leadership with students in these and other ways, I don't have a totally egalitarian classroom. I take more leadership and have more power than any of the students. I have found that students need an arena in which to *learn* to take responsibility for themselves and the group. For many, this is a new experience. I no longer expect that they automatically come to class with those experiences and skills. Upper division women's studies students often come more ready for reciprocity, and in those courses the degree of my influence is less.

Instructors, too, can share leadership. For example, three faculty members team teach our introductory, interdisciplinary course "Women's Image."[4] While more time consuming than teaching alone, the benefits of each other's ideas and support increase the quality of the instruction. We stimulate each other's thinking, exchange perspectives from our various disciplines, pool knowledge to develop readings, share problems and possible solutions regarding our discussion groups, continually critique the course, and build in time for contact each week – something highly valued in a world of hectic schedules. In addition, lectures are given by numerous college and community women. These have included an attorney (women and the law), a psychologist (Freud and his critics), a social worker from Planned Parenthood (women's health issues), a coordinator of the local prochoice group (the politics of abortion), a local women's studio collective member (women in the arts), and the director of a battered women's law project (creating changes for women). "Women's Image" thus becomes a community endeavor with a wide variety of women sharing its leadership.

COOPERATIVE STRUCTURES

A classroom based on cooperative norms is desirable from both a feminist and an educational point of view. Ample research in education and social psychology points to the increased cognitive and affective learning gains of students in cooperatively structured classrooms.[5]

Cooperative goal structuring is one method that facilitates interdependence. An activity has a cooperative goal structure when an individual can complete it successfully if, and only if, all others with whom she is linked do likewise. The group sinks or swims together. For example, when students have done the assigned reading, they form small groups. (I talk with any student who has neglected her reading and provide her with a comprehensive assignment that must be completed before she can receive credit for the session.) Each group is then given a different question that compels them to integrate the material in a creative way. Thus, after reading initial chapters from Gordon's *America's Working Women* and Lerner's *The Black Woman in White America,* each group gets one of the following questions: (1) Compare Gordon and Lerner's approach to history with what you have learned in high school. (2) Compare the value and nature of women's work in the Revolutionary period and today. What accounts for the differences? (3) Imagine yourselves "factory girls" in Lowell, Massachusetts in the 1830s. You are writing a letter to a friend describing your life. What would you say? (4) What were the key similarities and differences in the lives of Black and white working women before the Civil War? In discussing the question, members must see that each person in their group is prepared to respond. They are allowed about thirty minutes. When students return to the large group, I ask any member to present her group's response and the group is assessed accordingly. I usually use a checkmark, checkmark-plus, or checkmark-minus. In this way, each member feels a responsibility to do the reading, critically analyze it with others, and share responsibility for her peer's learning.

The major problem I've had in using this method is reinforcing the expectation that it is necessary to do all the reading before coming to class – something that some students are not accustomed to. Once we use this process, it becomes clear to students that they must read beforehand. The visiblity of a number of non-participants dampens the morale of the group. This is usually only an initial problem because the norm to read before class becomes established quickly.

Other methods foster collaboration. Breaking the class into small discussion groups is one common approach. Assigning cooperative rather than individual term projects is another. In my interdisciplinary course, "Women and Work," students contracting for an A (see below) must develop a comprehensive collaborative action project. Last semester one group researched, wrote, and distributed to women in the community a handbook about the legal rights of women workers in New York State. Such a project might prove too demanding for a single student.

Personal and academic support groups are another vehicle for cooperation. "Education of the Self for Women" is a course that enables a student to (1) identify, study, and attempt to change dysfunctional patterns of personal behavior, and (2) define, analyze, and plan collective actions to change those social forces that contribute to the development and maintenance of these patterns. At midterm in that course, students join a support group of three. They meet to help each other better understand and alter one of their patterns for a portion of each subsequent class. While such groups are more natural for courses with explicit personal content, this method can be adapted to almost any course. For example, I might ask women to choose two goals for personal development that they want to address during the semester. "I want to speak up in discussion" or "I want to stop procrastinating and complete my work on time" or "I want to give feedback assertively to my peers and the instructor" are typical goals. In support groups, the students discuss their goals and contract to help each other meet them. I insure brief periods for support-group meetings two or three times during the semester and a longer session at the end. While drawing little time away from the major focus of a course, support groups integrate a cooperative structure for student development.

In most college settings, the grading system reinforces competitive norms. Sometimes, however, a pass/fail option is available for entire courses. I use this alternative in "Education of the Self for Women" since it is presumptuous of me to grade the growth of another's self-knowledge. Despite my fears to the contrary in this grade-conscious era, not only do students commend this pass/fail system, but they continue to do high quality work as well. I promise a letter of recommendation for anyone needing evaluative information not reflected in a pass grade.

When letter grades are necessary or preferred, a contract grading system takes most competition out of the evaluation process. In this system, I describe in the syllabus what requirements are necessary to receive an A, B, or C. Each student decides the grade she wants to earn and does the appropriate work. I set criteria for the quality as well as the type of work expected. While criteria vary with each course, important general ones for me are that the work (1) be thorough, (2) reflect an understanding of the appropriate content, (3) be well written, well organized, spelled and punctuated correctly, and argued logically, (4) show a critical analysis, and (5) relate, where relevant, to the student's experience. While I have set the criteria in the past, another alternative would be to develop standards with students at the outset of the course. Students appreciate such explicit expectations and, with the competitiveness eliminated, meet and often surpass the academic performance typical of classes graded in a traditional manner.

One mistake I made when initiating a contract grading system was to have too many of the assignments come due late in the semester. If work did not meet the stated criteria, I was hesitant to ask that it be redone since we were so close to the end of the semester. I have since learned that to make contract grading effective, assignments must be spaced periodically throughout the entire semester so students have ample time to improve the quality of inadequate work.

INTEGRATION OF COGNITIVE AND AFFECTIVE LEARNING

Feminism values both intellectual and emotional capabilities. Feminists struggle to change the overly rational premises of male-dominated social relations and institutions, and to incorporate priorities appreciative of human needs and feelings. Similarly, we wish to strengthen women's intellectual abilities, so long suppressed by sexist norms and institutions. Our teaching can synthesize both the cognitive and affective areas of human learning. Since many academic women are adept at teaching cognitive material, I would like to suggest ways to incorporate affective learning into the curriculum.

One common device is the journal. In "Women's Image," we require each student to keep a journal in which she analyzes the reading and lectures and then relates the material to her personal experience. While reading and commenting on journals requires time and sensitivity from the instructor, the value to students is significant.

Experiential activities – structured participatory experiences to draw out feelings – also enable students to relate personally with course content. Simulation games are a familiar example. In "Issues of Racism and Sexism in the Helping Professions," students participate in an activity which enables them to experience being on the "ins" and "outs" of a power group. I explain that we will do an exercise in which a volunteer, on the outside of a circle, will try to break into the circle. A person volunteers; all others hold hands to form a closed circle. The outsider usually tries a variety of strategies before she gets in or gives up. We process the activity by sharing how we felt during the activity and how that experience compares to the dynamics of racism and sexism in society. We explore alternatives that both those in the power circle and the outsider had available to them but didn't think of or decide to use. We particularly focus on the choices white people and men have but don't act on because an "authority" sets the norms of "the game." In discussing this activity, some students discover that they were thinking of challenging the norms but didn't speak out. I ask people to consider the ways their personal behavior in the exercise reflects their behavior in real life. Some students who were in the circle mention their willingness to conform to group norms, their lack of familiarity with thinking creatively of alternatives, and their fear of taking risks. Such an experiential activity elicits powerful personal and social learning.

Affective learning can be integrated into a cognitively structured course through questions about the material that require students to make personal connections. After reading *Daughter of Earth* by Agnes Smedley, I might ask: What are the contradictions that Marie struggles with as a woman? How do you relate to and deal with these dilemmas in your own life? Dilemmas that students point to include: (1) the tension between family responsibility and ties, and the need to escape their limits, (2) a woman's difficult search for a life that includes both independence and loving relationships, and (3) the sometimes conflicting priorities between personal needs and the need to be involved in meaningful social change. The poignancy and power of themes in the novel relate to students' experiences, and significant insights can emerge from a discussion of such processing questions.

Finally, to include literature, poetry, and songs in courses in any discipline infuses material with feelings unevoked by much analytical writing. Among the short stories used in "Women and Work" are: "Louisa" by Mary Wilkes Freeman, "I Was Marching" by Meridel LeSueur, "I Stand Here Ironing" by Tillie Olsen, and "In Search of Our Mothers' Gardens" by Alice Walker. Part of the last class in that course is spent singing some of the fine songs — many of them union songs — about the struggles of working women. I provide words, background music on records, and enthusiasm to urge on the timid. The camaraderie inspired by song is a new and rewarding experience for many of our "modern" students.

ACTION

As long as we live in a sexist society, feminism inevitably implies taking action to transform institutions and values. Perhaps the greatest threat to feminism in the university is the ease with which we can allow the curriculum to reflect thought without action.

Incorporating field-based action into my courses has been a difficult goal. Action projects are demanded for an "A" grade in "Women and Work" and required of all in "Issues of Racism and Sexism in the Helping Professions." In the latter course, students design, develop, and implement an antiracist and antisexist curriculum project, or in-service program, for a classroom or agency. They have written and used creative and provocative curricula, games and children's books.[6]

Currently, I offer "Fieldwork in Women's Studies." Here students intern in an existing feminist project such as the Battered Women's Shelter, Mid-Hudson Pro-Choice Action Coalition, Women's Crisis Center, or they can develop a program themselves. A biweekly seminar, incorporated into the course, focuses on strategies for social change and provides space for integrating theory and practice. They read sections of *Feminist Frameworks* by Jaggar and Struhl, discuss various approaches to change, and analyze the projects they work in from these perspectives. These discussions encourage them to look beneath daily workings of a program for its underlying, and often unstated, values and goals. Students not only take action, but through analysis engage in a dialectical process to improve both political perspectives and concrete grassroots efforts.

CONCLUSION

Feminism is taught through process as well as formal content. To reflect feminist values in teaching is to teach progressively, democratically, and with feeling. Such teaching rejects what Paulo Freire calls the "banking system of education," a system that assumess that one person with greater power and wisdom has the knowledge to dispense to others.[7] Feminist education implies that we enter into a dialogue with other students, meeting them as human beings, and learning with them in community.

Initially such teaching is not easy, because as products of traditional education, we must relearn. I have found exploring these changes a challenge to my growth as a feminist educator. My teaching and learning have become more enjoyable and stimulating. While ideally a course could reflect all five process goals discussed above, in practice this is difficult. What I've found important is to express openly to students the relationship between the process of the class and the feminist principles I espouse. Such discussion not only demystifies the uniqueness of some of these processes, but motivates students to analyze critically social relations outside of the classroom for their hidden underlying sexist values.

NOTES

1. Florence Howe, *Seven Years Later: Women's Studies in 1976* (Washington, D.C., National Advisory Committee on Women's Educational Programs, 1977).

2. Jonathan Kozol, *Free Schools* (Bantam Books, New York, 1972).

3. Thomas Gordon, *Teacher Effectiveness Training (Peter Wyden, New York, 1974).*

4. *Nancy Schniedewind, "Women's Image: An Interdisciplinary Introductory Course," Women's Studies Newsletter*, Winter 1978.

5. David and Roger Johnson, *Learning Together and Alone: Cooperation, Competition and Individualization* (Prentice-Hall, Englewood Cliffs, New Jersey, 1975).

6. See *Open Minds to Equality: Learning Activities to Promote Race, Sex, Class and Age Equity* by Nancy Schniedewind and Ellen Davidson (Prentice-Hall, Englewood Cliffs, 1983) for an example of curriculum for public schools that integrates feminist process and content.

7. Paulo Freire, *Pedagogy of the Oppressed* (Seabury Press, New York, 1970).

Black-Eyed Blues Connections:
From the Inside Out*

by Michele Gibbs Russell

POLITICAL EDUCATION for Black women in America begins with the memory of four hundred years of enslavement, diaspora, forced labor, beatings, bombings, lynchings, and rape. It takes on inspirational dimensions when we begin cataloguing the heroic individuals and organizations in our history who have battled against those atrocities, and triumphed over them. It becomes practical when we are confronted with the problems of how to organize food cooperatives for women on food-stamp budgets or how to prove one's fitness as a mother in court. It becomes radical when, as teachers, we develop a methodology that places daily life at the center of history and enables Black women to struggle for survival with the knowledge that they are making history.

One setting where such connections can be made is the classroom. In the absence of any land, or turf, which we actually control, the classroom serves as a temporary space where we can evoke and evaluate our collective memory of what is done to us, and what we do in turn.

In Detroit, I am at the Downtown YWCA. Rooms on the upper floors are used by Wayne County Community College as learning centers. It is 10 A.M. and I am convening an introductory Black

---

*A slightly different version of this essay appears in *All the Women Are White, All the Blacks Are Men, But Some of Us Are Brave,* edited by Gloria T. Hill, Patricia Bell Scott, and Barbara Smith (Feminist Press, Old Westbury, New York, 1982). Excerpts were published in *Women's Studies Newsletter,* vol. 9, no. 4 (Winter 1981).

studies class for women on Community and Identity. The twenty-two women who appear are all on their way from somewhere to something. This is a breather in their day. They range in age from nineteen to fifty-five. They all have been pregnant more than once and have made various decisions about abortion, adoption, monogamy, custody, and sterilization. Some are great-grand-mothers. A few have their children along. They are a cross section of hundreds of Black women I have known and learned from in the past fifteen years, inside the movement and outside of it.

We have an hour together. The course is a survey. The first topic of conversation — among themselves and with me — is what they went through just to make it in the door, on time. That, in itself, becomes a lesson.

We start where they are. We exchange stories of children's clothes ripped or lost, of having to go to school with sons and ex-plain why Che is always late and how he got that funny name, anyway, to teachers who shouldn't have to ask and don't really care. They tell of waiting for men to come home from the night shift so they can get the money or car necessary to get downtown, or power failures in the neighborhood, or administrative red tape at the college, or compulsory overtime on their own jobs, or the length of food stamp lines, or just being tired and needing sleep. Some of the stories are funny, some sad; some elicit outrage and praise from the group. It's a familiar and comfortable ritual in Black culture. It's called testifying.

The role of the teacher? Making the process conscious, the con-tent significant. Want to know, yourself, how the problems in the stories got resolved. Learn what daily survival wisdom these women have. Care. Don't let it stop at commiseration. Try to help them generalize from the specifics. Raise issues of who and what they continually have to bump up against on the life-road they've planned for themselves. Make lists on the board. Keep the scale human. Who are the people that get in the way? The social worker, the small-claims court officer, husbands, the teacher, cops, kids on the block. Ask: what forces do they represent? Get as much consensus as possible before moving on. Note that there is most argument and disagreement on "husbands" and "kids on the block." Define a task for the next meeting. To sharpen their thinking on husbands and kids, have them make three lists. All the positive and negative things they can think of about men, children, and families. Anticipate in advance that they probably won't have the time or will to write out full lists. But they will think about the question and be ready to respond in class.

Stop short of giving advice. Build confidence in their own ability to make it through whatever morass to be there at 10 A.M. the next day. Make showing up for class a triumph in itself. Because it is.

Try to make the class meeting a daily activity. Every day during the week. Like a language, new ways of seeing and thinking must be reinforced, even if only for half an hour. Otherwise the continuity is lost. The perpetual bombardment of other pressures upsets the rhythm of your movement together. No matter how much time you take with them or who they are, the following methodological principles are critical:

Take one subject at a time.

Treat the subject with interdisciplinary depth and scope. In a variety of ways the women in class have been speeding. Literally, they may either be on medication, be suffering from chronic hypertension, or be skittish from some street encounter. Encourage them to slow down. This does not mean drift — they experience that too much already. Have at least three directions in mind for every class session, but let their mood and uppermost concerns determine your choice. They have come to you for help in getting pulled together. The loose ends of their experience jangle discordantly like bracelets from their arms. You must be able to do with subject matter what they want to do with their lives. Get it under control in ways which thrive on complexity.

Encourage storytelling.

The oldest form of building historical consciousness in community is storytelling. The transfer of knowledge, skill, and value from one generation to the next, the deliberate accumulation of a people's collective memory, has particular significance in diaspora culture. Robbed of all other continuities, prohibited free expression, denied a written history for centuries by white America, Black people have been driven to rely on oral recitation for our sense of the past. Today, however, that tradition is under severe attack. Urban migrations, apartment living, mass media dependency, and the break-up of generational units within the family have corroded our ability to renew community through oral forms. History becomes "what's in books." Authority depends on academic credentials after one's name or the dollar amount of one's paycheck: the distance one has traveled, rather than the roots one has sunk. Significant categories of time are defined by television's thirty-second spots or thirty-minute features.

Piecing together our identity and community under these circumstances requires developing each other's powers of memory and concentration. When, as a teacher, you first ask women in class, "Where did you come from?" you will get spontaneous answers ranging from "my mamma" and "12th Street" to "Texas," "Africa," and "Psych. 101." They are scattered and don't know what question you are asking in the first place. Still, the responses say something about their associational framework. The most important thing about them is their truth. Build on that with the objective of expanding their reference points.

Formalize the process. Begin with blood lines. Share your own family history and have class members do the same. Curiosity will provoke diligence, and the abstractions of "identity" and "community" will give way before the faces of ancestry.

Historical narrative will be most difficult for the younger members of the class. Their knowledge of what it means to "take the A train," for example, will in most cases be limited to hearsay or music. They relate to TV. Minimally, you want to get them to a point where they will enjoy evaluating all their contemporaries on "Soul Train" or the three generations of Black women in "The Jeffersons" series in relation to all the family history of Black people over the last fifty years that they have been discovering with other class members. To start that process, convene the class (as a field trip) to watch "Soul Train" and "The Jeffersons." Then press for answers to the question they ask all the time, anyway, when watching each other: "Who does *that* one think *she* is?" In this setting, help history prevail over personality.

Or begin with one paragraph from a family album. Have each person bring in and tell a story just about that one picture. Go from there. One eventual outcome of such a project may be to encourage Black women to record these stories in writing, still an intimidating idea. Use a tape recorder to ease the transition.

To help increase their powers of observation and their capacity for identification, have each woman sit, in a location of her own choosing, for one hour and record what she sees. It can be anywhere: a shopping mall, a beauty shop, a bar, restaurant,

park, window. Whatever they feel most natural with. Ride an unfamiliar bus to the end of the line and be alert to the community it
attracts. Spend a week riding with domestic workers on suburban
express lines. Record the conversations. Help women learn how
to use the streets for investigation instead of exhibition. Have
them go out in pairs and compare notes, bringing the results back
to the group.

Give political value to daily life.

Take aspects of what they already celebrate and enrich its
meaning so that they see their spontaneous tastes in a larger way
than before. This means they will see themselves with new
significance. It also imposes the responsibility of selectivity on
the teacher. Embrace that. Apply your own political acumen to
the myriad survival mechanisms that colonization and domestica-
tion breed into subject peoples. Remind them of the choices they
make all the time.

No activity is too trivial for political analysis. Note that a number
of Black women, myself included, have begun choosing long
dresses for daily wear. In one class session, discussion begins with
the remark that they're more "comfortable" in this mode. What
does comfort consist of? For those who are heavy, it means
anything not physically constricting. For working mothers, comfort means "easy to iron." For the budget-conscious, "easy to
make." For some of the young women in class, comfort is attached
to the added respect this mode of dress elicits from brothers they
pass on the street. For a Muslim grandmother, cleanliness and
modesty are signified. For her daughter, also in the Nation, Africa
is being invoked. The general principle which emerges is that this
particular form of cover allows us greater freedom of expression
and movement.

Don't stop here. Go from their bodies to their heads. A casual
remark about wearing wigs can (and should) develop into a
discussion of Frantz Fanon's essay "Algeria Unveiled," in which
he analyzes the role of protective coverings, adornment, camou-
flage, as tactical survival modes for women in the self-defense
stage of a movement. Help them to recall the stages of consciousness they've all experienced in relation to their own hair.
When did they start to regard "straightening" or "doing" hair as
"processing" it. When did they stop? Why? If some women in the
class will change their hair texture, does that mean their *minds*

are processed, too? Read Malcolm on the subject. How do they feel about Alelia Walker in this context: the first Black woman in America to become a millionaire – for producing and marketing hair straighteners and skin bleaches. Take them as far as memory and material allow. Normally, there will be at least three generations of social experience personally represented in community college classes. Try to work with it all.

Go beyond what is represented in class. Recall all the ways, historically, that Black women in American have used physical disguise for political purposes. Begin with Ellen Craft, escaping from a Georgia plantation to Boston in 1848, passing as a white man. Talk about the contradictory impact of miscegenation on their thinking and action. Then connect this to class members' public demeanor: the variations they choose and the purposes at work. What uniforms do they consciously adopt? Focus on motive as well as image; make intent as important as affect, a way to judge results.

Be able to speak in tongues.

Idiom, the medium through which ideas are communicated and organic links of association established (i.e., community) must be in Black women's own tradition. When Black women "speak," "give a reading," or "sound" a situation, a whole history of using language as a weapon is invoked. Rooted in slave folk wisdom which says: "Don't say no more with your mouth than your back can stand," our vocalizing is directly linked to a willingness to meet hostilities head-on and persevere. Take the following description of a Black woman "specifying" by Zora Neale Hurston, for example:

> Big Sweet came to my notice within the first week that I arrived . . . I heard somebody, a woman's voice "specifying" up this line of houses from where I lived, and asked who it was.
>
> "Dat's Big Sweet," my landlady told me. "She got her foot up on somebody. Ain't she specifying?"
>
> She was really giving the particulars. She was giving a reading, a word borrowed from the fortunetellers. She was giving her opponent lurid data and bringing him up to date on his ancestry, his looks, smell, gait, clothes, and his route through Hell in the hereafter. My landlady went outside where nearly everybody else of the four or five hundred people on the "job" were to listen to the reading. Big Sweet broke the news to him, in one of her mildest bulletins, that his pa was a double humpted camel and his ma was a

grass-gut cow, but even so, he tore her wide open in the act of getting born, and so on and so forth. He was a bitch's baby out of a
buzzard egg.

My landlady explained to me what was meant by "putting your
foot up" on a person. If you are sufficiently armed – enough to
stand off a panzer division – and know what to do with your
weapons after you get 'em, it is all right to go to the house of your
enemy, put one foot up on his steps, rest one elbow on your knee
and play in the family. That is another way of saying play the
dozens, which also is a way of saying low-rate your enemy's
ancestors and him, down to the present moment for reference, and
then go into his future as far as your imagination leads you. But if
you have no faith in your personal courage and confidence in your
arsenal, don't try it. It is a risky pleasure. So then I had a measure
of this Big Sweet.

"Hurt who?" Mrs. Bertha snorted at my fears. "Big Sweet?
Humph! Tain't a man, woman nor child on this job going to tackle
Big Sweet. If God send her a pistol she'll send him a man. She can
handle a knife with anybody, She'll join hands and cut a duel. Dat
Cracker Quarters Boss wears two pistols round his waist and goes
for bad, but he won't break a breath with Big Sweet lessen he got
his pistol in his hand. Cause if he start anything with her, he won't
never get a chance to draw it. She ain't mean. She don't bother
nobody. She just don't stand for no foolishness, dat's all."

Talking bad. Is it still going on? Some class members do it all
the time. All know women who do. Some, with a concern for
manners, find the activity embarrassing. One woman observes
that it's getting harder and harder these days to find targets worthy of such invention. Another, bringing the prior comments
together, says there's too little audience for the energy it takes.
Whatever our particular attitudes, we all recognize in Big Sweet
a pistol-packin' mamma, conjure woman, voice of Judgment, and
reservoir of ancestral memory – all of which are the bases of a
fighting tradition also personified in Harriet Tubman, Marie
Leveau, Sojourner Truth, and Ericka Huggins. Discover the continuities in their words and acts, and in the deeds done in their
name. Emphasize how they transformed personal anger into
political weapons, enlarged personal grudges to encompass a people's outrage. When words failed, remember how Aunt Jemima's
most famous recipe, ground glass plantation pancakes, made the
masters choke.

Take the blues. Study it as a coded language of resistance. In
response to questions from class members about whether femi-

nism has ever had anything to do with Black women, play Ma Rainey singing, "I won't be your dog no more." Remind them of our constant complaints about being treated as a "meal-ticket woman," our frustration at baking powder men losing their risables and of going hungry for days. Know the ways in which Peaches are Strange Fruit. Introduce them to a Depression-era Bessie Jackson responding humorously, but resolutely, to our options for feeding ourselves when that period's diaspora forced us onto city streets. . . .

Bring the idiomatic articulation of Black woman's feminism up to date by sharing stories of the first time we all *heard* what Aretha was asking us to *think* about, instead of just dancing to it. Let Esther Phillips speak on how she's *justified* and find out if class members feel the same way.

Be able to translate ideological shorthand into terms organic to Black women's popular culture. Let the concept of internationalism be introduced. But approach it from the standpoint of a South African Miriam Makeba, an Alabama-born Big Mama Thornton, or a Caribbean Nina Simone all singing Bob Dylan's "I Shall Be Released." Concentrate the discussion on each woman's roots, her place of national origin. Reflect on the history behind the special emphasis each woman gives to phrases such as: "Every distance is not near," "I remember every face of every man who put me here," "Inside these walls." Ask: what kinds of jails are they in? And what happens when we start acting to effect our own release? Devote one class session to a debate over whether it is an antagonistic contradiction for Black women to use Bob Dylan's music as an expressive vehicle. Explore the limits of nationalism in this way.

The whole world is ours to appropriate, not just five states in the South, or one Dark Continent. Treat the meaning of this statement through Nina Simone's recreation of Pirate Jenny. Play the music. Know the history it comes out of and the changes rung: from *The Beggar's Opera,* through Brecht and Weill's *Threepenny Opera,* to the Caribbean and Southern situations everywhere that Simone takes as her reference point. Know the political history involved and the international community of the oppressed she exhorts to rise. Particularly notice the cleaning woman's role. Recall the rebellions of the 1960s, when Nina Simone was performing this song. We all lived through the rebellions, but how did we relate to them? At what point did class members begin associating Detroit with Algiers, Watts with Lesotho, the Mississippi with the Mekong Delta, Amerika with Germany? Share your own experience and growth.

Use everything.

Especially, use the physical space of the classroom to illustrate the effects of environment on consciousness. The size and design of the desks, for example. They are wooden, with one-sided, stationary writing arms attached. The embodiment of a poor school. Small. Unyielding. Thirty years old. Most of the Black women are ample-bodied. When the desks were new and built for twelve-year-old, seventh-grade bodies, some class members may have sat in them for the first time. Now, sitting there for one hour — not to mention trying to concentrate and work — is a contortionist's miracle, or a stoic's. It feels like getting left back.

With desks as a starting point for thinking about our youth in school, class members are prompted to recall the mental state such seats encouraged. They cite awkwardness, restlessness, and furtive embarrassment. When they took away our full-top desks with interior compartments, we remember how *exposed* we felt, unable to hide anything; not spitballs, notes, nor scarred knees, prominent between too-short, hand-me-down dresses and scuffed shoes. They remember the belligerence which was all the protection we were allowed.

We talked about all the unnecessary, but deliberate, ways the educational process is made uncomfortable for the poor. Most women in class hate to read aloud. So we relive how they were taught to read, the pain involved in individual, stand-up recitation. The foil one was for a teacher's scapegoating ridicule. The peer pressure to make mistakes. We look back on how good reading came to mean proper elocution to our teachers in school and in the church.

We remember that one reason many of us stopped going to school was that it became an invasion of privacy. Not like church, which was only once a week, an event you could get up for. School was every day, among strangers, whether you felt like it or not, even if you ran out of clean clothes for the ritual. Showing up was the hardest part. After that, it was just a series of games.

Then, of course, someone inevitably says, "But here we are, back again." Is that a joke on us? Is it still a game? What are we trying to do differently this time around? To answer those questions, have women devise their own criteria for evaluating the educational process they engage in with you.

Be concrete.

In every way possible, take a materialistic approach to the issue of Black women's structural place in America. Focus attention on the building where we are learning our history. Notice who's still scrubbing the floors. In response to class members who pin their hopes for the future on "new careers," pose the following questions: How is a nurse's aide different from a maid? What physical spaces are the majority of us still locked into as Black women who must take jobs in the subsistence and state sectors of the economy? Do we ever get to do more than clean up other people's messes, whether we are executive secretaries, social workers, police officers, or wives? Within what confines do we live and work?

Reflect on the culture of the stoop; the storefront; the doorway; the housing project; the rooming-house bathroom; the bankteller's cage; the corner grocery store; the bus; hotels and motels; school, hospital, and corporate corridors; and waiting rooms everywhere. What constraints do they impose?

If we conclude that most of our lives are spent as social servants, and state dependents, what blend of sex, race, and class consciousness does that produce? To cut quickly to the core of unity in experience, read the words of Johnny Tillmon, founder of the National Welfare Rights Organization in Watts, 1965:

> I'm a woman. I'm a Black woman. I'm a poor woman. I'm a fat woman. I'm a middle-aged woman. And I'm on welfare.
>
> In this country, if you're any one of those things – poor, Black, fat, female, middle-aged, on welfare – you count less as a human being. If you're all of those things, you don't count at all. Except as a statistic.
>
> I am a statistic. I am forty-five years old. I have raised six children. I grew up in Arkansas and I worked there for fifteen years in a laundry, making about twenty or thirty dollars a week, picking cotton on the side for carfare. I moved to California in 1959 and worked in a laundry there for nearly four years. In 1963, I got too sick to work anymore. My husband and I had split up. Friends helped me to go on welfare.
>
> They didn't call it welfare. They called it AFDC – Aid to Families with Dependent Children. Each month I get $363 for my kids and me. I pay $128 a month rent; $30 for utilities, which include gas, electricity, and water; $120 for food and nonedible household

essentials; $50 for school lunches for the three children in junior and senior high school who are not eligible for reduced-cost meal programs. This leaves $5 per person a month for everything else — clothing, shoes, recreation, incidental personal expenses, and transportation. This check allows $1 a month for transportation for me but none for my children. That's how we live.

Welfare is all about dependency. It is the most prejudiced institution in this country, even more than marriage, which it tries to imitate.

The truth is that AFDC is like a super-sexist marriage. You trade in *a* man for *the* man. But you can't divorce him if he treats you bad. He can divorce you, of course, cut you off anytime he wants. But in that case, he keeps the kids, not you.

The man runs everything. In ordinary marriage, sex is supposed to be for your husband. On AFDC, you're not supposed to have any sex at all. You give up control of your own body. It's a condition of aid. You may even have to agree to get your tubes tied so you can never have more children, just to avoid being cut off welfare.

The man, the welfare system, controls your money. He tells you what to buy, what not to buy, where to buy it, and how much things cost. If things — rent, for instance — really cost more than he says they do, it's just too bad for you. You've got to make your money stretch.

The man can break into your home any time he wants to and poke into your things. You've got no right to protest. You've got no right to privacy. Like I said, welfare's a super-sexist marriage.

Discuss what it means to live like that. What lines of force and power in society does it imply? A significant percentage of Black women have had direct experience with welfare, either as children or as mothers. In discussing "how it happened to them," all become aware of how every woman in class is just one step away from that bottom line. A separation, a work injury, layoffs, a prolonged illness, a child's disability could put them on those rolls. It is a sobering realization, breaking through some of the superior attitudes even Black women have internalized about AFDC recipients.

What other work do we do, and how does it shape our thinking? Read Studs Terkel's *Working* and compare Maggie Holmes, domestic; Alice Washington, shoe factory order-filler; Diane Wilson, process clerk. Study what women just like those in class say about themselves. Although, as with everything, a whole course could be devoted just to analyzing the content, process, and consciousness of Black women's jobs, be satisfied in this survey to personify history so that it becomes recognizable and immediate; something they participate in.

Have a dream.

The conclusion to be drawn from any study of our history in America is that the balance of power is not on our side, while the burden of justice is. This can be an overwhelming insight, particularly in times of economic stagnation, physical deterioration, and organizational confusion. Therefore, it is important to balance any discussion of the material circumstances of Black women's lives with some attention to the realm of their dreams.

In all other areas of life, we can talk about struggle, organization, sabotage, survival, even tactical and strategic victory. However, only in dreams are liberation and judgment at the center of vision. That is where we do all the things in imagination that our awareness demands but our situation does not yet permit. In dreams, we seek the place in the sun that society denies us. And here, as in everything, a continuum of consciousness will be represented.

At their most fetishistic, Black women's spiritual dreams are embodied in the culture of numbers, signs, and gambling. In every poor community, holy water, herb, astrology, and dream book shops are for women what poolrooms, pawnshops, and bars are for men. Places to hang on, hoping for a hit. As Etheridge Knight has observed in *Black Voices from Prison,* "It is as common to hear a mother say, 'I gotta get my number in today' with the same concern and sometimes in the same breath as she says, 'I gotta feed the baby' . . . In some homes the dream book is as familiar and treated with as much reverence as the Bible." In many homes, dream books produce more tangible results.

The most progressive expression of our dreams, however, in which mass liberation takes precedence over individual relief, and planning replaces luck, is occasionally articulated in literature. Sarah Wright provides such an example in *This Child's Gonna Live.* In that story of a Black family desperately trying to hold on to its territorial birthright and each other in Depression-Maryland, the most fundamental religiosity of poor Black people is recreated, its naturalism released. The landscape is made to hold our suffering and signify our fate. Particularly in the person of Mariah Upshur, the faith of the oppressed which helps us to fight on long after a cause seems lost is complemented by a belief that righteousness can make you invincible. Colloquially speaking, all that's needed is for God to send the sufferers a pretty day. Then, children will be cured of worms, the land thieves will be driven from the community, the wind will be calm for the oystermen, the newly planted rye will hold, and a future will be possible in a land of "slowing-up roads" and death. That is, if we're deserving. What does "deserving" mean? Discuss Richard Wright's approach to this subject in "Bright and Morning Star."

Relate the fundamental hopes and values of Mariah Upshur's dream to other belief systems through which people have been able to attain freedom. The concrete experience of people "moving mountains" is communicated by the story of Tachai in the People's Republic of China. The triumph of vision, perseverance, and organization over brute force to regain land is demonstrated in Vietnam and Cuba. Spell out the commonalities in all liberation struggles in this age which vanquish the moneychangers. Find examples in our own history where beginnings have been made of this kind. Make the Word become Flesh, so the new day that's dawning belongs to you and me.

As teachers, we should be able to explore all these things and more without resorting to conventional ideological labels. This is the basic, introductory course. Once the experiential base of the class-in-itself is richly felt and understood, theoretical threads can be woven between W. E. B. DuBois, Zora Neale Hurston, and Frantz Fanon. Then bridges can be built connecting the lives of ghettoized women of every color and nationality. In the third series of courses, great individuals can be put in historical perspective; organized movements can be studied. In the fourth stage, movements, themselves, may arise. Political possibilities for action then flow from an understanding conditioned by life on the block, but not bound by it. And the beginnings of a class-for-itself may take shape. But the first step, and the most fundamental, should be the goal of the first course: recognizing *ourselves* in history.

Self-Disclosure and the Commitment to Social Change*

by Evelyn Torton Beck

Question: "What are your feelings about a teacher's self-disclosure?"

Answer: "I think it is entertaining and helps pass the lecture time."

From student questionnaires, Fall 1979

MY INTEREST in the theoretical aspects of self-disclosure grew out of my experiences in teaching. For a long time, I believed that by introducing myself on the opening day of every new class, the students would better know what I was bringing to the material and what to expect from class. Therefore, on day one, it has been my practice to sketch out my intellectual history: how and why I came to develop the particular course, how I selected the material, and what I expect of students. I also give a quick overview of those facts of my life, past and present, which seem most relevant to that class. For example, I wouldn't dream of not being out in a class on "Lesbian Culture," and I always say I am Jewish to the class on "The Jewish Woman." Recently, I also began to add that I am primarily a cultural Jew after I discovered that students assumed I was orthodox unless I said otherwise. Clearly, whatever is the norm for any group will be assumed to be true of the teacher unless she declares her difference from that norm.

Satisfactory definitions for self-disclosure are difficult to find, and there is always the danger of oversimplification. What exactly constitutes self-disclosure? (The minute we open our mouths

---

*This article originally appeared in *Women's Studies International Forum,* vol. 6 no. 2 ("Women in Academe" issue, edited by Resa Dudovitz).

we self-disclose. On the nonverbal level, we do it even before then.) Where is the line to be drawn? And what about quantity? How much should we disclose on any given subject? In any given situation we may tell a great deal about ourselves without ever thinking of it as self-disclosure. We only begin to call it self-disclosure when we talk about ourselves in situations where one would not expect certain kinds of information to be announced.

According to patriarchal concepts, anything personal in the classroom would have to be considered self-disclosure. Socially unacceptable or difficult facts are almost always considered self-disclosure, too. Moreover, I think our own comfort level with information we give also determines whether we perceive ourselves to be self-disclosing or "just talking." When I talked about being Jewish in classes, I never thought it was particularly personal information. But the minute I add, as I have been doing lately, that I am a refugee from Hitler, it feels like real self-disclosure, whether I am in someone's living room, in the classroom, or at the Modern Language Association Convention. I suspect that our attitudes toward self-disclosure do not remain the same over time, but change as we change, as the times and circumstances change. If there were no homophobia in our society, coming out would no longer be an issue, and we would not have to worry, to paraphrase both Adrienne Rich and Audre Lorde, that the undisclosed will soon become the undisclosable.

My investigation of self-disclosure grew out of an ongoing dialogue I was engaged in with a colleague in the School of Social Work at the University of Wisconsin (Madison). Typically, our conversations went something like this:

"I think it is vital to tell students who I am. Women need role models and visible support. The more the students know about me, the more effective I can be as a feminist teacher."

"But if you tell them too much about your lifestyle, you will lose credibility, just as I would if I told my students that I had a son who was schizophrenic. Students will say you are biased."

This perpetual discussion had no natural end, so we decided to do a little experiment. When the appropriate topic came up, she would tell the students about her son, and I would continue to self-disclose as I had been doing. Then we would draft a simple questionnaire which we would distribute at the end of the semester, asking whether students thought we had, in fact, self-disclosed; if they found it helpful to their learning; and what their feelings about self-disclosure were. In all, we collected 161 answers; 125 from her large lecture class in social work, 36 from several of my smaller advanced classes.

Reading through these questionnaires, I was struck with the sameness of the answers, though neither of us had ever brought up the issue of self-disclosure as a topic for classroom discussion. Overwhelmingly, students thought the teacher's self-disclosure humanized the classroom and was important to their learning. They also said it encouraged openness in students, created a good atmosphere, brought unity to the group, validated diversity, and altogether made the class more meaningful. Only a handful were indifferent or actively annoyed by the self-disclosures (and these were all in the large lecture class where such behavior from a teacher was probably more unexpected). But, at the same time, dozens of these students also gave the same caveats: "Yes, but only if it is appropriate to the subject matter." "If it doesn't take up too much time." "If the teacher isn't doing it only to satisfy her own needs." "It depends on the teacher's personality and comfort level." I was impressed. The students (a mixture of graduate students and undergraduates representing a variety of disciplines) obviously saw that self-disclosure was positive, but that it did have its limitations and dangers.

While most of my students have responded favorably to my openness and said it helped them to learn (even before the questionnaires), I have also come to realize that in some classes, my self-disclosing so early in the semester alienated a few students (particularly those who had no previous experience with feminist pedagogy). By explaining the philosophy behind my feminist teaching (my belief in the importance of synthesis and wholeness) early in the semester, I consciously try to prepare the students for the emotional impact of this pedagogy on their lives. With such an introduction, even students unfamiliar with feminist teaching usually welcome the possibilities of the approach. But typically there are one or two who resist, even resent integrating the "personal" with the "academic," perhaps because it too deeply threatens their learned responses to the academy.

Because I have developed a reputation as a feminist at the university in which I teach, and because in recent years I have taught more electives than required courses, my students are largely self-selected. Thus, I get many more women than men, particularly in courses with "women" in the title. Those men who do sign up for my classes are, on the whole, open to a feminist analysis and respond well to feminist pedagogy. Nonetheless, given our socialization processes, the women tend to resonate more fully to my self-disclosure and to talk more easily about themselves. Both male and female students consistently report that the experience of a feminist class changes their lives and their relationship to learning.

Not surprisingly, I find that my ability to self-disclose comfortably is strongest in the small, advanced women's studies class and weakest in the large introductory lecture with a heavy concentration of "traditional" students. My comfort level on this spectrum varies and depends, in part, on the kind of feedback I get from students during the semester. There have been large lecture classes in which I have self-disclosed a good deal, and smaller ones in which I have not. Since classroom dynamics are always unpredictable, I know that there was considerable variation in my degree of self-disclosure even in those classes to whom I distributed the questionnaires.

Was the experiment a success? Can I now use these results to prove anything? Yes and no. Reading the forms made it very clear to me that the students had liked our classes. The question is: did they like our classes because we self-disclosed, or did they value self-disclosure because they had liked our classes? Which was cause and which effect? How to measure all these variables? Fortunately, because I am not a social scientist, I am free to leave this question unanswered, and can go on to equally uncomfortable questions that this topic raises.

Q: "Is it possible to talk about self-disclosure without self-disclosing? If so, how?"

A: "Easily. You can be abstract and theoretical and leave yourself entirely out of it. You can quote student questionnaires and report on the research you have synthesized, particularly the extensive work done in psychology that tests the effects of therapists' disclosure to their clients. The results are largely positive and support the validity of self-disclosure, not only for the client, but also for the therapist."

Q: "What kind of a parallel is that? You are not a therapist; you are a college teacher."

A: "But the therapist is a teacher, too. Sidney Jourard, the humanist psychologist who first opened this topic in the mid-fifties, conceived his task very much the way I conceive mine: 'Education is a subversive enterprise − it is a process of enlivening the creative imagination, sharpening prevailing orthodoxies.'"*

Q: "All right. I accept the parallel, but I still do not see the necessary connection between feminist pedagogy and self-disclosure."

A: "One of the purposes of feminist education is to challenge traditional ways of seeing and to implement new ways of learning − break down hierarchies, empower the student. But the teacher in a feminist classroom is still, by virtue of her position, an authority figure. As our questionnaires showed, students felt that self-disclosure humanizes the teacher and makes her more accessible. Thus, self-disclosure reduces the student-teacher hierarchy without undermining the teacher's expertise. At the same time, self-disclosure gives the teacher the opportunity to validate diversity and difference in terms of race, class, age, sexual preference, and ethnic origins, among other things, some of which are less easily categorized. If she discloses who she is, particularly if she stands in opposition to the prevailing patriarchal orthodoxies (for instance, if she comes out as a lesbian), then she is using herself and her position as a knower to help bring about social change, to break stereotypes and prejudices."

Q: "Is there anything we should never disclose to students? And what about timing? When should one disclose what? Is it possible that by disclosing too much too soon, you discourage some students from sharing their experiences if these differ considerably from what the teacher tells about herself? What kind of guidelines can you give?"

A: "The best guideline I can think of is to trust the process. Listen to the class with the 'third ear.' Be willing to take risks or to hold back. Trust yourself. A little self-disclosure might help to clarify this point. In one class where I laid out a very radical view of cultural politics, I believe that some of the students never fully heard what I had to say the rest of the semester, or were not as open as they might have been had I disclosed less on that first day. Some may even have defined themselves as being against my views. This realization made me rethink my relationship to self-disclosure and question its effectiveness under some circumstances. It also made me particularly sensitive to the question

---

The Transparent Self, Van Nostrand Reinhold, New York, 1964.

of timing. I no longer feel compelled to 'tell all' on the very first day. Self-disclosure can also be gradual and incremental, building on the trust that is developed in the classroom."

Q: "One other fact about self-disclosure. Once you have disclosed, you cannot *un*-self-disclose. So why risk it? I am not differentiating here between the risk of coming out in class as a lesbian for an untenured professor, who may be in immediate danger of losing her job, and the risk run by a tenured professor with relative job security. The difference in magnitude of these risks is so large that it constitutes a qualitative difference. This dilemma (which is more practical than theoretical) is not my focus here, but the problem and the dangers must be recognized in this discussion."

A: "Aside from the commitment to social change, sometimes it is more difficult to teach a certain subject without disclosing. How does a closeted lesbian feel when she is teaching about homophobia? How does it feel to have to say 'they' and to think 'we'? When I teach about the Holocaust, I find it painful to speak of my own experience but would find it much more difficult not to disclose. And I do not do this just for my own comfort, either. I think that this kind of teacher openness gives a great deal to the students. It certainly makes a difficult topic less abstract and keeps the students from distancing themselves from it. Not surprisingly, one of my colleagues reports that she received her highest teaching evaluations in those classes in which she has come out as a lesbian. Obviously, if the teacher feels integrated and whole, she can be more effective in the class."

Q: "What else can you conclude from your reflections and research?"

A: "First, and most significant, I have not changed my mind about the importance, the effectiveness, or the validity of self-disclosure. I still believe it is a powerful component of feminist pedagogy. However, I believe we must use it with caution, measure, and thoughtfulness. I must not forget that the longer I teach, the more I learn, the more I assume a feminist perspective as given, the harder it is for me to remember how the world once looked to me. By self-disclosing too soon, I may be depriving the students of their own process. In the future, I will focus more on what I am still struggling with and less on where I have arrived, at least in the beginning. I also cannot overlook the fact that self-disclosing has some real personal and pedagogical risks. If the students' value systems differ greatly from yours, they may judge you negatively. Or, once you start to disclose, they may ask more questions than you want to answer. Conversely, you may tell them things they do not wish to know. Or you may raise expectations about how close you are willing to be to students, how much time you are willing to spend outside of class. If you set limits, you may invite hostility, anger, or disappointment. By self-disclosing, you may also invite crushes, passions, dependencies. If you make yourself too human, students may forget that your papers really do have a deadline. Or, worst of all if least likely, you may get heady and lose your own sense of measure and appropriateness.

"Surprisingly, I have decided that what is most important is not necessarily the act of disclosing, but the state of being ready to self-disclose: to be in a frame of mind where self-disclosure is possible, when it seems to be most beneficial; to know that it is always in your power to decide when and what to disclose. That kind of readiness means an internal integration and a willingness to take risks that allows for the unexpected in the teaching process, including the possibility of self-disclosing. I think that such a stance toward ourselves, our students, and the material we teach creates a powerful synthesis where the point is not self-disclosure for its own sake, or for the sake of political correctness, but because telling seems important at a given moment when it is most congruent with, and most organic to the teaching act. Spending so much time with self-disclosure has also helped me to know something I have always believed: out of our lives, we make theories; according to our theories, we live our lives. And I do not know which comes first."

"What Are Rights Without Means?" Educating Feminists for the Future

by Jan Zimmerman

WHEN Rebecca Harding Davis asked "What are rights without means?" in her book, *Life in the Iron Mills,* at the end of the nineteenth century, she did not dream of the importance it would have for women contemplating the end of the twentieth century. For Davis, the question had an economic answer: what did it matter to have rights under the law if women lacked the money (or time) needed for clothes, food, shelter, education, job training, childcare, or even busfare. Although the economic status of women compared with men can hardly be said to have improved dramatically in the intervening century, Davis' question resonates with added importance in an increasingly technological society that embeds social values in technical design.

What does it mean to have the right to a job, even one that offers equal pay for work of comparable value, if there is no public transit to get from home to childcare to job and back again? What does it mean to have the right and the money to purchase contraceptives that cause pelvic inflammatory disease (IUDs), blood clots, and strokes (birth control pills), or permanent infertility (some of the new, inadequately tested, long lasting, implanted contraceptives)? What does it mean to have the right to enter careers in technical management when one has been subtly – or not so subtly – discouraged from learning to read a circuit diagram or use a computer?

As we rush headlong and headstrong into a future widely acknowledged, if not always applauded, for its technological character, it is essential for feminists to educate themselves about the place of technology in their lives today and tomorrow. We must recognize the central role of technology in social planning, consider the force of material reality in structuring women's lives and choices, assess technology's differential impacts on women's lives, and explore its potential for furthering feminist goals. Sadly, most educational programs in women's studies – whether formal or informal, academic or community based – neglect technical subjects as irrelevant or antithetical to women's goals.

TOMORROW IS HISTORY

With technological changes exploding around us – literally in the case of nuclear weapons, figuratively in the case of video games – it is impossible to provide a comprehensive list of all the negative impacts technology could have on women's lifestyles, role options, career choices, or daily existence. Let me, therefore, provide just a few instructional examples.

For those of you who haven't noticed, the microcomputer revolution is upon us. Your digital watch, your microwave oven, your self-dialing telephone, your calculator, and your bank's twenty-four hour automatic teller all contain computer circuitry. Even if you refuse to buy a home computer or play Ms. Pacman, it is impossible to move through an urban environment without being affected by the computer technology that adjusts traffic signals, stores your name and donation to the National Women's Political Caucus or any one of thousands of other organizations, types (and typesets) your daily newspaper (and almost every other book or publication you read), or records your checking and credit card purchases. You may feel anger or indifference toward these technologies; you may treat them with gratitude or hostility; but you can't avoid them.

Superficially, men and women are affected identically by computer technology – by its invasion of privacy; by its ever-increasing power to structure daily life; by its random, aggravating errors; by its impersonality and fixed logic (soon to change with artificial intelligence). But when it comes to controlling the computer, as contrasted to using one, there *is* a difference: far more men than women know how to operate a computer, know how to program one, know how to build one, know how to turn one off. Like the automobile of fifty years ago, the computer offers those with knowledge and access the power to define many aspects of their lives. That power is not equally available to men and women. Nor will it be in the future.

Even as women seek to enlist in the ranks of the computer revolution, they are finding them closed. Buying into the need to train themselves for supposedly lucrative computer careers, for example, women are finding that computer programming and operations are no longer challenging, creative, well-paid jobs, but are becoming more clerical, factorylike, routine, and poorly paid. The pattern of job segregation in this ostensibly neutral "new" field is only too familiar to women who watched secretarial and banking positions lose status and pay as they became "feminized." Women are hired to perform tedious data entry or word processing tasks, to insert variables into prepackaged applications programs, or to check paper and tape supplies, while men are hired (or promoted) as systems analysts and information managers. The discrepancy between men's and women's wages in the computer field continues to grow. As one data processing manager noted, "we don't pay enough to hire males, so 83 percent of our programmers are female." Like an endlessly receding horizon, good jobs in technical fields seem always one step away from women — and women are blamed for their own ignorance or lack of training.

Computer jobs are not the only place where the future looks disquietingly like the past. The marriage vows between computers and telecommunications pledge a brave new world of video shopping, telephone banking, and electronic piecework from the well-wired cottage. By combining cable television or telephone line connections with home computers or hand-held keypads, it will soon be possible to shop for bargains from video catalogs, read the daily newspaper, pay bills, research library materials, turn lighting and heating systems on and off, or send personalized computer letters to everyone on your Christmas card list.

With their feet tied this time with fiberoptic or coaxial cable, women will once again find themselves housebound, constrained to act only in the private sector. For some futurists, like Alvin Toffler, this is a cause for celebration, since married women will be able to work from home while caring for children. (Nary a word is said about *men* working from home and caring for children.) For white women, this will probably mean data entry for piecework pay; for Third World women tied into the global assembly line, it will mean assembling circuit boards for computer production, a far more hazardous task, but one also done on a piecework basis with the home as the new electronic sweat-shop. Unfortunately, as one female noted in a recent Atari Computer radio commercial, the computer cannot cook dinner — the much-vaunted computer revolution has yet to revolutionize women's traditional roles.

These roles are reinforced by women's prospects at the other end of the technological revolution. Appropriate technologists, who would willingly give away second-car transportation or microwave ovens, neglect women's continuing double burden at home and work. Author Margaret McCormack recalls "watching college students bury a gas guzzling car on Earth Day '70, thinking that they had never raced in such a car to an emergency ward on the other side of town at 3 a.m. with one feverish baby in the front seat and its healthy sibling sleeping in the back seat . . . Nor had they probably ever tried using bicycles to shop or do laundry with two kids in tow."[1]

Although public anxiety about an energy shortage has temporarily abated, the need to shift to renewable resources and encourage energy conservation has not decreased. All too often, however, this conservation is taking place at the expense of women, whose (free) labor is used to replace the increasingly high cost of traditional energy sources. Nuclear energy advertisements make a point when they show a woman defending her washing machine under the slogan, "Try telling the lady she'll have to start washing by hand." However appropriate it may be to oppose a nuclear solution, we must still learn to acknowledge women's needs. In the debate over allocation of scarce resources, often settled by utility companies unilaterally deciding whose power should be curtailed when, women's voices are not heard. As prices rise, the anguish of women, who head two-thirds of the families living below the poverty line, is a silent scream.

In the area of reproductive control, by contrast, one might argue that women are vocal and active. A woman's control over her own body is readily acknowledged by feminists as central to women's rights and power. But too few feminist voices are heard in discussions about the reproductive technology of tomorrow. Consumed with more immediate battles for abortion rights and against forced sterilization, women have had little time to address the implications of such techniques as test tube babies (*in vitro* fertilization), surrogate motherhood, Nobel Laureate sperm-banks, cloning, artificial wombs, and genetic engineering on women's role in reproduction. Currently, such high technology experiments are taking place on a limited basis, restricted to clinical settings and fairly wealthy participants (e.g. *in vitro* fertilization costs approximately $4000 per *trial;* surrogate services, $25,000 per pregnancy; rarely is insurance coverage available). Doctors, almost exclusively male, retain control over most decisions made about who has the "right" to participate, who has the "right" to bear children, and who has the "right" to select genetic donors. With the exception of some feminist health centers offering artificial insemination, actual alternatives in reproductive technology thus remain firmly within the male establishment.

Although the possibility of women becoming extraneous to reproductive biology is a far-fetched nightmare, it could become one from which we cannot wake up. Far more likely, though hidden from public debate, is the possibility of developing a class of mostly poor, probably nonwhite women, who will be forced by economic necessity to serve as the childbearing class for embryos conceived through the donation of genetic material from two (or even one, in the case of cloning) donors who happen to be of higher economic class. Rights without means, indeed!

Typical of most technological development, the rapid progress of reproductive engineering is occurring in a private arena, without debate in a political forum. The public is "informed" by "golly, gee whiz" announcements in the popular press, without any real understanding of the implications for the future. If past patterns hold true, by the time enough women understand those implications and try to influence their direction, the technology will be considered a *fait accompli* to be resisted only by ignorant opponents of "progress."

In this manner, an entire myth of "technological determinism" has been constructed to place the blame on Mother Nature for the path of technical development. In truth, technology is not an act of God, but one of man. Politics, economics, and social relations have far more to do with the particular choice of technological progress than do natural laws conserving the amount of energy and mass in the universe.

A SECOND LOOK

With all the negative connotations of technology, it is tempting for women to wash their hands of the whole thing; to denounce technology as another male power trip, another case of "the bigger the boys, the bigger their toys"; to refuse to deal with technology because it has been used to exploit the earth, dominate different races and classes, and enforce existing power relationships between sexes and between nations. But to condemn technology because it has not been "neutral" is to deny both woman's past and our future.

If "anonymous was a woman" in art, she is even less well known in the history of science and technology. Careful review of anthropological and archaeological evidence shows that women were probably the inventors of most tools essential for survival of the early human species. Everything from a sling to carry babies to a basket to carry berries, from horticulture to ceramics, food preservation to clothing design, probably resulted from female ingenuity, creativity, and intelligence.

Paralleling their absence in other fields of history, women remain invisible, but not nonexistent contributors to technical areas. Even those well versed in women's history would be hard pressed to name a woman scientist or inventor apart from Madame Marie Curie. The name of the Alexandrian mathematician Hypatia, like that of Grace Hopper, the inventor of the COBOL computer language, is unknown to most. Few know that Ada Byron Lovelace was the world's first computer programmer, or that Shaker women invented cut nails and a revolving oven. Therefore, ecofeminists who claim that technology is a purely patriarchal activity do so at the peril of losing our own history.

Women have the potential to develop and utilize technology that could meet our own needs. With the proper encouragement and training, including inspiration from the past, women could contribute designs that would dramatically alter the vision of tomorrow that is held out by men.

For example, women could utilize computers to create our own information data bases, taking back the power to name categories of knowledge that are important to us. Since no major data base on women is currently maintained, a coalition of women's organizations (including the Business and Professional Women's Foundation, the American Library Association, and the National Council for Research on Women) is exploring just such a feminist alternative. Similarly, women could utilize computers to maintain our own information networks, computerized mailing lists, and political alert systems. The National Women's Mailing List (NWML) in San Francisco has established a feminist context for a direct mailing list in which each woman has control over the use of her name. The NWML also teaches computer literacy courses designed for women and plans to open Ada's Data Center as a public access computer facility especially for women's groups.[2]

Other women may choose to follow in the footsteps of Frances GABe, a sixty-eight-year-old Oregon woman who is building a self-cleaning house because she says: "Women shouldn't have to do their work either on their knees or with their heads hanging in a hole."[3] To GABe, it is pointless to wait for a social revolution to change women's roles; she prefers to change technology. With a little applied effort and determined design, women could continue to invent devices that eliminate the need for upper arm strength as a precondition for blue collar employment (just as the forklift and the chain saw have made women's exclusion from loading docks and lumber camps needless). Or they may invent male contraceptives or meals that children can safely prepare and clean up themselves.

TOMORROW IS A WOMAN'S ISSUE

As persuasive as these examples may be, there are more reasons than self-preservation and self-aggrandizement for feminists to have a technological education. First, we must seek to end all artificial distinctions between women's and men's issues. For too long, women have been trapped in a social service ghetto of childcare, health, and welfare concerns, while "important" matters of energy, economics, and national defense have been reserved for men. Told "not to bother their pretty, little heads," women have turned (or been pushed) away from the central issues of planning, research, and development that determine the shape of tomorrow. Not until women confidently assert their opinions, unafraid of intimidation by "experts," and control the allocation of resources will they be able to alter the ultimate material structure of society. Although we must be ever conscious of being co-opted by patriarchal values in medicine, law, and engineering, we cannot afford the purity of noninvolvement.

Second, in academia as well as politics, oppressive value systems masquerade as scientific knowledge. Sociobiological theories, which supplant social explanations of sex roles with genetic or biological determinism, are now touted as the rationale for women's place in society. Like nineteenth-century craniologists who looked for differences in brain size to account for women's presumed intellectual inferiority, today's sociobiologists propose "math genes," "left brain/right brain" differences, or sex hormones to justify men's position of superior power. Without the scientific knowledge to refute these egregious explanations, accompanied by the historical knowledge of why these theories continue to surface, tomorrow's young feminist may find herself splashing helplessly about in a sea of false "facts."

Third, women's learned "technophobia," encouraged by a society that wants to keep control of technology in the hands of a select few, has serious consequences for women's development as full and complete human beings. Artist Sheila Pinkel, who uses a multitude of "high tech" tools to produce her images, notes that technologies as "extensions of nature . . . allow human beings to see and do things that surpass our corporeal physical capabilities." Without technical knowledge, women are denied that opportunity for transcendence, just as they are denied the tools for developing alternative, equally valid descriptions of the way the world works.

One of the best kept secrets of the scientific world is that crucial discoveries and inventions almost always involve great leaps of imagination, flashes of intuition, or acts of faith. Instead, we are fed a myth of linear, continually accruing progress in scientific thought, a perspective available only through the distorting lens of hindsight. Who knows what discoveries women might make, approaching the universe with concerns about interrelationships among living things or holistic environments, rather than with a determination to sort and categorize the physical world?

Totally different paths may be opened, totally different research choices made if feminist concerns in turn influence technological development. Women may move swiftly away from centralized computer services to expand two-way, decentralized communication networks that better serve their needs. They may choose to exploit the capacities of electronics for simultaneity, ambiguity, or randomness, instead of forcing the world into an imitation of binary (on/off; yes/no; 0/1) logic. Women may choose to reduce research expenditures on cloning in favor of research to reduce the mortality rate for infants of teenage mothers. Unfortunately, because of the academic chasm between women's studies and technical fields, relatively few of the already limited number of women who enter scientific or technological careers carry feminist values with them. Perhaps equally essential to reaching feminists with technological information is the need to present women technologists with information about feminist alternatives.

EDUCATIONAL VISIONS

In the hope that visions may become the first step of a self-fulfilling prophecy, I would like to offer some suggestions for incorporating education about technology into the education of feminists and vice versa:

• Provide supportive, all-female environments for women and girls to overcome math anxiety, technophobia, and computer illiteracy. Sex-role socialization, antagonistic peers, and parental opposition can only be confronted through a positive program of female role models, a "safe" learning situation, and the opportunity to err without embarrassment. Whether in an academic setting or a community one, whether run by women's studies programs, by counseling centers, or by mathematics/computer science departments, such environments will be crucial to bring women "up to speed" technologically. Equally important is the need to alter the pattern of junior high school girls losing interest in science and math.

• Incorporate courses in the history and philosophy of science into women's studies curricula and include women's issues in course offerings in other departments. Like other subjects in which mainstreaming or separation is an issue, the precise outcome will depend on the politial and academic structure of the individual institution. Similarly, courses in the sociology of science, the psychology of discovery, future studies, technology and public policy, or science and society need to be illuminated by a feminist perspective. Innovative courses in women's science fiction, women inventors and visionaries, or women and technology can stimulate student interest while validating the inclusion of a critique of technology in the development of feminist theory.

• Encourage joint appointments of faculty between women's studies and scientific and engineering disciplines. Try to locate department offices or classrooms in each other's settings to encourage communication and cross-fertilization of ideas. In many colleges, women's studies and technical departments are so far apart physically that students in one are often unaware of the existence of the other.

• Seek opportunities to connect women's studies programs with nonacademic community resources in technological areas. The American Association of University Women, for example, focused on "Taking Hold of Technology" as a key topic for two years. The Society of Women Engineers, Women in Data Processing, and American Women in Science all have local chapters that can provide resources to campus programs and that, in turn, could benefit from a dialogue with feminist speakers at their own meetings.

Any effort to place women and technology in the same sentence, let alone classroom, is, by its very existence, a ground-breaking one. Until we recognize the need for a feminist assessment of technology and gain the tools to construct an alternative feminist design, women will be condemned, like the Red Queen in *Alice in Wonderland,* to running faster and faster to stay in the same place. For reasons of self-preservation, self-fulfillment, and self-sufficiency, women can no longer rely on the technological hand-me-downs of their big brothers. We and the rest of the world, need another option.

NOTES

1. Margaret McCormack, "A Feminists Perspective," *Social Policy,* December 1977, p. 18.

2. National Women's Mailing List, 1195 Valencia Street, San Francisco, California 94110, 415-824-6800.

3. Frances GABe, a sixty-eight-year-old artist, inventor, and building contractor lives in the world's first self-cleaning house which she built on 7½ acres of forested plateau. For more information contact: F. GABe, Studio, Route 5, Box 695, Newberg, Oregon 97132.

Charlotte Bunch and Betty Powell Talk About Feminism, Blacks, and Education as Politics

Charlotte: In this book, we describe a variety of different places in which feminist education occurs, in university and nonuniversity settings. But one of the questions we are particularly interested in is how education involves a certain kind of attitude toward life – some people are educators as a central way in which they perceive the world and go about their lives both inside and outside a classroom. For as long as I've known you, you have been one of those people. I've heard you refer to yourself as a feminist educator, a Black lesbian educator. You have said that your perception of education and its importance to the lives of women politically is based on your experience as a Black woman, coming out of a Black tradition of seeing education as important to the race. Can you talk about how you came to see yourself as an educator?

Betty: I probably started referring to myself as an educator only in the last five or six years, although I've been teaching for nineteen years, but the attitude you refer to is something that has always been there – from the first time I stepped into a classroom, in kindergarden. There was this sense of educating oneself and educating the world that was seen as a part of lifting up the entire race in the Black culture of the forties. We had our little graduation in my kindergarten in 1945 in a Negro section of town in Miami, Florida – St. Agnes. One of our themes was faraway places, and while singing our hymns in five-year old voices, I remember the Father lifting me up and saying, "Young lady, you will go far. You will go far places for us." The belief was that every person who could was going to use everything that education had to offer in order to go that distance, not only for yourself but also for the race. Education was the way out, but it was also a way of being. Everybody had a sense of that. For example, as a central part of the culture, the church was a place where you tithed for all of the Negro colleges four or five times a year. We understood that as we were giving money at St. Paul's Church on that particular Sunday, people in Negro churches all over the South were also giving money for the schools. So we had a strong sense of contributing to the community through tithing for the education of the race. I believe this grew out of the leap to embrace education immediately after emancipation.

The educator was such an important person in the community that I remember thinking it was something I could never be. I teach a foundations course in the School of Education at Brooklyn College – the history, philosophy, sociology, and psychology of education. In covering the sociological aspect, I teach Black history within education and language by using a photographic essay book by Francis Benjamin Johnston, the nineteenth-century photographer. This is her book of photographs (1890) of the Hampton Institute in Hampton, Virginia, one of the first Black colleges in the U.S. Her photos capture that total dedication and commitment to education as the vehicle for lifting the race – students sitting at rigid, almost reverent, attention in their math classes, their science classes. The philosophy of education at Hampton Institute was a hands-on approach combining manual with intellectual training. So you see six or seven-year-old girls and eighteen and nineteen-year olds in long dresses hanging out in the lumber yards and in the fields taking notes. Those images are so real to me because they reflect what I experienced as a child growing up. The concept that education was important was integrated into the race through the schools and the churches.

Charlotte: You describe the educator in the Southern Black community when you grew up as someone of very high status, an important person because education was valued. When we look at U.S. society today, education doesn't have that value in mainstream white America, and yet it is still used by every class to pursue its interests. The upper class certainly uses education as a tool — Harvard and Stanford, for example, are clearly meant for training the upper class, usually white males, to control the world. When I was in college, I realized for the first time that some people are actually taught how to make things happen with the assumption that it is their responsibility and right to influence and control the world.

Betty: From the point of view of Blacks, it's not being trained to control the world but to have more control over how we *survive* in the world: expanding our access to things in the world and our economic well-being. But education was also about moral and spiritual well-being. It was very much understood that we were to be trained to be morally and spiritually effective in the world.

When it came to the gay civil rights movement, I brought this consciousness and approach as an educator with me. Here I was, thirty-two-years old, embracing my feminism and my lesbianism at the same time, realizing that I loved this woman and that meant I was a lesbian and the world doesn't like lesbians. So I said: "What, are you crazy? How can we go out and tell them about this? We've got to make them understand." That was totally out of my Black consciousness, my Black being. The sixties had given me an increased consciousness about blackness, but the attitude was already there, especially growing up in the South. I knew we had to set the world straight; we had to inform the world where it is ignorant, where it is morally stupid. There was just no question about the fact that one has to educate. I use the Latin definition —*educare* — to lead forth, to lead forth the truth that is there within the environment and within the person.

For me, when you do know something about the reality of the world that those who stand in ignorance do not know, then you can't not educate. That's not an arrogant posture. It's simply about reality. If you're Black, you know things about reality that whites do not know because you have experienced being Black. For example, if you're Black, you know that your brain is not smaller; you don't smell — you *know* that. And certain people are acting, standing in their ignorance, like you have a smaller brain. So clearly there is a dialogue of education that has to take place; you've got to lead forth the truth out of this ignorance. It was very easy for me to make that leap immediately around gay rights. I knew that I didn't have two heads, and that I was not this evil person attacking kids and so forth. And I knew you've got to lead people away from their ignorance and prejudice. So I immediately found myself on stages at the Gay Academic Union and doing television shows about being a lesbian. From the beginning, I spoke about the linkages between the Black liberation struggle, the feminist movement, and the gay civil rights struggle. Talking about that was really preaching and teaching to me. In fact, preaching and teaching are synonymous to me.

Charlotte: When I first met you, I felt this immediate connection to what you were doing but I didn't know what to call it. Now we talk about seeing ourselves as educators and communicators, but since neither of us is a classroom teacher of women's studies in the traditional sense, most people don't think of us as feminist educators. Yet, what is at the heart of feminist education to me is this very concept you're now talking about: looking at the world and feeling the need to call forth people's better instincts, to challenge people's ignorance and make them examine it; and to call forth, in particular from women, the ability to do something about the world. I realize that a lot of my approach to politics as education comes from becoming politicially aware and receiving my earliest political training in the civil rights movement in the South. Much of my approach to feminist education has been modeled on a Southern Black education model — that combination of being the educator/teacher/activist/preacher. Until I met you and heard you calling yourself a Black educator, I didn't realize the degree to which my attitude had its origins in the Black Southern experience.

Betty: As we're talking, I get clear how the whole concept of education (education almost doesn't fit sometimes) — this passion for changing the person and changing the world — was there from the time I was five or six years old, making little speeches at my mother's social club on Sunday afternoons. These Black ladies were sitting there, fanning themselves and waiting to hear and see this little child being well trained to give little speeches that had morals. There was a special kind of urgency and importance at having the truths that we knew sprinkled throughout our lives. In church we got it, in school we got it, in the social clubs and community activities we got it; it just permeated everything. We were being taught and groomed to teach in ways that were not formal — just to stand up and give a speech. I gave a lot of speeches.

Charlotte: Another issue I want to discuss is the assumption that people are educable, that people can be changed by being engaged with other views of the truth. I think that approach is important for any kind of political movement. When I look at what goes on with feminists, there seems to me to be some who approach a situation and say: all right, whatever is wrong and ignorant here, we have to figure out a way to help people see it differently. And then there are others who say: Those dumb idiots, let's forget about them. I think it's important for a political movement to see education as very political because if there is any hope for the human race, we have to believe that people can change. I wonder how much responsibility we can take for pushing the people that we interact with to make changes, just as we have been changed by people doing that with us. This doesn't mean that we don't confront or get angry, but it does mean that we do so as part of trying to educate and help them to change also.

Betty: I really want to respond to that. Because you preceive that people are educable and that there are things that you'd like to communicate to them doesn't mean that you are perfect and that you know all the answers. Sometimes people who have the notion that others are educable come off with an attitude of "I know, I've been through the entire process," which is condescending and the antithesis of real education. Blacks in this country have experienced this attitude when people appeared in an almost missionary fashion to "teach" them.

Charlotte: One of the struggles that goes on with feminists, as it has with Blacks, is over our effort to maintain a belief in a different kind of power for change than force and militarism. The question of education becomes central to political strategy, therefore, because we are dependent on the process of convincing and changing people. To get the changes we want, we've got to convince enough people to be willing to work to make that possible: first, the education of one's community to feel good about ourselves and to stop our own self-hatred; and second, the education of our communities in the tools for change. What's interesting about gay men is that they immediately use the tools of the system that, as men, they already have. They know how to work the economic and political structures. It seems that one of the big tasks of feminist education is to figure out what the tools are that women need to be able to shape something different in the world around us. Education is getting the tools to help you learn to be more than just a victim of the circumstances you find yourself in.

You teach education and linguistics, not women's studies or Black studies, so you don't teach the content of our oppression directly. Yet I know you are teaching oppressed people how to have tools to take control of their lives and to do something in the world. How do you bring that perspective into your classes?

Betty: Formally, I teach a range of subjects at Brooklyn College. My field is linguistics applied to education, so I deal with foreign language students, or anthropology-sociology students who want to learn the basic application of language to culture. I also teach the foundations course. But no matter what I am teaching, my primary goal is to get the students to see beyond any of the givens that they have, any of the constructs they have about language or history or philosophy of education. It's not the content of the subject but *how* you know, how you get at knowing, that I teach.

Students are used to saying: tell me what to do, and I'll take down all the notes. What I try to do is engage them in their own learning, have them participate in their learning. There's a lot of classroom strategies for that. People have basically been miseducated by the culture. One of my most important tasks is to try to strip away the blinders: to try to get them to imagine another way of learning, another way of seeing, another way of being. Then I teach the actual content, which involves a lot of alternative educational techniques and breaking down barriers between teacher and students.

When I teach about women, for example, my approach is based on understanding that the people I am working with have been misguided by the culture, too. I must show them how to reflect on what they have been given, hold it out in front of them, size it up with what I'm going to give them, and start questioning. One of the tools in basic thinking comes by questioning authority. We just question it all.

It is essential to do this questioning because, in the final analysis, what we want people to do is behave differently. That's our revolution, and it's very difficult. One of the crucial tools is the ability to question the essentials and to question them not as an intellectual exercise, but with the intent that if they come up with new answers, no matter how discomforting those answers are, they will change their behavior. What you need, of course, in order to question effectively is new information, new data. Feminists have been producing this material, which makes it possible to question better and to have our actions respond to that new information.

The mode of questioning is very important when you look at feminist education. I try to create different visions and a new way of looking at the world in my classrooms. I also realize that students need guidance, so I am constantly with them: "Why don't you try another question or just a little piece of it." "If you're going to stop right there, you haven't gone far eough." I do this sort of guidance with everything. In feminist education, we need to develop techniques of helping people see differently and question in ways that are not just rejecting what *is* but developing and learning to go beyond it.

Charlotte: I've mostly taught feminist theory, and one of the main struggles that I've encountered in doing this is how to teach people to think. Particularly, I struggle with how to teach women to think because women have been socialized to be passive, to please people rather than raise questions, to not use our minds actively. How do you teach someone to put down the book, put away all the pat answers, and just think? I had a history teacher in college who said that for his test, we were not to memorize anything in the books, but simply to read them and sit down and think about them. It terrified me. How do you teach thinking?

Betty: Serious thinking is missing from the culture. While I don't want to get into lamenting on a cosmic level, we must note that within this culture there is a giving over of ourselves to technocracy. We want to be technicians around everything, whether it's a philosophy course or the practice of medicine. Most kids in college in America today are not coming there because they want to think; they are coming to get training or a degree for jobs. Both men and women are terrified if someone tells them to think because nobody has ever taught them how to do it. When we talk about feminist education, we're doing so in a culture that, even within its most literate institutions, doesn't foster a lot of serious, original thought. Women resist thinking because the culture is so resistant to it. Clearly, this situation is part of the challenge of feminist education — to recognize there is no way that we can move forward without really thinking and analyzing. So much power can emanate from the kind of purposive thinking we're talking about.

I've had the idea of creating cells nationwide where we think for half an hour together; we would all do it at the same time. What if we knew that Thursday evening all across the country there were 300 cells that were meeting with maybe five or six or even ten or fifteen women in each cell focusing on the same issues. I tell you, the power would be enormous.

This idea has been with me since I did a paper in college on racism – or prejudice, which is what we called it then. I lived in an interracial house and after I had written the paper, I gave a speech in which my point was that we won't conquer prejudice just by Black folks talking about it to whites. I had a very clear sense, on one level, that resolving racial problems was really about white people getting together and doing it among themselves. And so my whole thing was that you need to organize cells in every community, and once a week, people would come together and they would really deal with racism. That was 1959 and my nineteen-year-old vision was just so unclouded: if all over American white people were meeting once a week and dealing with this stuff, thinking about racism and analyzing racism and talking about racism, then change would occur.

Charlotte: It's fascinating to me that you had this vision in 1959. Almost ten years later, when I was working in Washington, D.C. (where I had gone to do community organizing in the Black community), we – white folks – realized that what we had to do was education in the white community. We started the Center of Support which did white racism discussion groups in the suburbs. They were your little cells. But our approach to doing those sessions was very linked to the fact that we had lived in the Black community and still had the authenticity of the sixties civil rights experience. We talked about race based on the education about racism that we had been given by the Blacks we worked with. When Black people say "We can't go on educating whites for the rest of our lives," I recognize this as a woman and a lesbian. What's crucial is that the education process beget more education. As whites, we were able to teach another set of white people, but the process began with interracial interaction, that initial education that we got from Black people.

At some points, education about oppression does seem to require what Frances Doughty calls *mandatory presence*. It requires the presence of someone from the oppressed group, at least to get the process started, whether that's Blacks with whites or gay people making contact with straight people. For example, we know that what changes heterosexuals' minds most about homosexuality and affects their homophobia is knowing "one." That has to occur, and yet none of us want to spend our entire time being the lesbian taken to lunch. While most of us can do a certain amount of that educating, we have to set up processes so that the people we educate will be educating others. We have to say, now that you understand homophobia or now that you understand racism, you must take that back to the rest of your people so they will change also. Each of us has to pass that education on. That's where your concept of education as an ongoing part of daily interaction is so important, and so different from what most schools teach.

Betty: It was at the Racism-Sexism Conference cosponsored by Sagaris and the National Black Feminist Organization in 1977 that I first encountered the concept of mandatory presence. One of the themes there was looking at how each of us could do things very positively around race and sex after the conference. It was emphasized that you cannot always have this mandatory presence, and when it is not there, it does not mean that you do not deal with the racism issue. The assumption was: after the conference, we're counting on you to raise these difficult issues in every arena of your life.

Charlotte: If we could teach this approach, people might understand better that after you've had a primary learning experience about oppression, you have to become the presence yourself, whatever your race, sex, sexual preference, nationality, or class. Frances once called this being "one-woman coalitions" who raise all the concerns of our allies, whether they are present or not. I get angry with straight feminists when I see women who I know have been through education about homophobia, who still wait for a lesbian to raise those issues. I don't mind doing education the first time, when someone hasn't yet confronted an issue, but when you see people who have been through that and don't carry it on themselves, it's frustrating.

Not only does our culture not support these ideas, but it also has perpetuated, if not created, the very problems themselves. For example, our culture treats differences as something to be afraid of, something to distrust. Look at the myths about Black people, the myths about homosexuals, the myths about women.

All involve terror and distrust of someone who is different from the dominant norm – the other.

Education involves breaking down those fears. It's not just providing information about the inequality of women or the inequality of Blacks. It's not just letting people know that some people get a bad deal. It's also speaking to that fear of difference, that absolutely irrational and yet deeply imbedded terror of the other in our society. Fear, insecurity, and hierarchy are so entrenched that if someone is different from you, immediately there is a need to rank them as better or worse; to worry that they're going to get you; or that there's something very terrifying about their lifestyle. If we could learn from differences to see that they make life interesting, then those differences would open us all up for greater possibilities. More important than anything that I learned about the facts of racism in the sixties, as an eighteen-year-old in the white South, was the discovery that there was a whole different way of seeing the world. Race wasn't just about being oppressed; it was also about perceiving the world differently, interacting with it in various ways that we now call cultural differences. That is an experience that everybody could have in terms of learning from differences in race, sexual preference, class, etc., if people could open themselves up to receiving difference, instead of distrusting it.

Betty: When we talk about educating people into a different way of viewing difference, we must look at what the media does to keep people locked into those fears of difference. One media technique for controlling differences is the integrationist, or most accurately, absorption approach, such as in *The Jeffersons* on T.V. In order for white America to be able to take in Black America, Black America has to be presented as the Jeffersons, which is to say, the same as white America. There is no difference whatsoever. This denies the richness of various cultures and their potential to powerfully affect the world.

Charlotte: The irony is that when you look at what the white-male-ruling-class mode of being has done to the world, it's hard to see how anybody could help but realize that the world needs some different approaches. Instead of thinking that women should be more like men, or Blacks like whites, we must recognize that the world needs the insights those differences can produce.

Betty: Unfortunately, white men do have the power to determine what is acceptable and good, and they take the energy from these various human movements and create the image of the Jeffersons, the Cagneys and Lacys. If we are really talking about looking at different modes of being in the world as experienced by Blacks, women or gays, for example, then presenting them as they are begins to diminish the power of the white male mode which is based on seeing itself as superior and dominant.

Charlotte: One task of feminist education, then, is to teach people to understand the differences in how things are viewed: differences based on race, class, sex, sexual preference, religion, culture, as part of the substance and variety of human experience. This is not to say that we are going to approve of everything just because it's not part of the dominant culture, but we do see learning from differences as positive. So, Betty, concretely, you've got all kinds of different people in your classes at Brooklyn College. How do you teach them to understand differences?

Betty: The first thing I do in all of my classes is start breaking down the barrier between teacher and student, and the barriers between students. Brooklyn College is in an urban setting. My class this summer had Black women, one Haitian male, Jewish women and men, one Hispanic female, Italian men and women, and very few WASPS. In terms of class, there was a wide range of experiences.

First, I have them introduce themselves and say one thing that they're really good at. I begin with "I'm Betty Powell, and I am very good at teaching, but I'd like to be better at tennis." So they start immediately having to come with their person to the classroom, not just their heads. Part of dealing with difference is to begin to have each person expose her or himself so we can see what we are here, what's the configuration. Then they must say who the people were before them. If this is a hard task, I say, "Just imagine if there were eighty-six students and you had to remember them all." It immediately engages them. First, they get a little uptight. I point out that education is about paying attention, and what we're doing now is introducing ourselves to each other, so they should pay attention. An initial appreciation of who each person is starts developing just by saying that's so-and-so and that's what they do.

Then, I do other exercises where they interact with each other, depending on the particular subject. A number of these are autobiographical things, such as giving three instances of having learned something, how they learned it, who they learned it from, where they were in terms of their family, environment, neighborhood, schooling. They write down these things and then share them in small groups. A lot of breaking through differences is having students share the commonality of their experiences. The variations on those commonalities for a Jewish kid growing up in Brighton or a Black kid growing up in Crown Heights are also great. Seeing that our experiences are very different, yet the same, is something I consider vital.

In terms of classroom techniques, feminist education can draw a lot from the human potential movement within education. We don't have to reinvent the wheel. There are many texts, programs, and workshop materials, whether you're dealing with 100 ways to increase self-concept within the classroom, or techniques for enhancing the setting of cultural differences. The Teachers/Writers Collaborative* has a lot of this kind of material.

Charlotte: You were teaching innovative education before you became a feminist. In what ways has being a feminist affected your teaching?

Betty: First, it's made me more convinced about the importance of getting people to question assumptions and to break down their own concepts. It just strengthened my conviction that if we are to learn, we do need to work differently and to learn to see differently. Second, my references to women and the condition of women in life come into my teaching all the time. Since I don't teach "women's subjects," I announce very clearly that they'll have to get used to the fact that I am an ardent and vocal feminist. Some are a little anxious, and comments go back and forth about that, but the consciousness gets set up within the first week.

As we're discussing the philosophy or sociology of education, I point out that it's been men who have projected these modes of thinking that we're talking about. Women have only just begun to give their vision of how we ought to be educated. Obviously, therefore, much is lacking and there's lots of room for my students to give their input. Thus, while it's not a course on feminist education, it's very clear that they have got to respond in a way that's more enlightened than how they came into the classroom.

---

*Teachers/Writers Collaborative, Inc., 84 Fifth Avenue, New York, New York 10011.

Another illustration is how I discuss pronouns after they submit their first paper. I say, "Some of you really struggled very hard with those pronouns, didn't you, using s/he." Some write it once or twice and then don't know what to do, and some of them don't do it at all. I tell them that as a linguist, I know that the problem has not been solved, that it's very difficult, but that they have to be conscious of it. They have to decide the best way to handle pronouns in their writing. Sometimes I'll give them an example or indicate a preference, but the main point is that they have to decide something about it.

Having established that kind of awareness in the first few weeks, I am free to make reference any time to women or to the lack of women in this place, or to the condition of women when you talk about adolescent development, and so forth. All of my topics give me room for making observations, or having them make observations, that clearly come out of a feminist consciousness. Most young women really do appreciate having that space to make their own comments about this or that.

Because feminism is so much a part of me, there's no way that I can teach without me or my students being affected by it. There is nothing that you can say for any length of time without running into sexism, so I just open it up every time and see where it takes us.

Charlotte: What you're doing teaching as an explicit feminist in the Education Department is injecting feminist education into that part of the curriculum. Unfortunately, a lot of women, especially those who are not white or middle class, are either afraid of women's studies or see it as frivolous or irrelevant to them. Unless we get feminist education into ongoing courses like yours, especially in fields like teaching where there are a lot of women, we're not going to reach these women. How do you think we can reach more women who don't respond to women's studies?

Betty: What I think would be good, and this has happened at Brooklyn College, is to get the faculty for women's studies to have program workshops for all the other female faculty, where we could talk about these issues. For example, I would like to go to some workshops with other faculty members from physics, from psychology, from anthropology, and share with them just what I've shared with you – some of the things I do with my classes. But I also want to get beyond what I do. I am still frustrated at not getting enough feminism in. I'd like to discuss how to balance feminism and my commitment to teach applied linguistics and my responsibilities to teach students how to think. We could deal with practical things, like teaching students how to write and how to read, which I often have to do in the first few weeks. After eleven years at Brooklyn College, I believe that these kinds of workshops where feminist teachers could get at some of these common problems would be enormously helpful.

I'm discussing reaching out to female faculty because I see that as the best way to reach students who will not take women's studies courses. If they're not going to take a course, they probably won't come to a lecture or anything else where you can get to them directly. But one could reach at least some teachers in those various departments and help strengthen their presentation of feminist issues through their courses.

Charlotte: How can feminist education be more relevant to the lives of Third World women in a place like Brooklyn College?

Betty: As a Black woman, I know that Black women in ever-increasing numbers are articulating what it means to them to be feminists and what their concerns are. Yet it's still difficult, and feminism continues to be looked on by many Third World women as not addressing the major concerns of their lives. Black women in college today, by and large, are not imbued with the same sense of education as an ideal that I had when I went to college. The culture has changed in these twenty years, and the culture today instructs them to get in there and get that piece of paper in order to get a job. That's a broad generalization, of course, and I do meet many students who just really want to learn. At any rate, it is very important for feminist education to deal with issues of racism and the insights of Third World women and have that in the curriculum. Women's studies also needs to have a consciousness of the particular situation of the Black and Third World women students on the campus, so that effective outreach can be made to them. There are many specific things one could do, like coordinating student programming with the Black Studies Department or with Puerto Rican studies. Such programs need to start with some topic that's very interesting to the students, like sexuality, but the agenda would be to talk about women's studies and what it can give them. Then you can have Third World feminists like me talk; that is my role. In a sense, it's kind of token, but it's an important visibility and presence. For women students to see a Black or an Asian-American faculty member saying, "I am a feminist," is important.

Charlotte: Following up on that, I think that women's studies and feminist education must take into account the life experience of women of different race and class backgrounds which may affect what they want out of a course. For example, in a working-class college, where many students come from poor schools, I've found that what women often want to learn first is how to read and write, as a necessary prerequisite to doing women's studies. So, teaching women to read and write can be feminist education. If feminists act as if learning those skills is not very important, we've lost many women already.

To reach those who aren't already feminists, it's crucial to know what each woman feels she needs to survive better in the world. Then we can both address that need and teach a critique of patriarchy through relating to that need. If we know why someone is taking a course, we can move from that starting point to a greater understanding of what feminism has to say or needs to know in that area.

Betty: Yes, if we don't pay attention to those needs, it only reinforces some women's suspicion that feminism is irrelevant to their lives. When a young Black woman is screaming that she has got to learn to play this society's game, that she's got to learn how to survive in this world, a women's studies course that disdains this misses her. A lot of my colleagues will complain that the students can't read and write, but they won't put any energy into changing that.

The important message to get across is that feminist education is not, and must not be, just the education of the few elite so that they can go out and play with boys. That's crucial. We can't move into the next phase of the contemporary women's movement without such an understanding, or without a significant number of Third World women really committed to feminism. But with such an approach and a broad base of feminist support, so much more is possible in the world. This is our challenge.

Friends and Critics:
The Feminist Academy*

by Elizabeth Kamarck Minnich

I USE THE TERMS "feminist academy" and "transformed academy" almost interchangeably, but I have chosen to focus on the *feminist academy* because it makes more explicit *how* we wish to transform what is into what we are finally ready to come out and say we want.

The problem in talking about the feminist academy is, as always, to decide what we mean by "feminist" – no small task, it would seem. But since I believe that it means what we are making it mean – that it is a term still in process, just as we are people still in process – I shall proceed by looking behind what we are doing and how we are doing it to see what we are, together, creating.

What is it that marks our work as feminist? On the most basic level, I think that feminism has to do with a cast of mind: a way of thinking, and a movement of heart and spirit; a way of being and acting with and for others. The cast of mind is fundamentally one of critique; the movement of heart is toward friendship. Both are strongly personal in that they must first be chosen and then developed by each one of us on her own, and both enable as well as require us to stand on our own, even as we stand with others. Both also unite the personal with the social and the political by questioning, and then refusing barriers (intellectual and actual)

---

*A revised version of the Keynote Address delivered at the Fifth Annual Great Lakes College Association Women's Studies Conference, November 1979.

between kinds of acts, ways of being, kinds of people that have been strictly labeled as private or public. And this refusal is, of course, very important because it is by refusing people access to the public, to the political, that those in power keep power and deny those they exploit crucial personal as well as political sources of identity, of experience, of strength. It is time we returned the distinction between what is private and what is public to its proper status as a useful intellectual distinction and broke its hold as a harmful political prescription with very serious consequences for every part of our lives – including, of course, education.

Let me first speak about the cast of mind and then about the movement of heart I take to be feminist.

The cast of mind is one of critique, is critical in the technical sense. Feminist thought takes nothing as given or settled for all time. It accepts no truths as revealed and holds none to be directly reflective of what is "natural," and so unquestionable. It sees the prescription in apparently descriptive statements. It is radical: it seeks the roots. And it is radical, also, in that it evaluates even the roots to see whether they are sound or rotten, with the determination to learn how to make new roots if necessary. (I know that's an odd twist on the metaphor: you can't *make* roots, can you? They are natural things.) But critical thinking, feminist thinking, is in quest of just such fundamental – founding – metaphors and refuses to accept them passively. "The roots of the tree of knowledge," for example, is a metaphor carrying with it the unadmitted, and therefore unargued, unexamined impression that knowledge is something natural and, like a tree, grows only by increment – inch by inch and at its own slow place. Trees, mind you, can only change within certain limits, or they protest by dying. *Is* knowledge like that? Hardly.

We have rediscovered what the guardians of knowledge have wanted us to forget: that knowledge and all the methods we have of obtaining it are human constructions. They are, indeed, man-made and so could be human-made. Of course they are. What else could they be? No one "discovered" the scientific method, the forms of rhyme, the methods of the historian. They aren't out there growing away, ready to be stumbled on, or laid claim to, or planted with our name and our flag. They were developed and discarded according to whether, and then how well, they served a purpose. The critical attitude leads us to seek the deepest level, the level of unquestioned assumption (which not at all infrequently turns out to be in metaphorical form), and then asks of the unquestionables *what* purpose they serve – and *whose* purposes they serve.

We have been critical in this sense when we have asked questions about the curriculum as a whole and about the content of the courses in it, and the results of our questions have led us to realize that what is taught is neither natural nor necessary. It isn't even particularly traditional, since most so-called traditional liberal arts subjects have developed very recently indeed and bear no resemblance whatsoever to the *quadrivium* and the *trivium* of the original liberal arts: to rhetoric, dialectic, grammar, mensuration.

We started by asking a few innocent questions, such as "Why are no women mentioned in history courses?" To our surprise, we not only found no answers (acceptable *or* unacceptable), but a refusal of the question itself, a clear indication that we had hit on a very important question indeed. Bit by bit, we uncovered the roots of history. We saw for ourselves the white male scholars picking out what was "worthy" of remembrance and what constituted an explanation. We were excluded from both the story and the analysis. It *was* his-story. We had found the limits not only of the garden but of the guardians of the garden, the rootmakers themselves. And we learned something genuinely liberating: it is very often precisely what is most important to those in power that is labeled "nonpolitical" (meaning not open to negotiation), or "nonacademic" (not open to discussion), or "natural" (not open to change).

The so-called lack of legitimacy of the women's studies courses that have grown out of our initial questioning, the doubt so readily and audibly cast on their necessity, indicate that they *are* important. No one says American studies are unnecessary because "*man* covers us all," or objects that it would be "divisive" to study European history. No one objects to classes on child development by saying children are covered in "regular" psychology courses so we don't need a separate course. No one says we shouldn't have separate courses on Flemish or French painters because "we study all the great artists and shouldn't demean anyone by giving them a special label." But they say these things about courses on women. Studying us is not considered legitimate because *we* are not considered legitimate, and that reveals to us just what the terms of legitimacy are and whom they serve.

Feminist thinking crosses the line between the personal and the political and then goes farther. It steps outside the limits and sees them not as given but as imposed and, therefore, as open to change. The full meaning of this vision is very important. We have begun changing the very definition of knowledge, challenging its status, thinking critically about its methods as well as its results. We are already in a new era, perhaps too new and overwhelming to keep us from naming and claiming it yet. It is often easier to see what we are up against than it is to recognize how much we have already accomplished.

But it is time we did so. Our era has in common with other great turning points in civilization a combative, critical, creative spirit that lets loose and requires every resource of mind, of heart, of imagination, of courage we have and can develop. And how very different these qualities are from the qualities of mind and spirit characterizing the familiar safe sanctum of the absent-minded professor, protected by academics offering unbreachable job security (because that is what tenure, which was designed to protect freedom of inquiry, has become). A feminist academy, having critique as one of its animating attitudes, will have to cherish not security but struggle. The safe, the proven do not need protection; those who take risks do. It will be a long time (a time that perhaps should not end) before feminism can be defined in any way that removes struggle from its very core. The feminist academy will have to protect struggle consciously and carefully, even when the struggle is within ourselves and with each other.

And that leads me to the second basic motion of feminism, the motion toward friendship. If the maintenance of struggle sounds like a paradoxical subject with which to bridge critique and friendship, it is indeed time we thought these things through.

I take friendship to be a relationship between equals and to be public more than private. It grows with being shared and cannot be betrayed by the taking of new people as friends because it is non-exclusive. It delights in difference, in separateness, demanding the honesty of full, mutual recognition, of seeing and being seen. Friendship, like the critical attitude, rejects the need to move in so close that we cannot be seen. It cherishes less than it admires and comforts less than it challenges.

As feminists, we *have* moved out and taken our own space. As we have done so, we have also discovered friendship; have begun to learn to value distance and difference, and the struggle that always comes with them, as much as we value closeness. We have learned what the experience and not just the concept of equality means. Equality is not comforting like intimacy. It discovers and protects — cannot exist without — differences (it makes no sense to say that identical things are equal); and so, to be maintained, equality requires an honest and critical intelligence that evaluates and that is not afraid of judgment.

Friendship and criticism go together, each being a condition for the other. Those who teach women's studies already know how this argument relates to a discussion of a feminist academy. In a good women's studies course — a good feminist course — who we are, what we know and don't know, what we think, and what we unknowingly assume emerge, are seen, are questioned, are challenged. We learn to be most critical of what seems most obvious and to accept only what challenges us to be more than we have previously been allowed to be.

The feminist academy will be one in which the engagement of friends is central. I keep repeating "friends" because I am also trying to substitute that kind of relationship for models taken from the family. I believe we should no longer be mothers and daughters, or even sisters, to each other any more than to our male teachers, colleagues, and students. Friendship is a relationship that is chosen, not a "natural" one. We are strong enough now not to need the coercive closeness of the family, of the private world, where inequality, not equality, is basic — the inequality of age, of dependence based on natural physical needs (and not-always-natural emotional needs).

Let me also emphasize that, like the turn of mind to feminist critique, the turn to friendship involves being willing to make judgments — something of which we have, rightly, been leery. It is time we stopped being protective and did openly what we never stopped doing privately. Friendship asks us to raise questions, make selections, fight for what seems best; and in doing so, to make every effort to be appropriate, to be sensitive to truth and to caring. We are called on to destroy distinctions that are harmful in order to make distinctions and judgments that are true, useful, meaningful. In this spirit, we will not mistake distinctions for judgments, or judgments for evaluations of worth: we will not assume that to say something or someone is different is simultaneously to say it or they are less. We will not mistake descriptions for prescriptions or vice versa: we will not assume, for example, that because a group of people can truly be described as powerless, it ought to be powerless. We will not assume that judgments proper to one specific area carry over to others: we will not assume that those who have more education are therefore smarter, or that those who make more money are worth more on any other scale.

What I am saying is that the crude intellectual distinctions and judgments behind racism, class prejudice, homophobia – and less obviously, perhaps, but just as surely, behind a great deal of what presently passes for knowledge in the nonfeminist academy – are not only alien to the precise and questioning spirit of feminist critique, but also to the open and demanding caring of feminist friendship. People who seek truth, like people who seek friendship, not only are not cruel enough but are not stupid enough to accept social stereotyping or the exploitation it creates and justifies. But we *will* make judgments and distinctions because we want to be clear and to find and fight for what is good. We just won't do so stupidly.

Little by little, perhaps without our fully realizing it, as we have discovered the cleansing thrill of the question that opens everything up and the excitement of freely chosen friendships, we have been transforming the academy. We have done more than we know. We know that we have added programs for women, taught old material in new ways, made it possible for new groups of people to join us. We also know that what we have done is not enough and is not at all safe, let alone established. Sometimes it seems as if we work all the time just to stay where we are. But in trying to do these things, even when we have lost, *we* have changed, we have changed others, and we have let loose a new spirit that will not go away.

How can we *not* know that? It cannot be our little programs that are making people so angry with us. It cannot be the extra work we do that exhausts us, because our tiredness is emotional as well as physical. It is time to stop reacting to the anger of others and clutching our (genuine) exhaustion to ourselves, and recognize the fundamental changes – in ourselves, in our work situation, and in those around us – that we have made and are making all the time. What is exhilarating beyond exhaustion is the new life we are creating out of ourselves, out of our own struggles, and bringing into the dusky, divided corridors of good old dim and safe academia.

So that we may realize just how much we have done, let us think for a minute about what the nonfeminist academy has been like.

Colleges have their place between the dark privacy of the home and the bright glare of the public world, thriving in a kind of half-light. They have been where young people (half-children, half-adults) were initiated into the "community of educated people," meaning males, of course. And this initiation was carried out by adults, many of whom had themselves never left the half-light of the school room. For years, white male faculties guarded their peaceful world against intrusions from either the private or the public world. They fought desperately against having women in "their" world, women whom they saw only as mothers, wives, lovers, caretakers. They fought against having anyone who served them join them. Because we were so absolutely essential to their private bodily and emotional needs, we were profoundly embarrassing and threatening to them when we appeared before them, as people do in public, simply as people.

They fought, too, against the entrance of people from the public sphere. Experience has never counted in academia. In their world, in their academy, they wanted a space free from both the private and the political/public worlds. This way, they thought, they could protect themselves from the threatening "darkness" and "femaleness" of "natural" needs, on the one hand, and the threatening "maleness" of the public world where only deeds counted, on the other. They called protecting themselves "protecting the freedom to think." There is some truth to that, of course. Surely we do need time away from the pressures of both necessity and action if we are to think freely and fully. *All* of us need it. But equally surely, the best thinking has been in touch with necessities, has been moved and inspired and torn by feelings, has been challenged and tested by action. Not all at once, all the time, in every case, of course, but sometimes, often at crucial times. The academy, wrapped in its tattered shreds of monastic scholasticism, trailing the religious and class and race and sex biases of its founders, has rarely been a place for passionate thought. How could it be, when so much and so many have been excluded? Protecting yourself takes too much time and energy to allow for real passion.

A feminist academy cannot be a retreat. In that fact alone lies a great deal of what is threatening about us. We have already pierced the half-light of the gentlemen by refusing to leave our feelings at home or our politics in the street, just as once we refused to be kept out of schools altogether. And we have also breached the walls of the monks' cells, the neat disciplinary and departmental structure of the retreat. In doing so, we have gone all the way back to the spirit of Diotema (from whom Socrates admits he learned his method): the spirit of questioning in the passionate light of Eros.

What does this radical change mean for teaching in a feminist academy? For one thing, it certainly means that the form of the classroom should follow its purpose rather than vice versa. That is not mysterious when we know what the purpose is, and by now we do. We ask of classes that they impart knowledge while raising critical questions, that they consciously explore rather than suppress the feeling and imaginative dimensions of knowing and thinking, that they help both students and teachers know themselves better for having talked together and met the people represented through the books and other material taught. We ask that our classes be more like intensely moving conversations than like workshops where masters train apprentices, or monasteries where priests initiate novices. Sometimes our purposes will suggest that one person talk for a while to give a model of consistent, coherent thinking; to cover basic information effectively; to make herself, her methods, assumptions, interests, passions, visible. Sometimes they require discussion so that there can be a mutuality in the interweaving of knowledge with analysis, of questioning with defending, and so that the teacher can find out not only what she has said but what has been heard.

We should be free to choose when we will work in which way, and we should add to this freedom the full recognition of our differences. Some people speak well; some lead discussions well; some can do both. Some will develop new ways of teaching. If we care about excellence and about each other, we will help teachers work as they work best because that is for everyone's benefit. We will seek the help, the critical help, of our friends who teach with us, as well as of our students. We will accept the frightening, liberating challenge of being seen.

What will we teach in our new ways? That is hard to say because we are still in the questioning and building stage. But already we have cracked the walls of the so-called disciplines, discovered that they are ways of knowing — tools — and that we can use them in new ways that then help us redesign the tools themselves. What I mean is probably already very familiar to you. Think of what happened to history when we set out to look for women. We had to redefine the proper subject matter of history when we discovered not only where the women were, but how central to all of civilization-building were their activities: building and maintaining homes, communities, schools, hospitals, welfare agencies, the arts. It began to seem absurd to think only of politics, wars, and tariffs as the forces and controllers of what happened.

We have whole new fields to develop, whole new sets of methods to define. What we are doing is comparable to Copernicus shattering our geo-centricity, Darwin shattering our species-centricity. We are shattering andro-centricity, and the change is as fundamental, as dangerous, as exciting. We will have to teach our new students and ourselves how to think, not just how to "master" what has already been prepared. We will have to develop in them, as we are developing in ourselves, strengths beyond those required of people except in times of major personal and cultural turmoil. Our teaching will demand independence and strength and rebelliousness as necessarily as the old teaching demanding acceptance and submission.

What do we do in the meantime while the new strengths, the new tools, the new knowledge are growing? That, too, is not a real problem. At first, we will teach what we know, but now we will do so from our new perspective, in our new ways. Our teaching will also be our learning. We will work on it together, using such familiar devices as team-teaching to help us work beyond our own disciplines, faculty seminars, and speakers or consultants from outside of the academy to help us evaluate both the substance and the process of our work. We will develop these devices and others, and use them comfortably because we will have jettisoned the pervasive (though rarely acknowledged) notion that we should teach only what we learned in the past, as we learned it, if we are to be "respectable." At least part of the impulse behind teaching will have to change from the drive to exercise authority – to profess what one knows – to the desire to learn together. Like most revolutionary goals, that, too, is an old and a dangerous one.

And do not forget that in our academy we must get back to the most basic questions of all. To do so, we not only have to be critics. We have to bring into the realm of inquiry a fact about humans that has rarely been included among those we call basic: we are sexual creatures. At the base of the complex edifice of our knowledge about ourselves as a species are certain givens: that humans are mortal, are rational, have five senses, have the use of language. All of these have been carefully studied in the name of self-knowledge. Assumptions about how these give us shape – and even set standards for human lives – underlie almost any statement made in any course, in any text. But that we are sexual, that we are male and female, has been ignored. "Human" has been taken to mean "male." We hear and say that a lot. Now let us face and never forget again just how fundamental an error it is. Our awareness that "man" does *not* include us is the touchstone by which we are transforming the academy, and our world.

Obviously, I do not mean that the differences between male and female have been ignored on a daily level. Quite the contrary. They have even been legislated. But they have not been examined, debated, or questioned with anything like the intensity and determination that the equally basic facts of our rationality and our use of language have been. Precisely to the degree that we are obsessed by the supposed differences between "male" and "female," we have refused to question them.

In the continuing spirit of criticism, it is interesting to ask why our obvious sexuality has been so consistently ignored by those who have made it their business to know. I think it is because the oppression of the female is at the very heart of civilization. This is a strong statement *and* one it is time for us to think about very seriously. The differences between "male" and "female" as politically and socially defined have been so important to the maintenance of the prevailing order that they have been proclaimed nonpolitical, nonacademic, and "natural." That these differences are *not* natural is obvious if we look, for example, at those laws which force us to act "naturally" in our sexual relations. No one passes laws forcing us to use language, or have five senses, or be rational. Clearly, someone has been served and served well by the enforcement of the differences between the sexes as presently defined. Long-maintained contradictions usually point right at the heart of the matter, at what we are unwilling to face.

Let me give a parallel example. It is only now, when we no longer need to exploit animals for food, for shelter, for clothes, for amusement, that we are beginning to take the risk of discovering that they are not as fundamentally different in kind from us as we have thought. Not long ago, it was heresy to suggest that the "dumb" beasts also have complicated systems of communication it is hard not to call language. It was heresy to suggest that they are rational rather than ruled by the mysterious forces we call instinct, for that would have suggested that they have souls, heaven forbid. Only now, when we do not *need* to exploit animals, have we approached our knowledge of them critically and the animals themselves with something like friendship — that is, openly, with a willingness to see what is there without prejudgment.

I suggest that the parallel with the study of women is not at all far-fetched. As long as we were conditions for the life of men, it was too dangerous to their whole way of life and peace of mind for them to get to know us outside of our domesticated state. We are here now because something has already changed. It is not feminism and feminist scholarship that are threatening the old need and dependency-based relationships between men and women within the family. It is the destruction of — or our liberation from, if you prefer — the traditional family that has made feminism and our scholarship possible. Our traditional roles are not so necessary to simple survival any more, and so our oppression has become more visible.

We have to go back to the most basic levels of knowledge, the levels of definition and of metaphor, to shape what we will teach in our feminist academy. We will have to be philosophers and poets and scientists in all our scholarship, drawing on analysis, observation, empathy, and imagination in all that we do.

It is no accident that women's studies courses often develop internships, use journals as well as papers, include nonacademicians as teachers, use supposedly outmoded techniques such as in-depth interviews rather than quantifiable "instruments," are turning to oral history — to people — as well as texts and other written resources. Nor is it any accident that many women's studies courses are problem or topic centered rather than being disciplinary *or* interdisciplinary.

We are already working in new ways. In a feminist academy, these ways will be central rather than peripheral. For example, I can see the familiar disciplinary studies being offered as supports, as service courses, for new, exploratory nondisciplinary classes whose topics change, develop, focus as the whole community moves in and out of them as teachers and as students.

We have also already begun to include the excluded as students, for *who* learns is certainly as important an issue for us as what is taught. Again, it is no accident that continuing education programs and women's studies have often been born together, or have supported each other. A recent study showed that returning women are now making up the majority of students in many women's studies courses. This coming together that breaks the mold of the "traditional" student is also radical and will have as far-reaching effects as the other changes we have considered. The "nontraditional" student started as an add-on just as the first "women-in-history" courses started as add-ons. *Both* have proceeded to transform the academy.

We know that the people who want to learn are the students we want to teach, and that having been a mother does not incapacitate you from learning, that working with your hands does not destroy your head, that doing more than one thing in your life does not mark you as inferior any more than being useful makes you inferior. We have already changed. We welcome all who want to learn. We do so for selfish reasons as well as on principle: all of us need all the help we can get if we are to break out of our cultural, class, race, and sex biases. We need critics among us.

This openness to the challenge of including new people does something else for us. It forces the deinstitutionalization of the school. We will have to offer classes at different hours, provide daycare as routinely as we provide mixers and football games, and welcome part-time teachers and administrators as we are finally beginning to welcome part-time students. We will have to let form follow purpose here, too. The fetishes of the nine-to-five day, of single-use space, of rank and hierarchy will simply have to go. We can't afford these barriers to the realization of our purposes.

If we want good learners, we should look for them wherever we can find them. If we want the best possible teachers, we should find them wherever they are and be flexible enough to shape working conditions for them. If we want to study the greatest minds and spirits and the best of the products of our civilization, we need to look for them – *and* to be willing to recognize them when we find them, even if that means changing our long-unquestioned models. How curious that the people who have dealt with life and death and sickness and love and healing and caring all are uniformly crippled in soul, while the people who have made wars, built economic empires, run inquisitions, exploited all who served their needs are those among whom all greatness resides. Surely we are not rejecting standards when we reject such nonsense. And of course we will make judgments. Some things and some people and some ways of doing things are always better than others in certain specifiable ways. The point is to know what those ways are and then to avoid the sloppy intellectual error and the cruel human act that makes of a specific judgment a general one. What we will *not* do in our feminist academy is to mistake one kind of excellence for excellence itself.

Think for a minute of the idiocies of which we have already rid ourselves. We are too intelligent to believe that human means male, that learning is the same as wisdom, that the excellence of any one kind of work can be made the standard for all, that people who can afford to do only one thing with their lives are better than those who must do many, that what is useless is better than what is useful, that critical analysis is male and intuition female, that love is effeminate and friendship masculine, that what has been should be. Minds and hearts that are bound by errors such as these are literally crippled, but we want full, growing people in our academy. We transform the academy by naming errors, not merely to dismiss them, so we are free to move beyond them.

Will we make it? Is it possible to deinstitutionalize education, to support and preserve the struggle of critical friendship, and to do so without ourselves creating a new orthodoxy? Probably not. The sadly familiar destruction-creation-protection-persecution rhythm of change may well catch us, too. But that is all right. We do not seek to found a new order; we seek to find a new way to be, to think, to live freely. That means we welcome change and struggle and can admit failure in order to avoid being stopped by it. And when we look at what we have already become, beyond what we have done, it is clear that more is possible than anyone wants us to know. It is time *we* knew it. The feminist academy, the academy transformed, is not some edifice awaiting us in the far future. It is here now when we work together, knowing that our work comes directly out of who we are, even as it moves us toward who we want to be. The transformed academy is us at our best – *all* of us working to be sure that none of us is trivialized, ignored, excluded, or oppressed any longer. We have come out – a phrase that applies to us all – and we are not going back in.

Resources

The following resources include extensive bibliographies of materials relevant to feminist education. We recommend consulting these sources.

All the Women Are White, All the Blacks Are Men, But Some of Us Are Brave: Black Women's Studies. Edited by Gloria T. Hull, Patricia Bell Scott, and Barbara Smith. The Feminist Press, 1982.

Building Feminist Theory: Essays from Quest. Edited by Charlotte Bunch, et. al. Longman, Inc., 1981.

Feminist Frameworks: Alternative Theoretical Accounts of the Relations Between Women and Men. Edited by Alison M. Jaggar and Paula Rothenberg Struhl. McGraw, 1978.

Issues in Feminism: A First Course in Women's Studies. Edited by Sheila Ruth. Houghton-Mifflin, 1980.

Lesbian Studies: Present and Future. Edited by Margaret Cruikshank. The Feminist Press, 1982.

New Feminist Scholarship: A Guide to Bibliographies. Jane Williamson. The Feminist Press, 1982.

Nice Jewish Girls: A Lesbian Anthology. Edited by Evelyn Torton Beck. Persephone Press, 1982.

Radical Teacher. P.O. Box 102, Kendall Square Post Office, Cambridge, Massachusetts 02142.

This Bridge Called My Back: Writings By Radical Women of Color. Edited by Cherríe Moraga and Gloria Anzaldúa. Persephone Press, 1981.

Women and the Politics of Culture: Studies in the Sexual Economy. Edited by Michele Wender Zak and Patricia A. Motts. Longman, Inc., 1983.

Women in Development: A Resource Guide for Organization and Action. ISIS Women's International Information and Communication Service. ISIS-Geneva, 1983.

Women's Studies Quarterly. The Feminist Press. Box 334, Old Westbury, New York 11568.

331

About the Contributors

EVELYN TORTON BECK, Associate Professor of Comparative Literature, German, and Women's Studies at the University of Wisconson-Madison, is the author of *Kafka and the Yiddish Theater: Its Impact on His Work* (1971), co-editor of *The Prism of Sex: Essays in the Sociology of Knowledge* (1979), and editor of *Nice Jewish Girls: A Lesbian Anthology* (1982). She teaches a variety of courses including "Women in the Arts," "Minority Women in the Arts," "Lesbian Culture," "Feminist Criticism," "The Jewish Woman," and "Women in Literature."

NOEL PHYLLIS BIRKBY, co-founder of WSPA, is presently teaching at New York Institute of Technology at Old Westbury, Long Island. She is a practicing licensed architect in New York and California, where she also taught at the University of Southern California in Los Angeles. Since the Copenhagen Forum of 1980, she has made several lecture and networking tours in northern Europe, speaking on feminist education in design and on woman-identified architecture.

BETTY W. BROOKS, Ed.D., was/is a part-time Assistant Professor in the California State University at Long Beach Women's Studies Program and a well-known women's movement activist.

CHARLOTTE BUNCH, teacher, activist, theorist, and public speaker, has been organizing for feminism since 1968. She was a founder of *Quest: A Feminist Quarterly* and has edited six feminist anthologies. She is presently with Interfem Consultants in New York, where she works primarily on issues of feminist public policy and global feminism.

BARBARA HILLYER DAVIS, Director of the Women's Studies Program of the University of Oklahoma, holds a Ph.D. in English Literature from the University of Wisconsin. Her present work concentrates on building connections between academic women's studies and the wider feminist community. Her research interests focus on the experience of women with disabilities and women caregivers in relation to feminist theory, and on feminist pedagogy.

SUE DOVE GAMBILL, writer, quilter, and organizer, was born in Paintsville, Kentucky in 1951.

SALLY M. GEARHART, a radical lesbian feminist, chairs the Department of Speech Communication at San Francisco State University. She wrote *The Wanderground* and *A Feminist Tarot* and has appeared in the gay documentary, *Word is Out.* She is committed to political action, particularly to animal rights, and is addicted to Aikido and barbershop harmony.

DIANE F. GERMAIN, B.A. 1964, M.S.W. 1975, is a social worker, counselor, feminist educator, performance artist, humorist, and a working-class ethicologist. She is a Califia collective member and a member of the Lesbian Referral Service in San Diego.

BARBARA HAMMER, experimental filmmaker, has made over thirty short films which are distributed by Goddess Films, P.O. Box 2446, Berkeley, California 94702. Partly as a result of this essay which she submitted with her resume, she was recently hired to teach creative production and feminist film survey courses at the State University of New York at Binghamton.

TERRY L. HAYWOODE, sociologist and women's studies scholar, has a long-term interest in issues of feminism, class, and community. She is a community activist and a single parent, and teaches at Baruch College and the national Congress of Neighborhood Women's College Program.

FLORENCE HOWE, Professor of Humanities, State University of New York at Old Westbury, is Editor of *Women's Studies Quarterly* and chief administrator of The Feminist Press. She has written, lectured extensively, and served as consultant on a variety of issues related to education and women's studies.

GLORIA T. HULL, Black feminist writer and critic, teaches English and Black women's studies at the University of Delaware. She co-edited *All the Women Are White, All the Blacks Are Men, But Some of Us Are Brave: Black Women's Studies* (Feminist Press).

RUTH ISKIN, active in the Woman's Building and a co-editor of *Chrysalis* magazine during the 1970s, has an M.A. in Art History from Johns Hopkins University.

ANDREA FREUD LOEWENSTEIN, a lesbian feminist writer and teacher, taught English and Creative Writing at Framingham prison for three years. She now teaches in and directs a small educational program for women in a housing project in Cambridge, Massachusetts. She is finishing a novel, *This Place,* set in a woman's prison, and continues to struggle to find time for her own writing.

ELIZABETH KAMARCK MINNICH, Ph.D. (Philosophy), is a member of the faculty of The Union Graduate School, a nontraditional Ph.D. program that encourages feminist work. She also writes, speaks, and consults on the critical importance of feminist scholarship and teaching.

MARILYN MURPHY, feminist activist, teacher, and writer – with one mother, four sisters, four children, three grandchildren, and twelve nieces and nephews – enjoys being a Lesbian-Come-Lately living in California with her Companion Lover.

SANDRA POLLACK, feminist organizer, teacher, and researcher, is employed as Associate Professor at Tompkins Cortland Community College in upstate New York. This past year in addition to editing this book, she lived for four months in the Soviet Union as part of a faculty exchange program, learning about Soviet working mothers.

BETTY J. POWELL, feminist activist, Professor of Education at Brooklyn College (CUNY), sees her involvement in public speaking and political organizing as some of her most important educational work.

MICHELE GIBBS RUSSELL, born on the South Side of Chicago, Illinois in 1946, learned to think fast and stand tall in the company of such women as her mother Paula Gibbs, Margaret Burroughs, and others. Her published writing spans the past fifteen years and covers critical reflections on the Black liberation struggle in the U.S., women in the social division of labor, popular culture, and pedagogies of the oppressed. She has worked as a political activist, community organizer, teacher, and artist throughout the 1960s and 1970s. She is currently continuing her life and work in Grenada, West Indies.

JACKIE ST. JOAN, co-founder of Antelope Publications in Denver, Colorado, continues to be a student of radical feminism. She also practices law and works with the Colorado Coalition for Justice for Abused Women.

DIANE SANDS, active in feminist education as a women's studies instructor, is director of the Montana Women's History Project and co-director of a women's employment project. She is currently working on an oral history of illegal abortion in Montana.

NANCY SCHNIEDEWIND, Associate Professor of Educational Studies and Coordinator of Women's Studies at the State University of New York at New Paltz, is co-author of *Open Minds to Equality: Learning Activities to Promote Race, Sex, Class, and Age Equity* (Prentice Hall, 1983) and *Won For All,* a cooperative board game about women and minorities in American history (Women's Education Equity Action Program, 1983).

SUSAN SHERMAN, editor and publisher of *IKON* magazine, was a member of the faculty of Sagaris, Session II. Two of her books of poetry, *With Anger/With Love* and *Women Poems Love Poems,* are distributed by Crossing Press.

SHARON L. SIEVERS, Ph. D., is the former chair of Asian Studies and Interim Director of the Women's Studies Program (CSULB). She is an authority on Japanese women, and feminist criticism of politics in the nineteenth century.

CARMEN SILVA, Chicana feminist, has lived and worked in Los Angeles most of her life. She is an educator, writer, and political activist with a vision of a feminist community that would work for everyone.

BARBARA SMITH, founding member of Kitchen Table: Women of Color Press, lives in Brooklyn, New York. Her most recent book is *Home Girls: A Black Feminist Anthology* (Kitchen Table Press).

JUDY SMITH, coordinator of the Women and Technology Project, recently developed a "Feminism and Peace" course for the Women's Resource Center.

LESLIE KANES WEISMAN, Associate Professor of Architecture at the New Jersey Institute of Technology, is a past faculty member of the University of Detroit and the Women's Studies Program at Brooklyn College. She has been active in the women's movement since the late 1960s and is currently writing a book about women, space, and society.

TERRY WOLVERTON, a white lesbian writer, performance artist, and community organizer/educator, has had her work published in *Voices in the Night: Women Speaking About Incest* (Cleis Press), and in *Heresies, Sinister Wisdom, Fuse, High Performance,* and the *L.A. Weekly.*

JAN ZIMMERMAN, editor of *The Technological Woman* (Praeger, 1983) and author of the forthcoming book *Once Upon the Future* (Routledge & Kegan Paul, 1984) writes and speaks frequently about the impact of technology on women's lives. She was named by *MS.* magazine as one of "80 Women to Watch in the '80s."

Learning Our Way: Essays in Feminist Education, Edited by Charlotte Bunch and Sandra Pollack, is part of The Crossing Press Feminist Series. Other titles in this Series include:

Feminist Calendars
Folly, A Novel by Maureen Brady
Lesbian Images, Literary Commentary by Jane Rule
Mother, Sister, Daughter, Lover, Stories by Jan Clausen
Motherwit: A Feminist Guide to Psychic Development by Diane Mariechild
Movement, A Novel by Valerie Miner
Movement in Black, Poetry by Pat Parker
Natural Birth, Poetry by Toi Derricotte
The Notebooks of Leni Clare and Other Short Stories by Sandy Boucher
The Politics of Reality: Essays in Feminist Theory by Marilyn Frye
The Queen of Wands, Poetry by Judy Grahn
True to Life Adventure Stories, Volumes I and II, Edited by Judy Grahn
Zami, A New Spelling of My Name, Biomythography by Audre Lorde